THE SOCCER COACHING BIBLE

National Soccer Coaches Association of America

Project Coordinated by Tim Schum

Human Kinetics

Library of Congress Cataloging-in-Publication Data

The soccer coaching bible / National Soccer Coaches Association of
America.

     p. cm

  ISBN 0-7360-4227-X (softcover)

  1. Soccer--Coaching--United States. 2. Soccer--Training--United
States. I. National Soccer Coaches Association of America.

  GV943.8.S65 2004

  796.334'07'7--dc22

2003022881

ISBN-10: 0-7360-4227-X
ISBN-13: 978-0-7360-4227-7

Copyright © 2004 by Human Kinetics, Inc.

Developmental Editor: Cynthia McEntire; **Assistant Editor:** Scott Hawkins; **Copyeditor:** John Wentworth; **Proofreader:** Jim Burns; **Graphic Designer:** Robert Reuther; **Graphic Artist:** Tara Welsch; **Photo Manager:** Dan Wendt; **Cover Designer:** Keith Blomberg; **Photographer (cover):** Courtesy of the Home Depot Center; **Art Manager:** Kareema McLendon; **Field Diagrams:** Brian McElwain; **Line Drawings:** Tim Offenstein; **Printer:** Versa Press

Contributor photos are used with permission from the contributors.

Human Kinetics books are available at special discounts for bulk purchase. Special editions or book excerpts can also be created to specification. For details, contact the Special Sales Manager at Human Kinetics.

Printed in the United States of America   10 9 8 7 6 5 4 3

Human Kinetics
Web site: www.HumanKinetics.com

United States: Human Kinetics
P.O. Box 5076
Champaign, IL 61825-5076
800-747-4457
e-mail: humank@hkusa.com

Canada: Human Kinetics
475 Devonshire Road Unit 100
Windsor, ON N8Y 2L5
800-465-7301 (in Canada only)
e-mail: orders@hkcanada.com

Europe: Human Kinetics
107 Bradford Road
Stanningley
Leeds LS28 6AT, United Kingdom
+44 (0) 113 255 5665
e-mail: hk@hkeurope.com

Australia: Human Kinetics
57A Price Avenue
Lower Mitcham, South Australia 5062
08 8277 1555
e-mail: liaw@hkaustralia.com

New Zealand: Human Kinetics
Division of Sports Distributors NZ Ltd.
P.O. Box 300 226 Albany
North Shore City
Auckland
0064 9 448 1207
e-mail: info@humankinetics.co.nz

THE SOCCER
COACHING BIBLE

CONTENTS

KEY TO DIAGRAMS

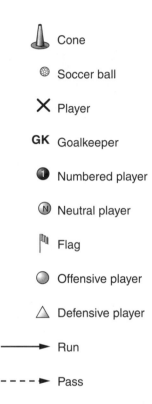

    Cone

    Soccer ball

    Player

GK   Goalkeeper

    Numbered player

    Neutral player

    Flag

    Offensive player

    Defensive player

    Run

    Pass

I

Priorities and Principles

CHAPTER 1

Sharing a Love for the Game

C. Cliff McCrath

Successful coaching is getting people to believe it's in their best interest to help achieve someone else's goal. Parents who get their children to go to bed on time without World War III breaking out are successful coaches. Managers who get their employees to achieve company goals are successful coaches. Teachers who motivate their students to improve their learning in a subject they resisted are successful coaches. Consider the following three examples: Coach B, Coach Danny, and Coach Legend.

Coach B

Coach B was a quiet, thoughtful, somewhat mysterious man. He coached soccer at a small Midwestern college that competed with the likes of Indiana, Michigan State, and Purdue because there weren't enough schools of its size with teams to form a league.

Coach B's soccer teams were always the most feared and, over the long haul, the most successful. His very presence inspired the players on his squad. He had soda-bottle thick glasses that made it difficult to determine the color and outline of his eyes. He always seemed larger than life and appeared to loom over others like the Chief Justice on the Supreme Court. Had he not been such a good man, such features would have made him look sinister or even evil.

Coach B's habits, speech, and ideals for living were so far above reproach that he seemed flawless. People truly wondered if he ever sinned. Players worshipped him and played their hearts out for him. While some coaches feel compelled to shout and belittle players, Coach B sometimes just looked at his players. His style was to speak softly, but his words carried a strength that transformed stray dogs into show dogs.

Danny Quick was one of those stray dogs. Danny was a wild-eyed, whirling dervish whose athletic skills and instincts were honed in the streets and back alleys of Detroit. They didn't even play soccer in the Motor City—or if they did, few knew about it. In this city, the Lions, Tigers, and Red Wings ruled. Unless you were on the streets, as Danny was. On the streets, one of the games played was "Buicks versus Fords," which was a daily challenge between the Brewster Roosters and the Alfred Street Gang. Wars were fought with hubcaps from "abandoned" cars (usually without consent of the owners). Opponents flung the dented discs at each other like Frisbees; the objective was to score a "hit" while yelling out "Bop!" "Crash!" "Bang!" or "Pow!" in the spirit of Captain Marvel, the cartoon hero of the day. A roar of "Shazam!" indicated a direct—and temporarily disabling—hit on one of the opposing team members. Danny was a gold medalist in the haphazard world of Buicks versus Fords and other street sports.

One day, Danny was ambling across campus among the late-afternoon shadows when he heard a familiar shout. He spun around to see his roomie, Mike Easterling, heading his direction. "Where ya' headed, Pascal?" Danny asked. "Pascal" was a name he and Mike had adopted for each other in Philosophy 101 when they had first heard the name Blasé Pascal. Whoever spoke first was usually addressed as Pascal, leaving Blasé for the other. The names were interchangeable.

"Hey, Blasé. I'm turning out for soccer," Mike answered.

"Soccer?" Danny scoffed. "Isn't that what girls play at recess?"

"Nope. This is a game they play all over the world. I'm turning out to get in shape for basketball. Want to come?"

"Okay, I'll play along," Danny relented. "If it involves some running, I'll use it to get in better shape for hockey."

The equipment manager handed the Pascal brothers their gear, including huge rubber bands to hold their socks and shin guards in place. These rubber bands were wide enough and strong enough to strangle elephants. The shin guards were ancient, beastly contraptions made of reinforced cloth with tubes for bamboo sticks that slid down the front side of the heavily reinforced pads.

Moments later, the two boys jogged over to Coach B, who was several minutes into his practice session. That's when Danny remembers seeing the Coach B "look" for the first time. It wouldn't be the last. Coach B directed Danny to join the backs and Mike to join the goalkeepers. Ironically, Mike would go on to become a two-time All-American goalkeeper, and Danny became his protector, an All-American center halfback in the old WM formation days.

It's been said that Coach B was a religious man, and Danny recalls trying to describe his coach to someone back home. "I never saw him with a Bible in his hand, but I know he must have read it often. I never saw him pray, but I think he knew how."

Young coaches often ask how to motivate their players. The answer is simple: Get organized and live a proper life. Coach B's practices were always meticulously organized and clear as crystal. His life was a living, breathing definition of motivation. He rarely, if ever, raised his voice. He merely expressed his desires—quietly, as if asking for a napkin in a restaurant—and his players stepped on each other trying to please him. He went on to become a president of two universities and through his very existence inspired hundreds of players, professors, and students. In one of his inaugural addresses, Coach B gave part of his definition of success, asking, "Of what significance is the victory if the challenge is too small?"

Coach Danny

Danny, shockingly, succeeded Coach B at his alma mater. Not so shockingly, Danny's coaching style was anything but quiet and studious. Indeed, Danny's life was a study. He was an interim coach, taking Coach B's place when he left for sabbatical studies to complete his PhD.

Danny was one of seven graduating seniors (three of whom were All-American players) whom Coach B had informed of his plans before notifying the public. The seven were huddled around their coach when he quietly said, "Fellows, I'm leaving. I have a sabbatical."

Danny had never heard the word "sabbatical" and thought that Coach B was sick. "Is it terminal?" he asked. As frequently happened, his coach and teammates thought he was joking, and the ensuing thigh-slapping provided just the cover Danny needed. The transition was in place, and he jumped to the next question. "Who's going to coach next year?" I'm sure he was thinking, *Who's the poor slob stuck with this bunch of leftovers?*

Coach B didn't bat an eye. "You are," he said. And he meant it.

The *Chicago Sun Times* previewed the season and predicted that the reign of Coach B's team had come to an end. The team was decimated by graduation, and the coach was leaving. The team was now in the hands of a raw-boned, borderline lunatic who had never coached a day in his life. The *Sun Times'* prediction: zero wins and last place in the Big Ten Conference.

Preseason practice resembled something between the *Twilight Zone* and *Animal House*. Two-a-days seemed like two-a-years. But the team survived. Sort of. In two nonconference games at the start of the season, more goals were scored on Danny's teams than had been scored in all games combined over the previous two seasons. The next game was a conference game against defending Big Ten champion Indiana University.

Depression reigned. Preseason speeches and fiery tirades mocked every new move and every word Danny uttered. The *Sun Times* was right. Or were they?

On the night before the conference opener, the team was just going through the motions, preparing for the impending slaughter. Danny tried to rally the troops but to no avail. He looked on his team in silence until he could no longer contain his rage.

He blew his whistle. "Line up along the touchline! When you hear the whistle, sprint to the opposite side and then jog back!"

No one remembers exactly how many times they ran back and forth. What they do recall is that they finally stopped after 15 players had stumbled out of the ranks vomiting and clenching their sides. At this point, Coach Danny screamed, "Huddle up and listen up! We're standing here a half-mile from the squad room" (where the team always met for focus the night before a game). "Since I can outrun all of you, I'm going to give you a one block head start to the gym and the squad room. Anyone not there when I get there can turn in his uniform!"

He blew a final blast on his whistle, and his team was off, some stumbling but all of them frantically clawing their way toward the squad room. True to his promise, Danny waited until they rounded the corner at the opposite end of the field and then started his own run, fueled by some sense of personal insult or perhaps embarrassment. After all, everyone who knew him knew he gave 100 percent 100 percent of the time. There was no "I'll try" or "I'll do my best." It was more like the motto of the Marine Corps in World War II: "That job won't take long, did it?"

He was deep in thought, brooding, hurt, and pained. What had gone wrong? After all, weren't his enthusiasm and personality enough? Didn't they understand that there was no room for failure?

His brooding suddenly ended and he snapped back to reality when he realized he was just a few feet from the last player, and they were still about 200 yards from the gym. He slowed down and searched for the right words. What could he say? His mind was a kaleidoscope of darting thoughts and emotions that he knew came from the combat zone of his storied childhood. Together they flooded his body. For a second or two, even he felt like throwing up.

He paused outside the squad room door, desperately trying to gather his thoughts. Any thoughts. Steam and waves of heat and gasping sounds emanated from the room. He entered and stepped up on the pallet that served as a podium and supported the lectern. In front of him was a sea of faces, blanched from lack of oxygen and whitened even more by fear . . . the great motivator!

Then it all gushed out and made sense. "Gentlemen, no one in his right mind makes a team do sprints for 30 minutes the night before the biggest game of the year. But since you all know I have never been in my right mind, I won't waste any time trying to vindicate myself.

"I accepted this job because Coach B told me I was going to be the coach. And when I got over the shock of being named the coach, it occurred to me that there were only two things I really knew about how to approach this task. One, I knew that demanding your respect was something I would never do. I grew up knowing that respect isn't something a person can demand.

It has to be earned. You have never heard me say that you need to respect me, and you'll never hear me demand it.

"What I can demand is 100 percent of your effort, 100 percent of the time. Every returning player in this room knows that, as a player, I gave 100 percent all the time. And if you new players haven't discovered that by now, there are still some openings on the sewing team.

So what does this mean? "You read the *Sun Times*? A rookie coach and a team of leftovers. A team without seven of the best starters from last year. A conference schedule that features players from all over the world. Who are you kidding? Hey, I am an interim coach. I don't have to win one game!! Do you hear me?"

The silence beat his words into their ears and down into their souls like gunpowder rammers and swabbers preparing cannons for battle. His words suddenly seemed well rehearsed. They flowed smoothly and quietly. There was an eerie, yet comforting moment when his style and tone echoed memories of Coach B.

"Here's the way I see it, guys. Even though we have always been up against much more talented players, the pride of this program has always been our fighting spirit. We have always played with fury and pride. What I saw out there on the practice field was indifference and defeat. Guys clowning around as if they didn't care. In this case, believing the press clippings. Obituaries of gloom. Well, hear this: We have a choice!

"We can believe what they say and muddle through what will always be known as the season that wasn't or the year of the goat—make that "goats." If this is your choice, then I have a proposition for you. Today was the last practice of the year. We won't waste any more time practicing!"

The players were transfixed; all eyes were on Coach Danny.

"There will be no further practices because it doesn't take any practice to lose!" The words entered each player's mind like a laser and went to the very bottom of his soul. "If we're going to be lousy, why be stupid as well? You can if you choose to be, but it's not for me. I can go paint houses and make some extra money."

"On the other hand," he continued, "if we all make some sort of commitment to each other and dedicate ourselves to making every game the last thing we do on earth, then we can die with dignity and respect. If the opponent beats us, so be it, but at least every team that takes the field against us will know they'll never face a tougher challenge in their entire life. It's your choice."

Danny left the room and stood a long time in the shower in the coaches' locker room. He never knew what happened after he left. But he knew something was right the next day when the ragpickers defeated Indiana 4 to 0! They had scored a victory over the perennial conference champions—something Danny and his former fellow All-Americans had never done.

Danny also knew something was right the next spring at the annual athletic convocation held in the school's chapel. To a hushed crowd, with the team and interim coach lined up on stage behind him, the president of the university read a telegram from a PhD candidate studying at, of all places, Indiana University: "Congratulations! Great season! Great championship! Great team! Great coach!—Coach B."

Coach Legend

To Coach Legend, life was soccer, and soccer was life. It seemed from the moment he was born, the blood in his veins flowed to power his play and fuel his passion for the game of soccer. No one garnered more victories as a player. No one enjoyed a longer or more illustrious career as a coach.

Indeed, what this man-marvel represents to the spirit and growth of soccer might require a special archive in heaven or at least an eighth day of creation to accommodate his achievements.

In fact, the eighth day of creation might well have occurred on July 1, 1894, when Coach Legend was born in Dundee, Scotland. He began playing soccer with his first step and at age 93, two years before his death, he could still lock his ankle and put the ball in the back of the net.

In the words of a Philadelphia sportswriter, "If soccer enjoyed the same exposure as baseball, Coach Legend's name would be as well known as Connie Mack, Casey Stengel, and Babe Ruth." He was football's Knute Rockne, golf's Arnold Palmer, and Hollywood's John Wayne. He was pure legend.

Shortly after his birth, his family moved to Paisley and then to the Bridgeton area of Glasgow. He began playing soccer, or "fitba" as the Scots called it, for St. Clemens in the Churches League. At 15, he had a brief sojourn with the juveniles before being signed by the Scottish Junior League, sometimes called the nursery for famous clubs like the Rangers, Celtic, and Hearts. From there he went on to Shettleston, Vale of Clyde, and Kirkintilloch Rob Roy before his promotion to the Scottish Second Division with Bathgate and Clydebank. His final game as a Scottish professional was a 1 to 1 draw against Glasgow Celtic.

From Scotland, he immigrated to Canada, and in 1920 he signed to play for the Toronto Caledonians of the National League. In 1923, he moved to Philadelphia, where his presence was immediately felt and his impact as a player and coach would skyrocket. Indeed, he left his imprint as a tutor and mentor on the lives of literally thousands of boys and girls.

Upon his arrival, he signed to play for the Philadelphia soccer team in the old American Soccer League (ASL). The team later went bankrupt, and he joined the Fairhill F.C. team in the Allied League of Philadelphia, where he played and coached from 1925 until 1953. In 1942, Fairhill purchased the Philadelphia Nationals and named him head coach.

His first act, in his own words, was to "can" all the foreign players and enlist only American-born players for his team. He was foreign born himself but believed to the bottom of his soul that the United States was going to be a world power in soccer. Moreover, he believed to his last day on earth that it should—and would—be done with American-born players.

Little wonder that the Nationals proceeded to win three consecutive ASL championships. They lost the next year by one goal but came back the following year to win it all again. During the same era, his teams won the Lewis Cup three times and were the only team in the 36-year history of the Cup to win back-to-back titles.

While coaching professional teams and doubling up with youth and novice teams, Coach Legend was also asked to step in for the ailing David Gould, coach of the University of Pennsylvania freshman team. He did, and thus began one of the most remarkable coaching careers in secondary and collegiate history.

After pinch-hitting for one year, he assumed the reigns at the Episcopal Academy, where he remained for the next 12 years. His success there caught the attention of the people at Haverford College, and soon Coach Legend entered the collegiate ranks as the "Ford's" head man. After 23 years, he reluctantly stepped down. He had exceeded the retirement age of 65 by a mere 13 years.

Not to worry, for less than a tick of the clock passed before the enterprising administrators of nearby Girard College announced the hiring of Coach Legend, their new 77-year-young soccer coach. There he coached with the same energy and vigor of his earlier years and didn't step down for the next 12 years when, at age 89, his legs would no longer do what his laser-quick brain told them to do.

But the story doesn't end here. All this time, Coach Legend served as coach of multiple youth teams, two of which were the famous Lighthouse Boy's Club teams, known as the Nationals and later the Spurs. He coached each of them 10 years, and both won the championship every year. That's 20 championships in 20 years! In addition, during the record-setting era of Coach Legend, he served as coach of the United States National Team for the 1956 Olympic Games in Melbourne, Australia, where the team finished with an astonishing record of six wins, four losses, and one tie while compiling the first winning record in soccer in United States Olympic history.

No individual in the history of American soccer has compiled such a staggering record of achievements. He played the game for 45 years and coached an additional 38 years. As a player and coach, he won over 120 awards, including his 1954 induction into the United States Soccer Hall of Fame. His teams won a total of 111 championships.

Coach Legend, James "Jimmy" Mills, died before the 2002 World Cup, but I bet he was watching when his beloved United States took the field against Portugal on June 5, 2003, in North Korea. If anyone could pull that off, it would be Coach Legend.

CHAPTER 2

Competing With Class

Joe Bean and Layton Shoemaker

Say someone asks you, "What does it mean to compete with class?" Initially, you might struggle for an answer. That's because it's usually easier to think of competitive scenarios in which someone *lacks* class. Refusing to slap hands after a match because you lost, for instance, lacks class. But if you *do* slap hands after the loss, is that enough to say you have class? After all, everyone, or nearly everyone, slaps hands after a match, right?

So, just what is class? We suggest that it's a hard concept to define or explain but that we recognize it when we see it. Let's get some help with nailing this down. Ann Landers, from newspaper advice column fame, wrote an excellent description of the chief characteristics of class. Here are some basic tenets, adapted to sports, based on her description:

- Class always respects teammates, coaches, officials, and spectators. It always sacrifices self for the greater good of the game.
- Class oozes with confidence, never cockiness.
- Class has an element of pride without being proud.
- Class has nothing to do with status, position, or wealth. It bespeaks an aristocracy that has nothing to do with ancestry or accomplishments. Some wealthy "blue bloods" have no class, while individuals who are struggling to make ends meet are loaded with it.
- Class knows you need not extinguish another's candle in order to let your own shine.
- Class does not need credit for getting the job done.
- Class is never self-seeking and always looks for ways to praise others.
- Class is void of excuses. It learns from failure and moves on.
- Class is doing unto others as you would have others do unto you.

- Class has a sense of humor and knows that laughing at oneself is essential for positive well-being. Laughter lubricates the machinery of human relations.
- Class cultivates good manners, recognizing them as a series of small, inconsequential sacrifices.
- Class is equally comfortable with nobility and the blue collar crowd.
- Class is authentic. It loathes duplicity.
- True class has no rivals. If you lack class, whatever else you have is inconsequential.

When you think about it, hundreds, maybe thousands, of sport-related examples can be plugged into these common tenets of being a person with class.

The challenge to coaches is to carefully assess the importance of developing and sustaining class as one of the most important ingredients in creating and maintaining a successful program. Maintaining class is more important than winning. Somehow when we learn how to win or lose with class, the final score becomes far less significant. It's a case of process taking priority over product. Often when we become product driven, the process becomes distorted or compromised. Maintaining class is a continual process. It will influence the product, but is never compromised by the desire to win or to be the best.

When asked what she would consider a classy coach, one woman responded without hesitation, "Someone who doesn't wear a sweat suit to work every day." Wrong. Class has much less to do with appearance than with actions. Some of the classiest coaches never won a conference championship. In fact, some of them lost more games than they won. But they were and are the types of coaches that all soccer coaches should emulate.

Consider the examples of Hall of Famer and former coach Irv Schmid of Springfield College and one of his protégés, Alden "Whitey" Burnham of the University of Delaware and Dartmouth College. While playing at Springfield, Whitey learned from his mentor not only the rudiments of the tactical approach to the game but also the style of coaching Irv possessed and modeled for his teams.

During a game, Irv sometimes looked disinterested in what was going on. He would sit impassively on the bench, not raising his voice or yelling instructions to his players. He rarely questioned a referee's call. His teams were always completely under control and well schooled in the fundamentals. They were never out of any game. Over the years, Springfield College won many more games than it lost and was always among the best teams in New England.

As for Whitey Burnham, to know him is to love him. He exudes class in every way. He's polite, gracious, articulate, and witty. A gentleman's gentleman. Coaches who have played against Delaware or Dartmouth teams will tell you that Whitey was as classy a coach as his mentor. Although his teams were not always above .500, Whitey always maintained class in his coaching style.

Integrating Class With Sportsmanship and Ethical Conduct

Sportsmanship and ethical conduct must be integrally linked. It would be nice if they were linked in a way that made it impossible to have one without the other. Unfortunately, this isn't the way it always works. For example, in soccer it's considered good sportsmanship to knock the ball out of bounds when a teammate or opponent has been injured but the official has allowed play to continue. We also consider it good sportsmanship when play is restarted to restore possession to the team that knocked the ball out of bounds. Although this sort of behavior shows class, it should not be confused with ethical conduct.

Say the same team that knocked the ball out of bounds to show respect for the injured player also engages in regular shirt tugging to gain an advantage. They view it as part of the game and rationalize their conduct as acceptable because everyone does it. This might be viewed by some as poor sportsmanship, but it's really inappropriate ethical conduct because it's an intentional, overt violation of the rules. It's done with the intent to gain an unfair competitive advantage. We suggest that players or teams that have class do not engage in the common practice of shirt tugging.

Another example is the tactical foul. It's common practice to take opponents down when, through exceptional play, they have slipped past the last defender but are still outside the penalty area. Taking these players down shows poor sportsmanship *and* inappropriate ethical conduct—not to mention a complete lack of faith in your goalkeeper! In our view, taking players down after they have beaten you is playing soccer without class.

The example we just looked at raises the issue of situational ethics. In this kind of scenario—when we take down an opponent on offense before he reaches the penalty area—do we consider the current situation in the game before engaging in such an act? Would we commit the same act in the first five minutes of the game with the score tied 0 to 0? How about in the last five minutes of the game when we're winning 1 to 0? What if we're winning 4 to 0? What if were *losing* 1 to 0? No matter what numbers you use, once you start considering what you should do based on the score or other situation, the ethics become situation oriented rather than principle oriented. And that's wrong. Class teams and class individuals are principle oriented and are not swayed by the circumstances of the situation. Taking a player down because he or she has beaten you and might score is wrong on principle, so you shouldn't do it no matter what the score is.

Something else you often see is players trying to influence the decisions of officials. When a ball goes out of bounds over the endline or sideline, it's not uncommon for a player to raise an arm to indicate the subsequent direction of play with the intent of influencing the official. Doing this is poor sportsmanship. Do you ever see players raise an arm in a manner that would influence the official in favor of the *opponent?* Players and coaches should refrain from any behavior intended to influence the decision of an official. Showing restraint in this area is an example of competing with class.

As a coach, how do you instruct your players to set the wall? Almost invariably, players will set the wall closer than the prescribed distance with the intent of gaining a competitive advantage. These situations usually occur within 25 meters (27 yards) of the offending team's goal. One must remember that the offending team has just, intentionally or unintentionally, thwarted the opponent's attack. Allowing them to organize and structure their collective defense now rewards the offensive team. They then take additional advantage by setting the wall closer than prescribed. This is unsportsmanlike conduct. Those who compete with class refrain from such behavior.

Treating Opponents With Dignity and Respect

The vast majority of coaches respect their opponents, but the rub comes when they are expected to treat their opponents with dignity. What does that term really mean when applied to coaching against another team? Does dignity imply we are to be condescending or play soft in our games? That is something we as coaches would never want.

Actually, the two terms coincide with most coaching philosophies. If you respect a team, you will play them hard, fair, and within the rules. Thus, dignity enters into the picture. Dignity will show through the esteem your team has for the opponent. Shirt pulling, tackling from behind, unnecessary delay tactics, and other forms of gamesmanship will not surface during the game.

There are great rivalries at all levels of the game in which teams fight tooth and nail from start to finish. Yet at the end of the game, they not only shake hands, they embrace each other. Think of when Army plays Navy. These teams respect each other to the utmost. They play the game for all its worth but honor the traditions of the rivalry. They meet at midfield, embrace each other, and proceed to face the attending cadets and midshipmen to sing their respective alma maters. This wonderful display of sportsmanship and mutual respect is a model for coaches looking for ways to instill tradition and class into their team and league.

Treating Officials With Dignity and Respect

This aspect of a coach's responsibility is often overlooked. First, remember that the game can't be played without officials. Admittedly, there's a range of proficiency among the officiating fraternity, and some games might be affected by an official's lack of correct decision-making or knowledge of the rules. However, the coach must set the tone before, during, and after the game to ensure that the officials are treated with deference. If they don't set the tone, the team might show a lack of respect for the officials, and the game will deteriorate.

If an official is either unprepared to work a game or shows the inability to handle a game properly, it should be brought to his attention after the game in a calm, constructive manner. The coach needs to keep in mind that the game is over. No matter how frustrating the game might have been, it won't be replayed. The coach needs to keep in mind that this official might benefit from some honest constructive critiquing of his performance. If the criticism is communicated in a nonthreatening, civil manner, free of profane language, it can benefit your team and the game in the future. Coaches have tried this, and it works. Recognizing that you're dealing with another human being, not just someone in a striped shirt, makes all the difference.

Treat officials as you want to be treated. If you do, the game is the winner. All coaches recognize that there's a shortage of officials. We must be grateful for those we have and do our part to help develop more and better ones.

Influencing Positive Spectator Conduct

As soccer grows in popularity in the United States, teams need to attend to the fans that support the team, both home and away. The coach becomes an important element in the proper conduct of spectators. Of course, the administration of the game should provide game-management restraints, including fencing, ropes, or stands to keep fans from interfering with play. The coach, however, needs to address any problems with the administration if the facilities available for games are not up to proper standard or fail to provide game safety.

A spectator statement of conduct should be read over the public address system or printed in the game program before every game. Proper security personnel should be on hand to ensure that any unruly or overly exuberant fans are controlled. All coaches would like to see as much support for their team as possible. They can plan ahead by developing student sections for seating and even organize a sale of team scarves or caps and other positive ways to show support.

Integrating Class With Competitive Recruiting

When it comes to recruiting, the best advice is an old adage: If you can't say something good, don't say anything. To run down another school and its coach while recruiting a student athlete is unethical and usually without merit. If you have to resort to undermining another program to gain an edge in recruiting, then you shouldn't be in the profession.

Learn ethical and professional ways to impress a young recruit with your program. Inform recruits of the strengths of your institution. Introduce them to people they'll interact with if they attend your institution. Give them reasons to want to come to your school. If you spend time bashing another school, your potential recruits will question your integrity and wonder why you're not saying more about your own institution. Most young people today are sophisticated enough to assess the viability of a person acting in his or her own self-interest.

Cultivating Team Relationships

Any successful program is built around solid and meaningful player relationships. If teammates don't like each other off the field, they probably won't respond positively to each other on the field.

The coach should provide extensive opportunities for players to interact with each other. Try giving newcomers to the program "big brothers" or "big sisters" when they arrive on campus. These upperclassmen are responsible for welcoming the new players to the team and helping them get oriented during the first weeks. They help new players acclimate to the campus and find classrooms, the post office, the student union, and so on. They also aid in the process of building team morale.

Another way to build close relationships is to have a team activity, such as a bowling night or golf outing. Even a group date night that ends with a pizza party can be beneficial. Coach involvement in such activities indicates to team members the value you place on bonding with your players. Also try to entertain players in your own home as much as you can and make them feel part of your family. After all, you are their family away from home. Remember a team that stays together, plays together.

In many ways, the coach is an extension of the institution he or she represents. The coach is exposed to many more people off campus than many other faculty members are. Think of the number of away games a team has and the many people they encounter. Restaurant and hotel employees and guests, airport personnel, alumni, parents, prospective students, and many others are assessing you and your program by your behavior. The right decorum and behavior by your team positively influences the general public's attitude toward your institution. All members of the team can become good ambassadors by wearing proper attire, using appropriate language, and by being polite, helpful, and thoughtful. Nothing makes me more proud of my team than when I hear, "Wow, what a well-behaved group. Where are you from? What sport do you play?" What a good feeling it is to say proudly, "We're from Wheaton College, and this is our soccer team." Make public relations a priority for your team. Class wins friends and influences people!

Ambassadorship

Soccer is still gaining the acceptance of the American public. We've come a long way, but there's still much to accomplish toward winning a greater share of public acceptance and recognition. You can adopt many strategies to increase public awareness. One of the best is to conduct your program in a way that shows others that soccer is a sport they want to be a part of.

We need to learn from the mistakes of others in the sporting community. People notice when you do it right. People also notice when you do it wrong. Unfortunately, the negative creates an opportunity for the pundits to discredit much of the good being accomplished.

Coaches have an enormous responsibility to establish and promote programs that are dominated by outstanding sportsmanship and ethical conduct. Every soccer coach, from the youth level up to the professional, should be a soccer ambassador. One of the most critical components of this ambassadorial role is the adoption of the highest standards of sportsmanship and ethical conduct.

The NSCAA sponsors team sportsmanship and ethical conduct awards granted on the basis of the number of yellow cards accumulated by a collegiate team during the course of the traditional fall season. The impetus for the awards was the exemplary manner in which the Messiah College men's soccer team subscribed to extraordinary levels of sportsmanship during the late 1980s. Over the course of three seasons, including during advancement to two final four appearances, these Messiah teams played 49 consecutive games without receiving a single yellow card. Now that's setting a standard for conduct that's hard to replicate.

Leading With Class

Coaches should always be aware that they're the ones who establish the atmosphere for the team's standard of conduct. Everything the coach says or does is scrutinized, analyzed, or criticized sooner or later. Thus, it behooves a coach to weigh every word carefully and think through every action. Your positive example will ultimately be assessed, and you hope your players will respond to your proper example.

One of the best examples of model behavior was Dr. Bob Baptista at Wheaton. Bob's team was playing Lake Forest for the conference championship and the right to go to the NCAA regional playoffs. It was a home game for Wheaton and closely contested. Late in the game, Lake Forest just missed what would have been the tying goal. The game ended with Wheaton winning by a goal. As Bob checked in with the players after the game in the locker room, he overheard his goalkeeper inform a teammate that he thought the shot by Lake Forest actually had gone in the net and out a hole in the back. Instead of ignoring these comments, Bob inquired further and took the player to the field to check the net. Sure enough, there was the hole in the net.

What to do? Forget it? After all, Lake Forest had already returned home. Who would know the difference? That wasn't the way Bob Baptista thought or lived. His sense of fair play and integrity came to the forefront. He called the Lake Forest coach the next day and told him of the situation. The Lake Forest coach was willing to forgive and forget. He thanked Bob for his honesty and was about to hang up when Bob said, "I think we should play the game over." The Lake Forest coach told him that he had already collected the equipment from the players plus they couldn't afford to come down to Wheaton again. Bob insisted on replaying the game, and to do so Wheaton would come to Lake Forest the next day. The Lake Forest coach agreed to the replay. Wheaton won again—now they were the true and justified winner of the game and the valid representative for the NCAA playoffs.

Talk about delivering the right message to your team. Wonder why this story has gone down in soccer circles as the all-time example of true sportsmanship and integrity? The next week Bob had a chance to share the whole scenario with the student body, and he closed his talk by telling the students, "We had a lot more to lose than a game. We had our reputations as a Christian community on the line."

Would you have made the same decision that Bob did? It's a good question for all of us coaches to ask ourselves. One thing is for sure: Bob's team never doubted his character and integrity; he set a standard of conduct that would never be questioned. Leading by example—that's the key!

Through its ethics committee, the NSCAA has adopted a Code of Ethics and Conduct that contains guidelines for coaches to develop acceptable levels of sportsmanship and ethical conduct (see chapter 23). Although the code is intentionally stated in very general terms, it remains an excellent reference for developing more specific applications. Generally speaking, the NSCAA recommends adopting a set of inviolate principles to serve as personal guidelines for developing character that produces class behavior. Remember that principles dictate conduct, and conduct reveals character. Game situations do not develop character—they reveal it.

Mentoring

A mentor is an experienced and prudent adviser. To fulfill this important role with his players, a coach must perform a self-evaluation. First, ask yourself if you're capable of offering advice to someone in such a way that it will be useful and meaningful to that individual. Age and wisdom alone don't necessarily qualify you to be a mentor. Ask yourself if you're willing to be a mentor. A person needs to be willing to spend the necessary time to develop the proper relationship with the person being mentored. If this is the case, a meaningful dialogue can evolve.

For the mentoring relationship to prosper, a player must open himself. He or she needs to see in the mentor the characteristics he wants to have in his own life. This could be the catalyst that causes the player to approach you for this relationship. Many coaches get to experience having former players as assistant coaches. These times are great opportunities to guide, influence, and encourage them to become future head coaches. This is a rich, rewarding experience for any coach, and it is one of the neatest events in a coach's career.

During their run to the NCAA Division III national championship in the fall of 2002, the Messiah College men's team left an indelible impression on the players and parents of their quarterfinal opponent. The following was posted by a parent of one of the players on the opposing team:

> After the GC-Messiah game, I was drained. This was my son's senior year, and the loss, for a moment, just took it out of me. Then I was lucky enough to watch what was happening on the field. Messiah had celebrated, and rightly so. It hurt, but they earned it, so my hat was off to them. After the teams went through the line, I saw my son walk away from the others. He just knelt on the field, spent from the game. Knowing it was his last game, I wanted to give him a moment alone. Then something happened that I will never forget. The entire Messiah team came over to him. There were handshakes and hugs. Three years he has battled against this team, and even in defeat he had their respect. There were things said, no taunting as is so popular in sports today, but good things. And give Messiah all the credit in the world; they had the presence of mind and sportsmanship to do what they did. My son has told me he will remember that day for the rest of his life and hopes that if he is ever in the same situation he can handle victory with the class that Messiah did. Wins and losses come and go, but respect of your peers lives on long after the thrill of victory or agony of defeat. This weekend four (let's call it five including the play-in game) very good teams took the field. One was left standing. Give that team credit. But give the other teams credit also. There were no easy games. All games were decided by one goal. All teams left the field, winner or defeated, with the respect of their opponents. The south regional was called the field of death. I see it now as the field of victory; victory for D3 soccer, victory for each team, victory for each player, victory for the fans in support. Thank you everyone for the experience.

That is a poignant example of class conduct. It revealed both the corporate and individual character of the Messiah players. It should be noted that class conduct of this type is not entirely inherent. Most often it needs to be intentionally taught, modeled, and encouraged. When pursued with integrity, players will gradually and more naturally recognize opportunities to implement what has been planted in the core fabric of their being. What people do is a result of who they are.

When thinking about the merits of creating, developing, and sustaining a class soccer program, it is probably helpful to incorporate thoughts about the alternative. Clearly, the alternative is to abort the concept of developing a class program. One might conclude it's not worth the effort; besides, the rewards are subjective, intangible, and temporary. For those inclined to think this way, we submit that the most fundamental responsibility of a coach is the development of the character of each player. The basis of determining success in coaching is measured by the influence the coach has on character development.

19

Creating a Legacy

The whole idea of a legacy is to leave something behind that's meaningful and worthwhile. Longevity is necessary for a legacy really to take root and be a part of a contribution to the community. Someone who leaves a legacy has shown consistency in performance over the years, has developed meaningful relationships, has promoted his or her program with enthusiasm and integrity, has provided opportunities for growth and development in players, and has stayed true to his convictions and philosophy.

Really, when you consider the idea of *creating* a legacy, it can't be done. A legacy must evolve over years, and then history must take over. History determines whether a legacy has evolved or not. All coaches can do is their best for as long as they can. They then must let others determine the legacy question.

Two fundamental principles must guide the development of a team's effort to compete with class. First, follow the golden rule: Do unto others as you would have others do unto you. Second, do the right thing, in the right way, at the right time, for the right reason. Assessing all conduct on the basis of these two principles leads to positive results with enviable consistency.

CHAPTER 3

Developing the Next Generation of Soccer Players

George Perry

Playing youth soccer is a fantastic opportunity for children to have fun and develop relationships with others their own age as well as with adults. Many children meet people who serve as role models. One great aspect of youth soccer is that every player has the opportunity to be successful. In youth soccer, the coach has an enormous responsibility in this regard. Through good organization, including the creation of an enjoyable environment, coaches can make soccer a constructive learning experience.

Where do the coaches of our youngest players come from? Often they get a phone call that goes something like this: "Mr. Smith, we have eight players, including your daughter, who won't be able to play soccer this season if we can't find a coach. Do you know of anyone?" One of the biggest challenges for recreational programs is to recruit, educate, and keep youth coaches. We must help beginning coaches understand that even if they don't have much playing or coaching experience, they can do a good job as long as they're willing to learn what's needed for children at specific age groups. Most caring adults can coach if they keep their focus on the essential outcomes of coaching and avoid being distracted by areas that are inappropriate and potentially harmful.

Have Realistic Expectations

Adults working with young children need to have realistic expectations of the children. Children begin playing soccer for many different reasons. Some want to play because it's fun. Others play because their friends are playing. Still others play because their parents signed them up without asking them first. Whatever it is that got them into the program, once they're in, it's important that their expectations are met. Identify what each child is looking for. Children enjoy activities in which they have fun, have success, play with friends, make new friends, and have chances to show their loved ones what they can do.

Physiological and psychological differences exist among age groups. This doesn't mean we must do different activities for different age groups but that we should *adjust* the activities, as well as the goals and objectives, so that they match the age group with which we're working. Physiologically, children develop larger movements before they develop fine motor movements. Their cardiovascular systems can put out a high level of energy for only short periods of time. After a short rest, they can continue the activity with the same high level of energy. We must take care not to overstress their skeletal systems. Too much stress can hinder proper growth.

Psychologically, it's best for young children to focus on a single task. Though they might perform many different tasks, we should help them retain a single focus. Children have a strong desire to impress significant others in their lives—family members, coaches, friends. They find it difficult to discern between effort and ability. They believe they always give their best effort and also believe what they do is correct and good.

Create a Fun Environment

Soccer is for the players. This is as true for the 6-year-old as it is for the 26-year-old. The 6-year-old, however, must first develop an enjoyment of the game. Standing around and listening to coaches talk or waiting in line for a turn does not enhance enjoyment. Children want to play. As a positive byproduct of playing the game, they can learn to play better. Our challenge as coaches of young players is to create gamelike activities that aid the learning process and provide enjoyment for the players.

As coaches, we should look at ourselves as facilitators. We try to create an environment for learning, success, and enjoyment. All of us can do this if we're willing to learn the needs of children, create activities that allow them to learn while they play, and support them during their participation.

Many of the mistakes coaches of young players make are easily corrected. We can't look at coaching in the short term but as an investment in the future of the game. The future is not only in individual player development but in their development as long-term supporters of the sport. Such support could be as coaches, administrators, referees, or spectators.

Coaches can aid this development by not making young players play specific positions. Beginning youth play should be a time when participants are exposed to all aspects of the game. More important, coaches should recognize that by telling players to stay in one space, they take away some of the spontaneity, and kids might get bored with the game. Youth coaches need to be careful when designing training activities. Kids shouldn't be standing around in lines waiting for their turns. As new activities are introduced or corrections are made, explanations should be simple and concise. Try not to talk too much.

In the first few moments after starting an activity, make sure what you expected from the activity is actually happening. If necessary, make corrections as quickly as possible. Adjustments might include changing the size of space, increasing or decreasing the number of players, or imposing restrictions (e.g., setting a number of touches on the ball to eliminate dribbling). These are just a few ways to change an exercise so that it achieves the outcome you're looking for.

Base the success of an activity on player performance, not on the final score of the game. Be positive and encouraging. If you have to say something negative, use the "sandwich" approach—start with a positive comment, follow with the correction, and end with another positive comment. For example: "Good job getting to the ball quickly! Once you get to the ball, make sure you look at it when you're shooting. That's much better—good job!"

Use the Instructional Process

It's widely accepted that players under the age of six should play organized games with a maximum of four against four. If this occurs, each game would have a maximum of eight players. Ideally, you want a coach for each game taking place, which means you need one coach for every eight players. So if you have 100 players in an age group, you need at least 13 coaches. Can your organization provide enough quality coaches to meet the demand? To do so, you need to offer plenty of required coaching clinics to ensure that all your coaches know your program's philosophy.

To achieve uniformity in the instructional process, some organizations rely on a lead instructor for each age group. This person leads the activities for each training session. In effect, he or she has 13 assistants. The instructional part of a session lasts 25 to 30 minutes (suggested activities will be discussed shortly). After the first segment of practice, players play games. Each group of eight players goes to a small field to play a game, accompanied by one of the assistants.

Another way to organize players is to have all the teams come at the same time, with no more than eight players per coach. The lead instructor organizes and runs the training part of the session. He or she brings all the teams together and demonstrates an activity. Then each group goes with its coach to work on the demonstrated activity. The process is repeated until it's time to play the game.

Incorporate Age-Appropriate Activities

You can use these activities no matter which instructional model your organization uses. As the coach, you must decide which techniques you want your players to develop. Typically, coaches focus first on developing players' confidence in dribbling the ball and striking the ball (shooting or passing). Don't get too caught up in technical execution. Instead, allow each player many chances to repeat the technique and achieve success.

Make your field the right size. Too small and the players run into each other. Too big and communication becomes a problem. Encourage players to keep the ball and themselves within the space unless directed otherwise. Always demonstrate an activity before they begin doing it. *Show* it, don't just tell it.

Have Confidence on the Ball

Fast footwork activities help develop confidence. Challenge your players to compete against themselves. They should ask themselves, Can I do it better this time than I did last time?

- **Step-ups.** Players execute light touches on top of the ball, alternating feet. This is similar to running in place, only the player also touches the top of the ball with each step. Ask players to think of the ball as an egg—don't step on it, just lightly touch it. Players can perform step-ups in place or while moving forward, backward, or sideways.
- **Pendulum.** Players pass the ball back and forth between their feet. Players can try for speed or distance. How far apart can players spread their feet and still pass the ball? How far can they move while passing the ball between their feet? Try relay races to modify this exercise.
- **Rolling.** Players move the ball around using the soles of their feet. They should lead with the inside and outside of the foot. Have them pull the ball backward and go in all directions. Remind them to alternate feet.
- **Tracing.** Have players trace different patterns with the ball. Can they make the ball draw the letter U? A square? Can they cut a pie?

Have players develop combined sequences of these exercises with the ball. For example, ask them to do three pendulums and then step across the ball and change directions. Repeat the sequence. As a challenge, have players count how many successful touches they can complete in 15 to 60 seconds. These activities develop ball control.

Change Direction and Speed

Encourage your players to look up after every touch or dribble. When they see a space, they should move into it as quickly as they can. They might have to change direction and speed to do this. After they get into the open space, they slow down until they find another space. Repeat the process.

- **Follow the leader.** Players divide into pairs. Each player has a ball. One player is the leader, and the other is the follower. The leader dribbles the ball in all directions within a confined space. The follower tries to imitate what the leader does. Every 30 seconds, change leaders.

- **Green light–red light.** Players stand in a straight line at one end of the space. Each player has a ball. Designate a finish line at the other end of the space. When the coach shouts "green light," players dribble the ball toward the finish line. When the coach shouts "red light," players stop the ball. Players who don't stop the ball quickly go back a predetermined distance. To make this activity more gamelike, hold up a green shirt and a red shirt instead of yelling "red light" and "green light." This helps players develop their vision of the field.

- **Body part dribbling.** Players dribble the ball into an open space and stop it with various body parts—left foot, right knee, forehead—as directed. If players are too young to distinguish left from right, just use the body part (foot, knee, forehead).

- **Speed dribbling.** Place cones around a 20 × 20 foot space outdoors. Players dribble inside the space. On the command "Go!" players dribble around one of the cones as quickly as they can. They then return to the middle of the space and continue dribbling.

- **Relay races.** Create teams of two to four players. Players work on running in all directions—forward, backward, and sideways. They can run with or without a ball. If balls are used, each player can have his or her own ball or use just one ball. If balls are used, players can dribble with the right foot only, left foot only, or weave around flags. (Flags are better than cones because players must navigate both the ball and their bodies around the flag.) Use your imagination to create challenging courses.

- **Tag.** All coaches are "it." Players dribble around the open space, trying not to be tagged by one of the coaches. If tagged, the player must perform a task, such as five step-ups, before rejoining the game. As a variation, have a group of players be "it." Be sure to rotate players because everyone will want to be "it." Don't allow tagged players to remain outside the game. Once they perform the task, they return to the game.

- **Freeze tag.** A group of players is "it." All other players have a ball. If a player with a ball is tagged, he or she "freezes" and must stand still with a foot on the ball. Unfrozen players can try to unfreeze frozen players by tagging them. Play for one minute, then change who's "it."

- **Hospital tag.** A group of players is "it." They try to tag the other players, who are dribbling. A player who is tagged must hold the tagged body part with a hand (e.g., if tagged on the right elbow, the player holds the right elbow) while continuing to dribble. If a player is tagged a second time, he or she must hold that body part with the other hand while continuing to dribble. If the player is tagged a third time, he or she goes to the "hospital"—a designated space outside the dribbling area. At the hospital, the player performs a predetermined task, such as 10 step-ups. Once all "injuries" are healed, the player comes back and resumes play.

- **Crows and cranes.** Set up the area with two lines in the middle about five yards apart. Divide the group in half; each half stands on one of the lines. Each player has a ball. When their team is called, players dribble to the closest endline. The other team tries to chase and tag them, moving without their balls, before the dribbling team can cross the endline. After each turn, regroup and call a different team.

- **Crab soccer.** Divide the group in half. One half is in the middle of the space in crab position. The other half lines up on one of the endlines; each player has a ball. On command, the players with the balls try to dribble to the other end of the space. The crabs try to catch the dribblers by trapping the balls between their legs and feet. When a crab successfully traps a dribbler's ball or the ball goes out of bounds, the dribbler joins the crabs. After all the players are trapped, the two groups change places.

- **Sharks and minnows.** The procedure is the same as crab soccer, but here the sharks are in the middle on their feet, and the minnows are trying to dribble. For a shark to "eat" a minnow, the shark must steal the ball and dribble it out of bounds. For safety, players should not kick the ball away. After the ball is dribbled out of bounds, the minnow becomes a shark.

- **Win the ball.** Divide the team into two groups. Each player in one group has a ball. All players move within the designated space. On the call of "Go!" players leave their balls and try to get another one. Those without balls also try to get one. Every 15 to 20 seconds, yell "Go!" again. Encourage players to go after the balls.

- **Big square–little square.** Create a small square in the middle of the playing space. Inside the small square stand three to four players without balls. All other players have balls and stand outside the small square but within the larger space. Players with balls try to dribble through the smaller square without one of the players inside the smaller square stealing the ball. If the ball is stolen, players change places. Vary the size of the square and number of players in the smaller square.

- **Crazy cones.** Set up cones randomly within the playing space. Each player has a ball. On a signal, players try to pass their balls to hit a cone. Have them count the number of cones they hit. Each time they play, they should try to beat their own numbers.

- **Marbles.** Everyone has a partner, and each player has a ball. The first player passes into a space. The second player tries to pass his or her ball to hit the first player's ball. Hitting a moving ball is worth two points; hitting a stationary ball is worth one point.

- **Between cones.** Two lines of players stand five yards apart. Have no more than three players in a line. Between the two lines, place two cones three yards apart. The first player in one line passes the ball between the cones to the first player in the opposite line. After the pass, the first player goes to the end of the opposite line. Count the number of passes between the two cones. Play one or two touch. When the sequence is stopped, start again and try to improve the number of passes.

• **Windows.** Use cones five yards apart to mark a space. Divide the group of players in half. One group of players stands between the cones that define the space, with one player between every two cones. These players don't have balls. The other players start in the middle, each with a ball. The middle players dribble to a player on the outside, pass the ball, and get it back. They continue to move to another player on the outside and continue the pass sequence. Players should try to go to a different side of the space with each pass. After one minute, have inside and outside players switch places.

Use Observation and Imagination

Perhaps the most important skill that new coaches of youth players can develop is the ability to use their powers of observation. The age-appropriate exercises presented here focus on individual ball control and passing and shooting. However, as you implement these activities into skill-development practices, observe how your players react to them. You might see ways to tweak the activities to make them either easier or more difficult. Ask players for suggestions on other ways to modify the activity.

Although it must be done with discretion, coaches might occasionally want to divide players by ability so that each small group can experience success based on their ability level. Doing this might build player confidence, though it has its obvious risks.

Role of the Expert Coach

There's little question that people with expert knowledge of the game can and should lend that expertise to the youth coaching organization, particularly when they have attended residential coaching courses and understand both coaching methodology and age-appropriate activity.

Many of these suggestions need oversight in terms of implementation. A good first step is for the expert coach to offer either an NSCAA Youth Diploma or similar course that stresses the basics of youth coaching including

- practice organization (warm-up, fundamental technical work, gamelike activity, small game, cool-down);
- coaching methods (coaching position, organization of players, use of helpers, introduction, demonstration of activity, corrective process, activity recap, rules instruction);

- safety issues (spacing of group, first aid and liability issues related to treatment of injuries); and
- team administration (equipment issues, game administration, scheduling, organization of teams for games, meeting with parents to discuss seasonal objectives and expectations).

While working on this chapter, I met a woman who started coaching youth soccer when her children played and who has remained involved ever since. When she saw the material I needed to copy, she asked what it was.

"Oh, I'm writing a chapter on coaching youth soccer for a coaching book," I replied.

Smiling, she said, "Well, I hope you tell them that the most important thing is that the kids have fun."

I couldn't have said it better myself. Fun *is* the key element in youth soccer because without it children won't come back for more.

II

Program Development and Management

CHAPTER 4

Organizing and Orchestrating a Winning Program

Anson Dorrance

What does it mean to have a winning program? One obvious measure of success is a positive win–loss record that is consistent over time. Less obvious measures might involve blending high-level athletics with academic achievement, producing professional or national team players, or even creating an environment conducive to simply enjoying the rewards of playing the game and being part of a team.

However, the true definition of a winning program is much deeper, yet in a sense, much more basic. By this definition, any and every program—male or female, any age, and at any competitive level—can be a winning one.

Often, thinking narrowly, we attribute the win–loss percentage or the number of championships as the definition of success in sports. But this kind of success is ephemeral and not truly profound if it doesn't translate to something greater and more meaningful.

The game of soccer can offer a larger experience. This belief is reflected in a short passage I wrote for the introduction to my book *The Vision of a Champion*: "Your heart doesn't understand systems or shape or tactics, but it bleeds an indefatigable human spirit and, if it's strong enough, it 'grinds' away in our game for 90 minutes, or sometimes 150, if necessary. This spirit goes beyond sport. It is the athletic experience at its best."

Maybe you think it's easy to make such a statement considering our winning records at the University of North Carolina (UNC) and with the U.S.

---

* Written with assistence from Gloria Averbuch.

women's national team. We're winners, regardless, you might think. The numbers prove it. But, no—I'd consider our program a failure if it didn't transcend mere championship titles and exemplify winning at a more profound level. What's more, I believe that it is because of, not in spite of, this larger view of winning that we can experience success on the field. That's because winning begins with the right attitude, philosophy, and core values.

No team wins all the time, not even UNC. But at UNC, we strive to recognize our victories, even in defeat. Lee Montgomery wrote a great newspaper article for the *Durham Herald-Times* about our NCAA championship loss to the University of Florida in 1998. The piece really captured my definition of victory in defeat. Montgomery interviewed one player after another and asked himself, "Where are the frowns, the tears, the disappointment?" The theme of the article was his surprise at the lack of reactions customarily attributed to a team following a close loss such as the one we had experienced. I was proud of the way the players graciously praised the victor that day. Their conduct and exhibited values marked our program's success. The reporter's conclusion to his piece painted a picture of what I consider a winning program: "If you believe that friendship and encouragement and love is what matters in your life, here's your team."

A winning program is based on the philosophy that for athletics to have real value, true winning must occur primarily in environments off the field. The value of the game is in its challenges and the adversities you overcome. These construct character that permits you to win in the important arenas in life. Sport in and of itself does not have deep value. It is what the experience of sports can lead to that gives it depth. Even long after your team has moved on, this kind of winning endures.

One of my favorite descriptions of our program is from Mia Hamm, who wrote the foreword to *The Vision of a Champion*: "From the beginning, I knew I had made the right decision to attend UNC . . . the true reason I went there was because it is through this game that we learn the importance of human relationships."

Winning On and Off the Field

Obviously part of the measure of success in athletics is based on how you organize people in order to win on the field. In addition to coaching knowledge and experience, as a coach, you need the ability to create a winning environment, which depends on how you focus and organize your time, how you relate to people, how hard you work, and how you inspire others to do the same.

Ultimately, establishing and conducting yourself by your philosophy of a winning program can translate to creating winners on the field. The best example of this happened in one of our games. We were coming off a loss to

North Carolina State and were down a goal against Clemson at the half. In this situation, a coach's first instinct is to construct a formula or method of motivation to get the players to win the game. You try to inspire them. You also make some tactical suggestions about how to break the other team. We certainly did a bit of that in the locker room at half time. But I also changed the emphasis to a personal integrity issue, which is a part of a coaching philosophy and a process that builds character. The goal presented to the team at the half was not so much to win the game; I actually threw that out as irrelevant at that point. The challenge I gave them was to elevate themselves as expressed by their ability to dominate whatever amount of space on the field they could. If they could dominate only the two or three yards around them, I made it clear that the others would have to pick up their slack and carry them. This emphasized a character issue of personal responsibility.

Ultimately, I wanted each player to dominate as much territory as possible within each zone and express her player personality. Thus far in the game I had seen the opposite—our team deferring to the player personalities of the opposition and "hiding" from the game. All I asked for in the second half was that the players find something within themselves that was worth expressing. I wanted them to express themselves in a dominant form, and thus cover as much of the field as they possibly could.

In the first half, shot totals were Clemson's 9 to UNC's 7. If memory serves, in the game after halftime, including a full overtime and three minutes of a second overtime (when we won 2 to 1 on a golden goal), shot totals were Clemson's 1 to UNC's 14.

After halftime, we looked at the game differently. We weren't thinking so much about winning as we were about creating ways to express what made us unique. What inspired this victory was an understanding that not only are domination and teamwork driving forces of success, but that the deeper human qualities of personal responsibility, self-expression, passion, and inner strength can be even greater factors. Like our "competitive cauldron," a purposeful but supportive competitive environment, the beauty of this mentality is that anyone can adopt it. By simply deciding not to emphasize winning in a traditional sense (because ultimately, of course, none of us can control that; that's the nature of this game), an environment is created in which everyone can triumph.

As coaches, we must understand our obligation. It's not so much to win games as to elevate people to their potential. If in the process of doing that we win the game, then that's how potential has been expressed. But there are many situations in which everyone is elevated to his or her potential, and we're still not going to win. Within those games there can still be triumph because we have succeeded to inspire the team to play the best that it can.

Four Steps to a Winning Program

1. Create a winning philosophy of personal responsibility.
2. Communicate that philosophy to everyone involved in the program at every opportunity.
3. Surround yourself with those who can help you implement that philosophy.
4. Get every player to be personally accountable and live by the philosophy of the program.

A Winning Network

A winning program is built on a foundation of people, those with whom you work and interact. When constructing a staff, choose carefully, including in your choices of assistant coach, goalkeeper trainer, managers, the secretary in your office—everyone you permit to affiliate with your team. Hire people with qualities that make them worth associating with—they too are going to be a reflection of your team.

Part of your responsibility as the leader is to set a standard in everything you do in your daily conduct and in the way you treat people. This should also be the case for your staff. You want a collection of people with class. The best definition of "class" I've ever heard was from one of my managers (which reflects why he's a valuable staff member). He said, "Class is demonstrated when you do something for someone who can do nothing for you."

Among those with whom you surround yourself, everyone will have strengths and weaknesses. In a leadership lecture by Doug Williamson, a national staff coach of the NSCAA, I learned something fundamental. Surround yourself with people who are strong where you are weak. The ideal staff is not necessarily made up of those who are exactly like you. In fact, you should select people who are different from you, incredibly strong where you are incredibly weak. Then let those people run the areas in which they excel; have the humility to defer to them in their areas of strength. In this kind of leadership environment, there might be some conflict, but it's not negative conflict. It's positive because it results in the best situation and a strong foundation for the program. We must all humble ourselves for the good of the team.

Finally, try to surround yourself with people you enjoy being with so that you look forward to every part of your association with them. This is true of all the people in your program.

A winning program also depends on your relationship with the administration and its support of you. Some coaches would like to feel they are above the politics of the environment, but they're not. The days of the Vince Lombardi style of coaching—dictatorial fiefdoms ruled with an iron fist in which no one could question anything, and no reasons had to be given—are long gone. The landscape has changed. Today, this style is an inappropriate and ineffective way to maximize people's deepest potential.

As a coach, you have to come to your own conclusion about what constitutes a valuable administration. My ideal is administrators who feel that it's their function to make me most effective. Sometimes, the type of people who sit in administrative positions of power set about making it clear how different or lower your position is. They lose sight of their true mission, which is to make you function better. Keep in mind that in athletics, the teams are the front lines. The stronger the front line, the better we can overcome the hurdles placed in our way to prevent us from becoming the most effective coaches.

Your task is to communicate to your administration that you're all on the same team, trying to go in the same direction, and that you should work together to establish whatever makes both your lives easier. If it's the administrator's emphasis that you run the program a certain way, it's your responsibility to do so. It's also your responsibility to communicate how administrators can, in turn, help you achieve your goals. In other words, working well together is a dual responsibility. Each person's ability to communicate is essential.

From early in my coaching career at UNC, I recall one rancorous dispute over the use and abuse of my playing fields by the football team. An associate athletic director at the time ultimately said to me, "There's a holy trinity: football on one side, basketball on the other, and the athletic director in the middle. If we take a telescope and look beneath us, we might see the top of your head." This adversarial attitude, although hilarious to me at the time, was not productive for anyone. After various disagreements and recriminations, I continued to communicate, both verbally and eventually in writing, to this associate athletic director and to our mutual boss. I emphasized how the position he was placing us all in was inappropriate and absurd. Ultimately, his demeanor changed, and our relationship benefited.

If you want to create a truly extraordinary community, you have to understand the forces and various personalities at work and recruit them to support your efforts. That means becoming a politician in a positive sense and working the politics of your environment. This includes the administration, players, staff, and all their family members—because they all interact with one another and influence each other. All of us who lead teams seek to construct positive environments. As best we can, we want to give family and supporters ownership, a part in what we're trying to do. If nothing else, this communicates to them that we value their roles and respect their places in our community.

Budgeting

Another important aspect of administration is budgets. Because it doesn't generate revenue, collegiate soccer is in a difficult financial position. We can have no delusions or illusions of grandeur. At UNC, for example, we recognize that we're living by the grace of football, basketball, and a generous athletic director. No matter how little funding you're allotted, however, you can still have a successful program. With enough initiative, your results can be rewarding beyond the money you raise.

A percentage of our annual girls' summer soccer camp profits goes to our program. Many of our coaches at these camps are current or former UNC players. We also supplement our budget by having the team work the UNC basketball concessions stand every year. What I like about this is that it teaches our players to give back. A big problem with some talented athletes is that they believe they deserve special consideration, that the world owes them something. Yes, they have a gift, but it's not an entitlement, and these young people need to learn to be gracious to those who have contributed to that gift. Working the concession stand builds team spirit, boosts our budget, and provides a great lesson in giving back.

A Winning System

A larger philosophy of winning affects how you conduct your program, no matter what the specifics, such as systems or styles of play. In all areas, you set standards for the core values described, values that are monitored in various ways. At UNC, we do this in a choreographed fashion. *Choreography* is the word I use because my wife is a dancer and because in our program we pride ourselves on methodical attention to detail, of which extensive scripting is a part.

Our system* is built on monitoring all aspects of player training, for the benefit of the players, so that they can concretely understand their progress. We call it the competitive matrix—a series in which all soccer skills and fitness tests are charted and posted for the entire team to see. There are well-defined, seasonal training blocks in all areas of the game that work in conjunction with the competitive matrix. The matrix and training blocks are an extension of the competitive cauldron created to address the perennial problem of female players not being socialized to possess the type of competitive drive we know to be a big part of success in athletics. However, this system of creating competition among teammates, and of keeping track of it, can be just as useful in men's programs. In fact, that is where I originally got it, from watching the legendary UNC basketball coach, Dean Smith, who always held his players similarly accountable.

---

* All of these systems are defined in great detail in my books *The Vision of a Champion* (Clock Tower Press, 2002) and *Training Soccer Champions* (JTC Sports, 1996).

As everything we do in our program is an extension of the core values described in this chapter, we believe our training system defines and teaches personal responsibility and accountability, commitment to one's self and to teammates, discipline, dedication, and the wonderful mental and physical intensity that are hallmarks of successful teams. Success, however, also comes from an understanding that we are first and foremost a collection of caring, sharing human beings. Our program includes a lot of personal support and socializing, and an open invitation to families and friends to participate as well.

As coaches, we are first and foremost educators—especially those of us who work in educational systems and academic institutions. The development of our core values happens year-round at UNC, on and off the field. In the off-season, we conduct classes and invite guest lecturers on topics such as leadership and self-development. Players have required reading, and we encourage discussion and self-discovery in these groups. These classes and meetings also contribute to our team bonding.

The Communication Key

Much like running a business, running a winning program depends on the foundation of frequent and effective communication. For us, this begins with our players.

In addition to group meetings, at least three times a year I conduct meetings with each team member to discuss both academic and soccer progress. The purpose of these meetings is to hold players accountable and to set goals and challenges. However, these are not dry sessions using merely matrix charts and GPAs. These meetings create and develop a connection. Part of what I want to share is my interest and concern for those involved. It is important my players sense that ours is not a bloodless community, but a community based on respect and affection.

Every aspect of your program will benefit from extensive and inclusive communication, which at its core should be positive. Communication helps address a myriad of potential problems, from playing time (I always preannounce substitution patterns so there are no surprises) to integrating new players into the team. It helps prevent whining, jealousy, or other potential threats to team chemistry. Communication should also happen all the way down the line, including the families of players when necessary. Even when players and parents are geographically separated, we know the strength of these family relationships from the youth soccer model.

I had a starting player who had been one of our leading scorers since her freshman year. The decision was made to bench her. I knew this decision would have a cataclysmic impact on her and her family, so before benching her, I called her parents to share with them what was about to happen and why, to prepare them for the tearful phone call from their daughter.

Because I believe one of the crucial qualities of leadership is the capacity to provide hope, I also told them what their daughter needed to do to win her spot back. I needed their support. The critical point was to see how this player reacted to this test of her inner reserves, so I recruited her parents to take part in the construction of their daughter's character.

Even though communication is vital, and I don't want to detract from its value, the most important quality to have is a fundamental understanding of your role, your values, and your motivation.

I'm a convert to the Mormon Church. I converted after missionaries came to my family with the simplest of messages. Before that, we had gone through about five sets of missionaries. Even though these people were very articulate, inspirational, and deep spiritually, they did not completely succeed. The irony is that the missionary who finally convinced my wife and I to convert might have been the least sophisticated and the worst communicator of them all. What he had was a passion that wasn't expressed through elaborate phraseology, so please don't feel that to be compelling, you have to be brilliant in everything you say.

As with this missionary, your word choices can be incredibly basic and simple but the message undeniably clear. Words aren't everything. All of us have known people who could be verbally compelling but not be admirable. Not all coaches have to be remarkable communicators. What you do need is a fundamental understanding of what helps people succeed. This can be conveyed through actions and deeds as well as words.

In addition, when you have a supportive staff in place and a consistent mission, your staff can be recruited to maintain a strong and active communication network.

The Ultimate Leadership Role

As a coach, you're a leader. Your model of leadership is one that extends to everyone, from your players to your staff and all those involved with the team.

A winning program is defined by the way all the leaders (coaches, players, administrators) handle triumph and defeat. It's in the way your leaders assume personal responsibility and accountability. It's in the style and level at which you set your standards and the way you aspire and motivate others to achieve them. All of these qualities are a part of the positive construction of sport. Successfully achieving them creates a winning program.

I heard a great talk given by Tim Carter, who at the time was the director of youth development for the U.S. Soccer Federation. He had just come back from a whirlwind research project in which he evaluated player development in some of the world's most famous soccer programs to gather ideas and bring them back to the United States. His conclusion was simultaneously very simple and yet incredibly profound. Obviously, these great programs were doing some things differently and had varying philosophies on player development, but this was not the most critical area. What was consistent among them was the quality of the people they had instructing. Based on interview and observation, Tim concluded that the prominent reason for their success was the ability of those who were coaching the young players. It boils down to strength of leadership, including enthusiasm, passion, commitment, connection—all the many ways that people inspire and motivate others.

Effective Leadership

- Be the guiding force that sets the tone for your program.
- Lead with your personality. Players and staff will benefit by seeing your humanity.
- Take personal responsibility for all failures with your program. This example will encourage your players to become similarly accountable.
- Communicate your compassion and enthusiasm.

Winning Programs Keep on Winning

Perhaps nothing better defines the success of our program than the wise and wonderful words of those who have gone through it. *The Vision of a Champion* includes powerful testimony on a range of topics by a dozen of the great players who have attended UNC. Here are some comments from one of them, Angela Kelly, that exemplify the idea that a true winning program keeps on winning long after the players leave it.

> Maybe we were just so lucky that at North Carolina we would have died for one another because we genuinely cared about each other. Expressing that on the field, working our butts off in practice and in games, day in and day out, was just our way of telling each other that we cared and everyone meant so much. No one would have dared to give any less than 100 percent when that Carolina shirt was on her back. . . . At the expense of talking for my friends, there isn't one of us—Vench (Tisha Venturini), Mia (Hamm), Lil (Kristine Lilly), or myself—who wouldn't love to have those days back. Just to feel connected again.

CHAPTER 5

Establishing a Successful Club Program

Charlie Slagle

A successful club program depends on five primary objectives. The first is to grow the game. The United States still lags behind much of the world in attracting and retaining the best soccer players. Although soccer has made great strides in becoming the starter sport for a certain segment of the population, another huge segment is still missing out. Clubs must reach out to the underserved soccer communities and take the game to them. Once clubs have attracted the children of these communities, they must retain them as they get older.

The second objective is to set standards of behavior that contribute to a child's personal development. Sport is a great way to instill values in our youth, and clubs must hold themselves to a high standard toward meeting this challenge. Positive values develop over time as children learn from their coaches and parents, referees, and other players. If clubs tolerate poor behavior, children learn that such behavior is acceptable.

Third, clubs should develop the latent soccer abilities of all players. Soccer is a lifetime sport; many players continue to play the game into adulthood. It's the club's responsibility to work to develop all players to their potential, regardless of their abilities. Eventually, these young players become the parents, coaches, and referees of the next soccer generation. These future leaders need a background that promotes the continued growth of the game.

Fourth, clubs must take the responsibility to foster a love for the game. This entails providing opportunities for children and parents to enjoy the excitement of soccer. Such opportunities might include traveling to regional tournaments and attending high-level soccer matches as spectators.

Fifth, and most important, clubs must always remember the importance of allowing players to have fun. Soccer is a game, not a chore. If children are having fun, many of your other objectives are easier to achieve. Children want to have fun, and adults want them to have fun. But too often adults unwittingly emphasize success or another objective over enjoyment. It's the club's responsibility to create a fun, healthy environment for playing this great game.

Creating a Full-Service Club

Typically, the most successful soccer clubs are full-service clubs that provide opportunities for all ages and levels, including Recreation, Challenge, Classic, and Adult soccer. Recreation soccer is important because it provides the building blocks of the game for young participants. As participants get older, Recreation leagues provide an outlet for less gifted or less committed players to continue to have fun and receive the physical benefits of the game. With research showing that young adults in the United States are becoming less physically fit, recreational soccer's value is increasing.

The Challenge program links the Recreation and Classic programs. Challenge adds a higher level of competition than Recreation soccer without equaling the commitment required for Classic soccer. Clubs and associations must be careful not to begin this level too early because the tryout selection process can be very difficult for young players to handle.

The Classic program provides an outlet for the most talented and committed players to continue their soccer development. This program should have talented and dedicated coaches leading these young, gifted athletes. The program should allow talented players to reach their full potential.

Adult soccer is a continuation of the entire process but also provides a place for recruitment of qualified coaches and referees. The Adult league allows interested former youth soccer players to continue to play the game they love but also provides for new adult players to learn the game. Many of these new players will be parents of the club's youth players. Their participation creates an appreciation of the game that their children are playing.

A full-service club has control of its officials. A well-trained group of soccer officials adds to the enjoyment and education of young players and their families. In contrast, a poor group of officials turns families away from the game. Clubs that control the referees for Recreation and Challenge leagues can emphasize particular aspects of the game and identify sideline behaviors that need improvement. A club that controls its own officials can require that older players in the Classic and Challenge leagues be certified at a certain age. Obviously, this increases the pool of officials but also produces a group of players who understand the rules of the game and the difficulties of refereeing a game.

A full-service club sponsors tournaments and summer leagues. Tournaments bring different competition to the local teams and are a source of income for the organization. Tournaments also help the local community appreciate the immensity of the soccer community. They are not simple undertakings. Much planning and many volunteer hours are needed to run a successful tournament. Summer leagues allow players to play with a new set of teammates and new coaches, which broadens the players' soccer experiences.

Full-service clubs should also sponsor spectator opportunities in the local community and surrounding areas. Young players should see higher levels of competition. A higher level of play might be found at a high school or older club game or, for older players, at a college or professional game. The value of watching the game of soccer is lost on many of our players in this country. It's definitely worthwhile for clubs to encourage attendance at spectator events and emphasize the learning possibilities of such events.

Clubs should also reach outside their community to provide clinic opportunities. Clinics with high-level players or college coaches bring a different focus to serious players. Clubs should offer camps or academies that provide excellent instruction. Such activities are needed to offer a different perspective to the game for young players.

Clubs should make an effort to include all groups. Outreach programs are needed in underserved or economically depressed areas. It's important to provide services in local neighborhoods so that communities begin to realize the positive impact organized soccer can have. It's equally important for clubs to reach out to the challenged individuals in the local community and provide opportunities for instruction and play in the game.

Full-service clubs must have quality fields accessible for their programs. This means acquiring land (ideally via donation) and developing it into quality pitches. It means partnering with cities, towns, and counties to provide space in parks for the use of the soccer community. It can also mean sharing space with schools and other sport programs. A successful soccer league works on field development on an ongoing basis.

Player Training

Running a successful full-service club requires a great deal of work in many areas. However, none of this matters if the club does not provide the proper training of its players at all levels. The development of players breaks into seven age categories: instruction age bracket, transition age bracket, separation age bracket, decision age bracket, preparation stage, continuation stage, and adult league.

Instruction Age Bracket

The instruction age bracket is from under 5 to under 8 years old. At this point, the club introduces the game to the participants. The overriding concern is that players have fun with the game. At the under 5-and-6 level, groups of 15 to 25 players should meet once a week for a little over an hour.

There should be adult supervision in about a 4:1 ratio. Parents of children in the group can supervise if they have been trained. A typical session is 30 minutes of fun instructional soccer followed by a series of mini-games of 3 v 3. No score is kept, and teams constantly rotate so that everyone gets to play with everyone. Use small pop-up goals or cones as goals. Praise children for all of their positive activity in the game. Games should be part of the overall learning experience of the event. Focus on the children having fun and staying active.

The under 7-and-8 level has teams that play other teams. There should be about nine players on a team. The game is played 5 v 5 with or without goalkeepers. If you use goalkeepers, the goals should be 6 feet by 12 feet. If no goalkeepers are used, use pop-up goals or cones. Coaches are allowed on the field and are encouraged to stop the game for teaching points. The score of the game and league standings are not recorded. Players practice once a week for about 75 minutes. Practices should stay active and include plenty of playing time in competitive games with team members. Once again, focus on the children having fun and staying active.

Transition Age Bracket

The transition age bracket includes children from under 9 to under 10. They practice once a week and play one game a week. Games are 8 v 8 and refereed by a single official. Teams have a maximum of 14 players. At this age bracket, the concept of winning as a team is introduced. Score is kept, and league standings are compiled. Because scores are kept, sideline behavior becomes a factor; strict spectator conduct rules should be enforced. Clubs need to be proactive at this stage to establish proper decorum guidelines that stay with the children throughout their playing careers. Clubs should hold clinics for parents; they should publish a code of conduct rules for spectators and should enforce these rules. Practices focus on a higher level of technique development and introduce basic tactics. Still make ample time for competitive games during practice.

During this transition stage, clubs should offer advanced training pools for the committed and talented children of this age bracket. These sessions allow players to get an extra session per week to improve their skills above and beyond their recreational team practices.

Separation Age Bracket

The separation age bracket is for children from under 11 to under 13. At this stage, players and families have the option to play at all three levels of the youth club. Parents decide where their child fits athletically and how well each level fits into the dynamic of their family. Children develop at different rates, so at this age level, no decision is necessarily a final decision as to where the child's soccer career will lead.

Players and families who choose to play the Classic level don't automatically stay at this level throughout their youth playing years. Many factors, including physical and emotional development, influence what happens over the next few years. The same is true with players and families who choose Challenge or who continue with Recreation soccer. A child might develop a strong desire to become a better soccer player and move into the next level, or the opposite could happen. These are unsettled years in a child's life, with many changes occurring.

At the separation stage, Classic teams start playing nearby travel games and participate in a few local tournaments. Practices are three times per week for 90 minutes each. Technique is stressed heavily in practices and games. Tactical work consists of general tactics only and should not be used as a shortcut to victories. Team success at this age is not as important as player development. Tactical shortcuts can hinder the development of individual technique. At this stage, success is measured by player development, not by wins and losses. Coaches at the separation level should be independent contractors paid by the club through monthly dues assessed to the families of the players.

Challenge teams at this age bracket play in the club's Challenge league, which is established with parity in mind. Player development is enhanced through competitive games. Players practice twice weekly and have one game per week. Coaches are qualified volunteers who have been trained in instructing the age group. Challenge players might play a few local tournaments and compete in the league. Once again, player development is paramount. Practices should be upbeat and emphasize technique. General tactics are taught, and each practice includes competitive games.

The Recreation teams at the separation age bracket will be diluted in talent because some of their more competitive former teammates have moved on. Many of the better players will opt for the Challenge or Classic level, and the talent pool is not as deep. This allows some of the better players to change their roles on the team. Players who were good players before might now be the stars of the team. This change in dynamic could lead some players to pursue the next level as they develop into committed and talented players. The Recreation level plays 11 v 11 and has one full-field game and one practice a week. Coaches are trained volunteers; the focus is on technique development and enjoyment.

Decision Age Bracket

The decision age bracket includes youth from under 13 to under 15. (Note that there's an age overlap with the separation stage.) At this stage, players decide what soccer means to them. Teenagers have more options available to them than they had earlier in their lives, and they need to make a decision on how important the game is to them. The club should still provide soccer at all levels.

The Recreation league becomes more of an intramural league in which players play for the fun of getting outside and having a good time with a group of friends. Score is kept, and coaches provide a fun environment for the players. These age brackets can play anywhere from 7 v 7 to 11 v 11, depending on the size of the club and the financial commitment the club can expect from the players' families.

The Challenge level continues with 11 v 11, but there are fewer teams because former players have found new ways to spend their time. Classic teams continue to increase the intensity as teams travel farther from home for games within the state and for tournaments outside the local area. The increase in intensity is reflected in practices, as technique development emphasizes a lack of time and space. More complex individual and team tactics are taught.

Preparation Stage

The preparation stage gets kids ready for the next level age bracket; this stage is for youths under 15 to under 18 and pertains mainly to Classic levels and, to a lesser extent, Challenge levels. This step at the Classic level is to prepare players for the next level, which, in most cases, is the college game but could also be professional soccer. Intensity and competition are at the highest levels. Coaches challenge players to reach their full playing potential.

Challenge players in this age bracket strive to play at the next level, which might be high school or, in some cases, college soccer. Challenge players should be pushed to reach their potential. At this age bracket, recreational soccer is still important but should be treated as a fun, well-organized intramural activity.

Continuation Stage

The continuation stage is for those players who are out of high school and are playing at some higher level. This group is provided playing and training opportunities during the summer. They are enlisted to help develop the next generation of the club's players by assisting with clinics and camps.

Adult League

The last stage is the Adult league, in which the club allows players to continue playing the game they love. If size permits, clubs provide both competitive men's and women's leagues and secondary men's and women's leagues to allow players of all ability levels to enjoy the game. If possible, over-30 and over-40 leagues are included. Clubs also should provide coed leagues.

Budgets and Public Relations

Providing all of the programs discussed is a mammoth proposition compounded by the need to mesh all of these facets together. Whenever a club has more than one level of play, there will be people who assume they are not getting their money's worth. To neutralize this perception, clubs must be up front and publish timely financial reports. Clubs should not force members to support another level of the club. Recreation-league dollars need to be spent for Recreation programs, Challenge dollars for Challenge programs, and so on. In fact, each age bracket of every level must pay for itself and not be supported by another age bracket of that same level.

Clubs need to detail where each dollar is spent and establish fees accordingly. Some items, such as state association fees, payment of referees, and salaries of personnel who run that level of the club, are easily calculated. Other items, such as field use (including wear and tear to the field), shared expenses, including shared personnel expenses, and revenue production require assumptions to be made and clarified. The club should publish this data and be ready to justify it. By publishing their fiscal data, clubs keep their members informed and secure, with the hope they become more loyal to the organization.

Each club must determine its own rules and, depending on the size of the club, make decisions on any exceptions to the rules. In general, the larger the club, the fewer exceptions that should be made. In the early stages of recreational soccer, many parents feel that their children are not playing at the appropriate level because they're more talented than the rest of the league. Leagues should not make exceptions to their rules if players are playing at the appropriate age or grade level by rule. If taken to the extreme, the under-7 level would be full of under-6 kids because once one child moves to an older age bracket, other parents feel that family and child received special treatment. The club needs to remember that at this age, youth soccer is as much about socializing as it is about soccer. Thus, children should play in their appropriate age or grade level.

Clubs should establish their rules after careful consideration and with the help of board members. The club should use its board members to establish policy because this helps create a feeling of ownership by the membership. Many clubs make the mistake of mandating rules from on high and leave themselves open to second-guessing by the membership. A similar policy adopted by a member board receives better acceptance by the membership.

Clubs must realize that they are providing a service for their members, and their members are paying for that service. Costs should be kept at a reasonable level. The administration of tournaments and fund-raising can help this situation. Clubs must realize that even though club soccer has become a business, there's great value in encouraging members to volunteer. Fund-raising and tournament events are more successful when staffed by dedicated volunteers. Clubs should use the resources of their membership to reach its full potential.

Another aspect that must be considered is member-based creativity in programs. Too many clubs repeat the same program until it becomes stale. A program is not always justified just because another club has done it before. Clubs need to be responsive to their membership. Members generally have plenty of great ideas for both the short- and long-term success of the club. (These ideas might be hidden in a deluge of many other not-so-great ideas, however!) The club needs to examine new ways of doing things. Taking suggestions to club staff and then to member boards helps sift out good ideas. In encouraging member dialogue, clubs should make decisions based on what's right for a situation, not based on what some other club is doing.

Staffing

A successful club's administrative staff includes registration, finance, scheduling, and support personnel. The staff should respond to members' needs in a timely fashion.

The next group is the coaching staff. The primary purpose of the coaching staff is to train coaches at the various levels. A systematic coaching curriculum should be devised and implemented. Coaching various ages and levels of play requires different coaching talents, philosophies, and demeanors. These fundamentals need to be taught to the appropriate coaches at the time they are coaching that age bracket. This systematic approach allows for a continuum that enhances the club in both the short and long term. The coaching staff will also set basic coaching goals for each level of play.

If possible, clubs also need a fund-raising staff. To make youth soccer as affordable as possible, funds need to be garnered from the local community. Many businesses and individuals will support youth soccer because of the benefits derived from participation. Businesses like to be aligned with positive youth organizations.

Clubs should encourage volunteers to help in all operations. All communities have many talented individuals associated with clubs who can make great contributions. In small clubs, volunteers fill many staff positions. The larger the volunteer base, the stronger the club.

Many clubs fear competition from neighboring clubs. However, strong neighboring clubs force good clubs to become great clubs. Of course, strong neighboring clubs can also force average clubs to become former clubs. Clubs need to stick to their child-development philosophy both on and off the field. If clubs stick to that principle and work at making their club the best it can be, they'll generally flourish.

To summarize, a successful club provides levels of play for all abilities and ages. Soccer is a great sport that can continue well into adult life. The foundations for continuance are formed in our youth leagues and clubs. Depending on the size of the club, some will be unable to provide full service in all areas.

A basic tenet for clubs to follow is to stick to its established principles. They should not take shortcuts to achieve temporary success and should not favor one level or group at the expense of another. Clubs might lose some families who feel they've been treated poorly, but if the club sticks to its principles and guidelines, it will gain and retain far more families than it loses, which, in the long run, is what makes the club stronger.

Clubs should make sure that governing agencies at the state and national levels are doing what's best for the youth game. The goal of youth soccer, or any youth activity, should be personal development. If governing groups lose sight of this goal, the club should take the lead in taking corrective action.

Finally, clubs must remember that what they're doing is for the benefit of the youth in the community. This is a time in youths' lives when they should be enjoying activities. Clubs must ensure that their overriding pursuit has their youths' interests in mind. If anything undermines this pursuit, the club needs to step in and correct it.

CHAPTER 6

Building a Recruiting Network

John Rennie and Mike Jacobs

"The carpenter is only as good as his tools." "Coaching is not just about the Xs and Os—it's also about the Johnnys and Joes." "You're not coaching soccer, you're coaching people."

These and other clichés tell the story that the quality of your players largely determines your team's success. If you think coaching ability is the key to winning, that your system or training methods are *the* answer, please share your secret with the rest of us.

As college coaches, we have a very short preseason and only a few days between games to prepare players. Once the match begins, we have less control over the actual game than coaches in any other popular team sport in the United States. College soccer coaches can make substitutions, shout at players from the sideline (and maybe be partially heard!), and make some changes or adjustments at halftime. The vast bulk of our coaching takes place before and after the game. Training sessions belong to the coach, but the game belongs almost exclusively to the players. If you want to be successful, you better have good players and, for the college coach, that means recruiting, recruiting, and more recruiting.

Recruiting is a never-ending process that involves a lot of hard work. It begins with your own personal philosophy on how you want your team to play the game. Then you go out and try very hard to find the players you need to make that vision reality. After finding the players, you try to blend your ideals realistically with their playing abilities. That's when you find out how good a coach you really are. As is often the case, the devil is in the details.

Effective Recruiting

Coaches who are effective at recruiting are able to upgrade weak areas of their teams, replace players who have graduated, and make their teams deeper in areas where they are already strong. Many factors must come together to make for effective recruiting. Knowing what a good player looks like is crucial. Everyone sees the game and players in different ways, so it's imperative to know what kind of technical, tactical, physical, and psychological aspects are important to you as a coach. You also need to know the playing standard of your team because the players you're recruiting have to compete at that standard.

Depending on your conference or nonconference schedule, you might be more successful if you look for players with specific skills rather than just look for the best players available. A player's technical ability is very important, but if your team plays in a physical or athletic conference, you might want to look for players with great physical or athletic ability.

The key is to recruit players who have the right blend of technical ability and athletic skill. The best teams have players who exhibit both of these skills, as well as "piano carriers" and "piano players." Piano carriers are the blue-collar workers on the team who do the heavy lifting. The piano carriers enable the piano players, the skillful artisans on the team, to effectively do their jobs. Every player has to understand his or her place on the team, and it's your job as coach to recruit the right players to fit into each role. A coach who recruits 11 highly technical but diminutive attacking players might find the team struggling defensively for physical reasons. The team that plays 11 big and strong athletic types might have problems scoring. You need to find the right balance in the types of players you recruit.

With the amount of diversity in tactics in today's game, you tend to find coaches looking for players who offer versatility. For example, a coach might try to identify a wide player who can play midfield in a 4-4-2 alignment or as a winger in a 4-3-3 formation. Such versatility is crucial as the game gets more transitional. The more multifaceted players are, the greater flexibility you have in terms of team tactics. As the technical standard of the game in this country continues to improve, the premium on recruitment of two-footed players has reached an all-time high for most coaches.

Your effectiveness in selling your program can be the defining moment toward building your program. Coaches who believe in the product they represent—be it their soccer program, their community, or their university—have the best luck in appealing to players. A genuine belief in your program's success and a sincere feeling about your players' well-being usually attracts players to a program. All student-athletes want to feel wanted by a coach, but what they want even more is to know that they're going to be part of something special.

Former North Carolina State and Iona College basketball coach Jim Valvano used to ask recruiting prospects to "dare to dream," challenging them to come to his university and help bring reality to the aspirations he had for his program. He was looking for players who wanted to help build and establish a program rather than just join a program with an established history or tradition. Because of the ability to sell his recruits on his image, Valvano was able to reach great success at every institution during his coaching career.

Successful recruiters know what they're looking for and where to find it. They also have something to offer players. Understand what makes your university and program special. The easiest programs to recruit to are the ones that have many self-evident features, such as well-established colleges or universities, schools with football or basketball teams that play regularly on national television, or schools that sell merchandise in shopping malls across the country. In the absence of those qualities, really exceptional recruiters are able to find special and unique qualities in their own universities and market those attributes to potential student-athletes.

An unfortunate dilemma that can emerge in the recruiting process is negative recruiting, which is downgrading a rival institution. Coaches using these tactics are usually insecure about their own situations and programs and feel the need to mask that feeling by denigrating other institutions. Prospective student-athletes and their families usually find coaches who use that recruiting style less credible. Often programs develop a bad reputation when coaches use negative recruiting methods.

Prospective student-athletes need to understand the aspects of your school that most appeal to them. Proximity to their hometowns and families, the size of the campus and student body, and areas of study offered by the institution are unlikely to change during the prospective student-athlete's four years at your school. Make sure they have this information. Identify prospects who fit your school's profile. Once you locate candidates who match the profile, explain to the prospects how distinctive your school is. Give the prospect a chance to experience student life on your campus, whether it's meeting with university faculty or staff, attending class, spending time with the student body, or attending a soccer match.

Finding Players

First, identify areas of the country in which you can recruit. Although a number of schools recruit nationally, most schools have more of a regionalized recruiting base. A good way to gauge the area of your regional recruiting base is through contact with the undergraduate admissions office. Most admissions offices keep a demographic chart of the student body. This demographic survey, along with your own analysis of your program's rosters from the past 10 to 15 years, gives you a good idea where your school has the most name recognition and appeal. This helps define the market area for your program. Identify your recruiting area as finitely as you wish. We both recruited in New York City, so we knew the possible pockets for potential players by borough—Manhattan, Staten Island, the Bronx, and so on.

Learn where to find international players. What international students do you have at your university? The NCAA publishes a book titled *The Guide to International Academic Standards for Athletic Eligibility*, which provides all the criteria for international student-athletes to gain NCAA eligibility. It lists standards by country and is an excellent initial resource for recruiting non-U.S. students. Develop a relationship with your international admissions office to determine additional acceptance guidelines and requirements.

Many other factors come into play when establishing a market area for your program, including the religious denomination (if any) of your school, your school's proximity to those schools your team competes against, whether your campus is in an urban or rural setting, and whether your college is a private or public university.

Many prospective student-athletes attend private schools with religious affiliations, and some schools find students attending for religious reasons. A list of high schools in which students have enrolled in the past might be helpful in developing your demographic market area. Guidance counselors or college-bound directors at high schools are often more likely to encourage prospective student-athletes to attend universities where former students have found academic, athletic, and social success.

A factor for most prospective student-athletes is finding the right college environment. The student-athlete might want to be in an environment similar to (or very different from) home. Find out if a recruit grew up in a major city or in a rural area. Certainly there are advantages to each way of life, and it's important to convey the strengths of your campus and show how the environment might match what the prospect is looking for.

Many prospective student-athletes want to go to school close to their hometowns so that their families, friends, and supporters can see them play. Some want to attend school away from home but want to know if they'll play close to their hometown now and then. When Southern Methodist University entered the Missouri Valley Conference, it made the very fertile Dallas, Texas, soccer community a viable recruiting territory for rival MVC schools because their prospects knew they would play in their hometowns at least every other year.

Once you have established your market area, learn where the best players are participating in those communities. Check out club programs, Olympic development programs, and high school programs. To assess players in competition, keep a list of teams participating in major tournaments or against other strong teams in these competitive environments. This means researching (1) which teams have been perennially competitive in the area's

state cup championships, high school state, regional, or district championships and (2) which players have participated in the Olympic development
program at the district, state, regional, or national levels. Names that appear
repeatedly on these lists reveal players who have been exposed to a competitive playing standard.

Recruiting Network

Once you know where these players are, the next step is to contact either
the coaches of those programs or the rival coaches. Identify the most competent coaches in the community and develop relationships with them.
Seek their advice, opinions, guidance, and assistance. A high school coach
once told me, "I might not be a great soccer coach, but I've coached enough
collegiate players to know what one looks like." Also, coaches might have
players on their own teams who could contribute to your program or who
have competed against players from other teams, clubs, or programs who
could help you. If you're going to look for exceptional youth or high school
players, why not go to the source of their development?

Another fruitful resource for the college coach is former players who are
now high school or youth coaches. Ask them to help you identify prospects.
They played in your program, so they have a good idea of the kind of players who could be successful.

Friends all over the country are another valuable resource. Even though
we have both relocated throughout our coaching careers, we have been
successful recruiting players from our native New York metropolitan area
because of the friends and connections we left behind.

Get to know and trust the evaluations of other coaches. For young prospects, the most important part of a soccer resume is the reference section.
Awards and accolades look nice on a mantle, but having a competent coach
brings immediate credibility to a player's resume. A number of high school
and youth coaches have prospects worth recruiting based solely on who
mentored them. Knowing who players have played under provides a good
idea of future expectations.

It's not a coincidence that a school's success is related to the presence
of strong club programs in its communities. Clubs provide these schools
a base or foundation from which to build their programs. Over a four-year
period at Iona College, the soccer team had about a dozen players from FC
Westchester teams and another dozen from the Eastern New York Olympic
development program.

There are many ways college coaches can evaluate youth coaches. Most
clubs and their coaches are measured externally by how many championships they win and the success of their players in Olympic development programs, on college teams, or in the professional ranks. Because of
the more extensive playing experiences of our country's youth and high
school coaches, more coaches can influence player development. Although

parents might value the medals won, the college recruiter is more focused on a youth or high school coach's ability to develop players.

The most significant factors in player development are the training environment created by the coach and the level of competition players are exposed to. Some top youth coaches pride themselves on teaching players to play in as many different alignments and in as many different systems as possible. They want to make their players' soccer education extensive so they can adapt and fit into any college program. We once needed to recruit a left-sided player and identified one who played as a left-wing in a 4-3-3 setup, as a wide left-midfielder in a 4-4-2 formation, and as a wingback in a 3-5-2 alignment. Because this young man played in both zone and man-to-man defenses and competed on a team that won a USYSA national championship, we knew he had the versatility needed to compete at the college level.

When coaches seek input on a player, they want an honest answer. Asking a youth or high school coach to assess a player can sometimes be the kiss of death for that coach. If the coach gives a dishonest assessment and the player fails at the next level, it colors his or her future evaluations. Some coaches promote a player mainly to promote themselves or their clubs. The youth and club coaches who are most trusted in recruiting are those who give reliable assessments of players and who won't recommend a player to just any college program. In the United States, we have people working at the youth level who have collegiate coaching experience. They certainly know what a good collegiate prospect looks like.

Depending on your conference or what part of the country your school is in, the style of play in college soccer could be very different from that at the club level. Having someone who already experienced coaching at your level is of more value than someone who has limited experience playing, coaching, or spectating collegiate soccer.

Most competitive youth clubs have someone working under the title Director of Coaching. Develop relationships with these individuals and the club's coaches. The director will know the promising players on teams in each age group as well as the team's tournament and event calendars. He or she might be able to give an objective assessment of the player and perhaps provide regular updates on the player's progress. Maintain these club relationships by attending events, watching team practices, or just staying in contact through phone or e-mail.

Feeder System

The relationship between the recruiter and the club coach or director is often mutually beneficial. Most clubs are excited about any college coach's direct involvement with their club. The NCAA restricts any member coach to regularly work with players who live outside a 50-mile radius from that coach's institution. Knowing this limitation sets up an excellent opportunity for the development of a feeder system.

A big plus in working with players within a 50-mile radius is giving players in your school's community a feeling of proprietorship with that school, coach, and soccer program. When players are raised as supporters of a program, it makes it that much more important for them to aspire to attend that college. Raleigh, Durham, and Chapel Hill—the triangle area—have provided a large local youth fan base for Duke University and its men's soccer program. Our program is regularly among the nation's leaders in attendance for Division I men's soccer; it's not uncommon to see children from our youth community at Blue Devil soccer matches.

Giving a club the opportunity to have college coaches and players work with their players, whether as clinicians or as team coaches, brings more credibility to that club's teams as well as exposure and insight into the college game. Because so many parents, families, and clubs focus on the potential for the club experience to open doors to play in college, they value the exposure to college coaches. While serving as a team trainer, coach, or board member, the college coach might also recommend the club's players to colleagues at other colleges or universities.

Depending on availability, the school's facilities might be able to host club training. For many youth players, this could be an early opportunity to visit a college campus and start to formulate an impression about campus life and a future in college.

Working directly with youth players at the club, state, regional, or national levels gives you the most honest assessment of a player because you can see them in a home environment. A college showcase or all-star game is not a natural setting for players. Seeing these players with their regular teammates and in comfortable roles allows a much more accurate assessment. Watching how they behave in training gives you a chance to assess their work rate and such attributes as how coachable they are. Seeing them off the field, whether it's during a meal or just hanging out in a hotel or dormitory, allows you to evaluate them in social settings.

Recruiting is hard work. For the best recruiters, it's a process that continues all year. The hours spent during this process might seem thankless at times, but you reap the benefits when the season kicks off and the emphasis is back where it belongs—on the players. After all, no matter how good a coach you are, the players will win the games.

CHAPTER 7

Marketing and Promoting Your Program

Joe Morrone

You can't run an athletic program without a clear and consistent coaching philosophy. You also must know your own personal strengths and weaknesses, trying to maximize the first while minimizing the second. You base your style on your athletic experiences, doing your best to avoid the negative approaches you've witnessed and to mirror the positive techniques of successful coaches and individuals you have admired.

At a personal level, coaches should ask themselves how they wish to be perceived and why they are coaching. At a professional level, every soccer coach should have a basic goal of imparting real-life skills to their athletes. To achieve this, the coach needs to assess the program and develop short- and long-term goals that sharpen life skills while promoting the program and the sport.

Developing the Program

The coach starts at the program's core—the players—then steadily moves out from the core to influence change and improvement within the school or club and expand the program's reach to the local community, the state, and even perhaps the country. Anything and everything is possible!

Marketing starts at the top. Are your goals compatible with those of department and school administration? If not (and most soccer coaches are in this situation), you need to be organized, creative, positive, and persistent. You also need a well-constructed marketing plan.

In most situations, you need to develop a close, loyal, confident support group. Start with an assistant coach with enough confidence to privately offer constructive criticism but publicly support you and your program. You'll also need a well-organized secretarial staff (perhaps aided by student help) to perform the myriad tasks involved in soccer marketing.

Before you can market your program with much success, you need a successful team. Whether you're in a school or nonschool setting, you need to recruit and keep talented players in your program. In a college setting, establish a working relationship with the admissions office. Understand the criteria established for admission of athletes. Make friends in the financial aid office. The amount and type of aid your program receives determines the success you'll have in attracting quality players. You need to understand what aid is available so you can take full advantage of all opportunities.

Once athletes are on campus, you'll need to interact with other university offices—housing, academic counseling, even food services—to improve your players' overall college experience. The more fulfilling the experience, the better chance each player will become a productive team member.

Scheduling Competitive Games

Try to schedule competitive contests to improve your team and excite the spectators. "To be the best, you must play the best" was our motto at Connecticut.

In 1972, we hosted St. Louis University in our football stadium; by 1975, I was arranging intersectional games between UConn and other New England opponents, providing a monetary guarantee, room, and board (usually in homes of soccer youth players). Our gate receipts allowed us to entice big-time sport schools to Storrs, where we attracted large crowds.

We also switched from playing games on Saturdays to playing intersectional matches on Sundays, avoiding conflicts with football. By separating from football, we gave the media an opportunity to cover both sports, which helped soccer gain press coverage. Most important, it gave our soccer program its own identity. There were now "Soccer Sundays!"

Expanding the Budget

There's never enough money, and without it your mission is a tough haul. Because of tradition, football and basketball will always have money. Soccer and other sports have to work for it. This was true at Connecticut in the early 1970s, when sports were classified as revenue producing or nonrevenue producing. Soccer was classified as nonrevenue along with such activities as swimming and lacrosse. Our budgets were always low.

To raise money, I suggested we erect a fence around our field and charge admission. People couldn't believe I thought students and townspeople would actually *pay* to watch college soccer. "Joe Morrone's fence" became a standing joke in athletic department meetings.

But in 1976, we got our fence. We were one of the first, if not *the* first, schools to charge for admission and parking. I can honestly say that was the single biggest catalyst toward our obtaining a fairer share of the budgetary pie and recognition within the athletic department. And spectators did come to watch, and they *did* pay. Americans tend to believe that if you have to pay for something, it has value; if you don't have to pay, there's no value. We were charging people, so now we had value. Becoming a revenue-producing sport also enabled us to fly annually to intersectional matches, add scholarships, and improve our facilities and equipment. Along with gate admissions and parking, other revenue-producing activities included the following:

- **Raffles.** We held raffles for the benefit of our soccer program, usually involving high-quality items donated to the program for free.
- **Videotapes.** Each season, a highlight tape was prepared as a fund-raising project. Individual game tapes were sold to parents who could not attend matches and even to a local tavern owner, who showed them to his customers. They were also used for recruiting and for keeping a historical record.
- **Food and clothing concessions.** Manned by "Friends of Soccer" volunteers, we set up tables to sell food, drinks, and soccer-related clothing at all home games.
- **Exhibitors.** Our annual two-day indoor tournament attracted many spectators, and we were able to sell exhibit space to vendors.
- **Gifts-in-kind.** Sometimes businesses or individuals don't have cash to contribute but are willing to donate something of value in return for membership perks. An example of this was a bakery that provided donuts for our hospitality tent at home matches.
- **Sponsorships.** There was little of this until the late 1970s, when gradually we attracted commercial support, including backing from Metropolitan Life for both our indoor tournament and our newsletter. Later, Adidas, Diadora, and Lanzera were aligned to supply shoes, clothing, and soccer balls. One of our most important agreements was with Monaco Ford from nearby Glastonbury. The firm had a strong interest in soccer and donated an automobile for my use. At that time, this partnership put soccer on the same level as Connecticut football and basketball.

Establishing a Support Group

Private fund raising is a necessity to supplement your basic budget. Expanding your internal support group to include outside volunteers to help market your program is essential. In our case, that was our Friends of Soccer (FOS) club. Remember, to promote and market, you must make people feel they are important to the program and that their help is invaluable. We did this by adding many activities to appeal to as many segments of the population as possible.

We established a hospitality tent. The FOS club purchased and enclosed two 20 × 20 foot tents. This brought members together at games for food, drink, and camaraderie. The tent areas helped develop a family atmosphere and served as an important perk for joining the club.

We hosted indoor and outdoor tournaments. The indoor tournament culminated the winter training program and brought new teams, fans, and sponsors to the campus. Club labor supported this major fund-raiser.

We kept in touch with former lettermen. A former team captain attended a home game with the first soccer coach at the school, whom I had befriended. Pleased with the attention paid to his old coach and the discipline the team displayed, including their manner during the playing of the national anthem, this gentleman eventually donated two endowments for scholarships and $350,000 as an endowment for the sport. The lesson here is that every aspect of your program is important because you never know whom your program is reaching. In this case, attention to detail meant over a half million dollars for our program. Remember that every graduate is a potential volunteer helper, recruiter, or donor. Lettermen games, reunions, informal functions at other athletic events, special correspondence, and public recognition helped the family concept work for our program.

We organized membership drives. We created computer-generated recruitment letters, including the names of those who bought raffle tickets, to solicit and sustain club membership. We put applications on vehicles in the parking lot. We created special game ticket plans. Special rates were established for families, senior citizens, students, groups, and for reserved seating.

We created special publications, souvenirs, and game programs. We distributed team-schedule posters, wallet-sized cards, bumper stickers, and window decals to promote the team. Themes were printed on the stickers and decals to emphasize a particular club objective. Game programs featured and promoted a different player each game. We published a FOS Newsletter six times a year.

We printed media guides and advertising flyers to promote our player-of-the-year candidates and mailed them to college coaches across the nation. The flyers made other coaches aware of what we were doing in the hope they'd incorporate some of our ideas into their own programs.

We involved the parents of the players. It's important to have a parent committee to act as a liaison between the coach and the players' parents. The committee was available if a parent wished to speak to someone about the program or the school from a parent's perspective.

Based on the total dollars contributed, FOS members could earn rewards including preferred seating behind the team bench; preferred parking adjacent to the game field; access to the hospitality tent and free food and drink; an invitation to the press box, where members could mingle with athletic administrators, game officials, and the press; a subscription to the newsletter, which covered news items from both the soccer program and within FOS; a copy of the media and recruiting guides, which provided facts about everyone connected to the program (donor and sponsor recognition as well); team banquet tickets; and invitations to club-sponsored social activities.

We conducted many activities for members to recognize their contributions, foster camaraderie, and tighten bonds to the program. Members were invited to pre- and postgame functions at school basketball games. They were invited to the club's annual meeting (a short business meeting followed by a barbecue). They were invited to travel to away games. Many members followed the team when they traveled. At some intersectional games, members would set up the hospitality tent. We also organized trips to U.S. National Team and international soccer games. When the team traveled to different areas in the country, the FOS club coordinated with the school's alumni association to participate in university-wide alumni socials. This widened our impact within the university community. Campus and community VIPs were invited to the coach's home to join the team after the last regularly scheduled game. This provided another opportunity to network on the home front.

With the advent of intersectional play, we began to stage joint team meal functions. These gave players and fans from both teams an opportunity to mix in a noncompetitive environment. It was nice to know that after battling for 90 minutes, we could enjoy a team meal together. Plus, these meals gave our younger fans an opportunity to meet the players. By staging this first-class event, we hoped to expand our recruiting horizons as well as aid future scheduling. We also hoped that our opponents would imitate our methods as a means of improving soccer's image. The work we put into every aspect of our soccer program showed everyone that, while we wanted to win, Connecticut soccer was being marketed from a distinct perspective that involved more than just gain for our particular program. We wanted to be ambassadors for the game of soccer.

The major sports all provided a first-class atmosphere for the media. With the aid of a hardware store owner who provided free materials, an architect who drew up plans, a building contractor who paid two foremen to direct construction, and free FOS labor, it took all of one summer to construct a 120-foot long press box valued at $150,000 at no cost to the university.

The facility provided the media a quality facility from which to cover soccer, and it gave the FOS an opportunity to invite selected donors to sit in the press box each game, where they could be acknowledged for their support.

FOS members help us secure scholarships. You must approach your athletic director (AD) to ask for assistance in this area. On the field success can help sway the AD to your side. Also, the perception that there's strength in numbers might work for you when the AD sees you have an organization (FOS) supporting improvement in your program. Your goal should be to get whatever assistance you can get from your administration, then set about raising funds from the private sector for player and team endowments. We did our solicitation for funds via a yearly scholarship appeal in the newsletter and through a series of letters from the scholarship chairperson. Additionally, the FOS membership application listed scholarship opportunities.

FOS members helped improve the facilities. Bleachers were put on one side of the field and eventually around the entire field close to the boundary lines to provide a quality environment for the game. FOS signage identified the special seating section directly behind the UConn bench.

If you want a half-decent playing surface, get the grounds crew on your side. Let them know your needs and communicate them so they understand how the site plays into the overall marketing program. Most important, be generous with your compliments when your needs are met! You want your playing facility to be clean and attractive and parallel the first-class status of other aspects of the soccer marketing effort.

Hosting Special Events

As coach, you must show your interest in marketing and promoting the program by initiating special events and functions, ideally with the assistance of the FOS. For example, we hosted media soccer games. A small-sided preliminary contest pitted the print media against the electronic media. There was a special game program created for the event. Each team had its own game shirts and was coached by a UConn team captain. An all-star team with MVPs was selected and received gear from our team clothing sponsor. Most media people don't know much about soccer. This game gave them an opportunity to experience the game first hand and see that soccer is not as easy to play as it might appear from the press box.

We hosted FOS games. The FOS game was played on the same weekend day as a varsity game. Teams were composed of FOS members and player parents. The format was the same as the media game, with awards to everyone involved.

We hosted alumni games and reunions, building activities around alumni, such as a lettermen social the evening before the game and tickets to other athletic events that weekend. We extended free pregame and halftime entry to the hospitality tent, hosted a brunch after the game, and presented each alumnus with a souvenir gift. We did all this to draw our past players back onto the field and let them know we cared about them. Of course we invited them to become involved with the program, if they weren't already.

We hosted preliminary games and halftime games. We reached out to the local, regional, and statewide communities and invited youth teams to play games before our games or during halftime. We selected teams from several communities to allow as many different teams as possible to participate.

We welcomed the teams to our campus and then promoted our program. Above all, we complimented players on their play and encouraged them to continue playing soccer.

The objective of these games is obvious: to give youth players an opportunity to play on a quality field within a quality atmosphere. This inspires them to improve their play and plants a seed in their minds to attend your school or camp. Give them bumper stickers, posters, or schedule cards to further market your program. Allow them to get autographs after your game.

One weekend game should be used to invite all the youth in the state to attend at no charge. All players through eighth grade fall into this category. Banner contests, soccer-related games in an adjacent field, and even tours of the campus are possibilities that day.

We hosted sponsor days. You should be marketing your program to any commercial entity that enhances your program and their company at once. This can be done in many ways, including adding signage on the field or printing the company logo, message, or name on posters, schedule cards, bumper stickers, Frisbees, individual player cards, media guides, stationery, clothing, equipment, shoes, and other handouts. Also provide company exposure via promotional giveaways—T-shirts, mini soccer balls—and through public address announcements at home games.

Senior recognition day is common in most sports today. We invited families of seniors to attend a specific game. We featured the seniors in the game program and had them walk to midfield after an introduction. We took photos and sent them to those involved. Families were invited to the FOS tent, and all were invited to the postgame meal. We wanted our seniors and families to remember the occasion and continue to be part of our soccer family.

Many team sports host a fan-appreciation day. Select a game at which to give special recognition to your fans. We provided plenty of inexpensive souvenir gifts to those in attendance. Prizes donated by sponsors, supporters in the community, and even the soccer program or FOS were distributed to the fans. Supporters were recognized in the game program, news releases, and on the public address system. In addition to the usual halftime game, fans were invited onto the field to participate in shooting and kicking contests. To directly involve the students on campus, the preliminary game for this day was an intramural game.

In our attempt to reach out to everyone, we offered our facilities during our spring training sessions to the referees in our state for referee clinics. We conducted four one-day tournaments involving four teams each. We gave the referees an opportunity to evaluate and test their new people. This brought the referees to our campus in a pressure-free environment and also provided us with free officiating.

We hosted coaches' clinics. Over the years, we were presenters at clinics and seminars for coaches at all levels. This enabled our coaching staff to espouse our philosophy and objectives while establishing a coaching network. In addition, every high school coach was sent an entry pass to all home games. We wanted to expose them to good soccer.

A meet-the-players event is a good way to introduce new players and reintroduce upperclassmen. Ours was a FOS membership social with pizza and soda. After a preseason exhibition match, the team would mingle with club members, introduce themselves, and share refreshments with those in attendance.

We held our annual team banquet at the end of our winter training; this was the culminating event for our program. The occasion allowed virtually everyone connected with the Connecticut soccer family to be recognized. We made sure players received maximum allowable gifts. Assistant coaches, team managers, trainers, and all other support personnel were recognized. Each FOS executive board member was given a token of appreciation and was publicly acknowledged for their contributions to the program. We recognized and thanked administrators, sponsors, and members of the media. Key community VIPs were guests at the dinner, which concluded with farewell talks by each senior.

Generating Publicity

The coach's relationship with the media is crucial to the success of the program. In many settings, the coach can influence how the program is perceived, communicated, and even promoted.

We had an event board promoting home matches erected near the field. Game posters were put on multipurpose event boards throughout the campus. We also used electronic boards. The student union had two such boards that always promoted our games. We also prepared game posters for every home game and posted them in the dormitories, the library, the bookstore, and all the classroom buildings.

We used campus resources, such as the newspaper and radio station. Initially, only the campus newspaper gave us coverage. Accordingly, I did everything I could to assist the editor and his reporters to get them on our side. The campus radio station is another good partner to have. We were the first college to have all our games carried by a radio station on a constant basis. This helped develop a fan base on campus and in our community.

With our team's success, it was not long before the nearby community newspapers began to expand their coverage to include our team. Finally, the *Hartford Courant*, the state's largest publication, began following us regularly and even put us in their main events section—a tremendous coup!

In six issues a year, the FOS Newsletter related all the positive stories about our program. The mailing list included FOS members, department and university administrators, the media, alumni lettermen, recruits, and secondary schools.

We received exposure on television. ESPN, which was then a fledgling network with a direct satellite link, covered all our soccer games for the first three years of the network's existence, giving us a small but national audience. Then New England Sports Network (NESN) began, and they chose to feature our program because they wanted soccer games with fans in attendance, and we were leading the nation in that regard. All of New England viewed our home games.

We initiated press conferences and luncheons for the 1972 intersectional game with St. Louis and continued to host one before the start of each season and before the start of NCAA tournament play. Press interviews were held after every game. As many neophyte reporters focused on match statistics and not game tactics, I made it a point to subtly teach the game to them.

Make use of public address and scoreboard announcements. We created a series of PA announcements, promoting the FOS program and upcoming activities. Later we expanded this to include announcements on the scoreboard's electronic message system.

Using the 12th Man

Every team in every sport wants and needs support from fans to provide a psychological edge over opponents. This was as true in the 1970s as it is today. I wanted to include our fans, to get them involved, to have them feel they were part of the team, to realize their involvement was crucial to our success. We did this in several ways.

For the pregame warm-up area, we set aside a location where fans would pass the team en route to the game field. This gave fans a chance to learn from what we were doing and, because of our keen preparation, gave everyone a feeling of confidence going into the game.

At the game entrance, the team always entered the field in an orderly fashion in a single line and jogged around three sides of the field, stopping midway on the far touchline. Here they would wave to both sidelines. On some occasions, each player would carry a long-stemmed rose and go up into the stands to present the flower to someone and thank them for their support. At the end of the season, we would unfurl a long sign that thanked the crowd for backing us. All these efforts were attempts to make a personal connection with our fans.

We took pride in our behavior during the national anthem. We wanted to be good role models. Everyone, including the wealthy alumni, appreciated the way we stood for the anthem.

At the end of the game, the team stretched at midfield then returned to the bench half of the field to sign autographs and mingle with the fans, who we allowed to come onto the field. This fostered many friends and helped nurture a true family atmosphere.

It was my goal to have bleachers erected around and close to the entire playing field to create a true home-field advantage. Students started to put pressure on the athletic administration to expand the bleacher seating. We also installed a four-foot fence to keep the crowd from the field of play. Our crowds swelled to as many as 10,000 paid, most of them seated! On their own, students started to congregate behind the goals, "chatting" with the opposing team's goalkeeper. During midweek games, when crowds were not as dense, students would move from one end of the field to the other. They managed to "help" the referees as well, often flashing red or yellow cards on perceived violations to their team. Some opposing goalkeepers challenged our students, but it was fun, and everyone enjoyed the experience.

One young man volunteered to organize fan cheering. His only distinguishing feature was a red bandana around his head. He had all four sides of the field cheering in various sequences, waving bandanas, and singing songs. He was great! Later, our school mascot, a student dressed in a Husky Dog uniform, added to the fun at our games, especially for our youngest fans.

Getting the Community Involved

Our object was always to establish a mutually beneficial relationship in which my team and I were anxious to help the community. We considered community support vital to our success.

At the beginning, there was no youth soccer in our town. Working with the townspeople, we established what became known as the Mansfield Junior Soccer Association to promote youth soccer. In time, youngsters in the program served as ball boys at our games, played in preliminary games and halftime exhibitions, and attended my camp, where they got to know our players even better. An unexpected benefit occurred years later when no less than five of the Mansfield boys helped Connecticut win its Division I National Championship in 1981.

We also set out to establish youth soccer in the state. No statewide program existed in the early 1970s. It was important to us and to the development of the sport to start a statewide youth program. I prepared a structure for such a program, and the few town groups playing soccer in the state were invited to an organizational meeting; at this meeting the Connecticut Junior Soccer Association (CJSA) was formed, with myself as president. Other college coaches contributed a great deal to the statewide development of our sport. During my eight years of leadership, the CJSA expanded to indoor competition and even an under-23 college summer league.

Soccer did not have the support it deserved throughout the state at that time. The Mansfield Junior Soccer Association, along with other local organizations under the umbrella of the CJSA, helped change the attitudes of our state populace toward our sport. This organization currently has over 150,000 registered youths and a $1 million annual budget.

The college programs in our state set a terrific example to follow. With little soccer on TV and with professional leagues struggling, the colleges were called on to lead the development of the sport, and everyone responded!

Organizing and leading camps was an important building block in the development of my program. The "Connecticut" in the Connecticut Soccer School (CSS) was intended to insinuate this belonged to the whole state, whereas the "School" in the title was to infer we would offer instruction at a higher teaching level. The school provided an opportunity to both teach and network with youth and high school coaches; helped youngsters improve their game by focusing on soccer-related games and activities; gave young people an opportunity to meet and bond with our players who were staff members (these relationships built interest in attending our games); created recruiting opportunities; and formed a close synergy between the CSS and the UConn soccer program. The CSS was a sponsor of the UConn soccer program.

It was always my objective to work for my players and our program as well as for the sport. You can't promote and market one without the other; they always go hand in hand. It was and still is important to volunteer your services to do the hard work, whatever that is, to get the job done. It means being the treasurer or the secretary or committee member. It means earning the respect of your peers so when you speak to an issue, your thoughts have meaning.

Marketing and promoting your players and program along with your sport requires a tremendous commitment and work ethic as well as the ability to communicate effectively, organize efficiently, be consistent, and be fair.

The promotion and marketing of our program took many shapes. We tried to reach every segment of the population, including youngsters, students, members of the community, parents, university administration, prospective students, and the media. You name a segment, and we tried to sell them on the idea that they were a part of us and that we needed them to be successful. We truly sought to be an expanded family.

We wanted our players to be good role models who learned valuable life skills in our program so they would be good, productive citizens after graduation. We wanted our program to set the standard for others to follow, knowing that these programs might some day be as good as or better than ours. We wanted to reach out as far as we could to change people's perceptions of our sport, to convince them that this was indeed the world's game but that it would and could also be our nation's game and be played by millions of young people.

We tried to be inventive on the field of play and consistently to put our best foot forward as a team and as the coaches of the team. We wanted to be first class in everything we did both on and off the field. Today, we feel we met many of our concrete objectives, and best of all, our program and our great sport no longer hold second-class status. There is still more to do, but those of us in soccer now have a sense of pride, both in ourselves and our sport. That was not the case many, many years ago.

III

Optimal Training for Learning and Performance

CHAPTER 8

Creating the Training Environment

Lauren Gregg

We need to approach each training session with the understanding that, as coaches, everything we do or don't do influences our players. The art is to achieve a positive outcome from what we do. Based on my experiences—including coaching the U.S. women's national to two World Cup championships, 1991 and 1999, and an Olympic Gold Medal in 1996—I'll try to show how to maximize your time together with your players. Many of the nuances and insights go beyond the Xs and the Os of the game.

What could be more important than the training culture we create for our players? Creating a training environment requires a clear understanding of what you want to accomplish, how you intend to accomplish it, and a plan to implement it. If you're not sure about the focus of the session, your players won't know what they're supposed to get out of it. By creating a consistent set of standards, empowering the leadership within your team, preparing sessions, and paying attention to details, you can unite your team in the pursuit of excellence. As a result, your team members will recognize that they can reach a higher level of training and discover an enhanced commitment to each other and the success of the team.

Several key factors are involved in creating a foundation of excellence in training, including preparing sessions, setting relevant objectives for the session, putting the session into context, establishing a training mentality, and developing team chemistry.

---

* Some passages adapted from *The Champion Within: Training for Excellence* by Lauren Gregg, 1999, JTC Sports.

An important part of establishing clear expectations and training standards for your team is also one of the most important qualities of a coach—consistency. Consistency allows players to know what is expected of them. It sounds simple, but I often see coaches impose different standards on players from day to day or week to week. The result is inconsistency in player performance. Consistency can also apply to time. If you say the team will train for an hour and a half, do you train an hour and a half, or does it extend to two and a half hours? When you keep the time of training sessions consistent, players adapt and bring great energy and concentration to each practice. If they're unsure how long they'll be out there, they tend to hold back, resulting in inconsistent, suboptimal training. Once your session planning is complete and the necessary equipment and fields or grids are in place, the art now lies in selecting the coaching moments within the session.

Preparation

Preparation, including knowing what you want to work on and how to create an optimal environment, is fundamental to a successful training session. For those who don't have the luxury of daily sessions, finite planning is even more important to maximize the time you do have. With the U.S. women, we coaches often spent at least as much time designing the training sessions as we did executing them. Think about what you want to accomplish. What message should the players get from the training session? The practice might have several objectives, but be sure they support each other and are woven together so they enhance the message, not complicate it. Know what elements of the game you want to emphasize. Communicate goals to players and design a session to teach or reinforce them. Write it out from beginning to end.

The training focus should make sense and be consistent with the team's short- and long-term goals. For example, if you're coming off a weekend match, does the session address the past match or the coming match? If it's late in the season and your players are fatigued, does the training session fine-tune or tax your players?

When preparing the session, be sure there is a natural progression, a rhythm or flow to help players get where you want them to be. Planning goes beyond what you do in the session. It includes such aspects as structuring team delineation in advance, knowing the exact field dimensions, and providing a timeline of exercises. On-field preparation entails laying out the scrimmage vests and the fields or grids in advance. This allows you to get more done in the allotted time. Precise preparation contributes to the players learning to train effectively for 90 minutes (or whatever the age-appropriate match length).

Determining a topic for the session requires a clear sense of where the team is and where it needs to go. The focus should make sense for that week and for the time of the season. Coaches must be clear in their own minds what they want to accomplish in each practice.

Match analysis is a wonderful source of information. For example, you might train in response to a recent match you played. Or you might focus on an upcoming opponent and how you intend to handle them. If the session is designed to be the hardest one of the week, then manipulate how things flow, the numbers of players you use in exercises, and so forth to that end.

Typically, activities with smaller numbers require more participation and can be more demanding. If your team needs to work on defending in the final third, then begin with smaller drills and build up to match-related conditions. Any session should progress through increasingly higher levels of match-related conditions. The better the plan is laid out, the more confidence players have in what you're trying to accomplish.

In addition to training topics that fit into the context of the team's short-term goals, teams and players should have an annual training cycle or rhythm. An annual cycle is a long-term vision for the construction of the team. An annual plan ensures that players get rest as much as it ensures focused training. It also helps players who play more that one sport. With the women's national team, we had a four-year plan, an annual plan, and a daily plan. We started planning from the World Cup and worked back to create a four-year calendar. Within that calendar, we had annual plans. As we got closer to the World Cup, we prepared a six-month plan. That planning block was further divided into several shorter blocks for the time leading up to the World Cup. Finally, weekly training rhythms were laid out. From that point, we selected daily topics as focal points for each training session.

Selecting a training topic is important. Matches provide a great deal of information for both coaches and players. Review as many matches as possible with your team. It takes only 15 minutes to dissect what the team did well and what needs work. Reviewing matches together helps ensure that everyone is on the same page. One way to analyze matches is to have each field unit (goalkeepers, defenders, midfielders, strikers) report to the group what they felt they did well in the match as well as what their unit needs to work on. Or you could have a different unit indicate what they felt another unit did well, which creates positive energy and respect among the team. As coach, you could address areas that need improvement so that only positive feedback comes from teammates. Another idea is to work together as a team to generate lists of what the team is doing well and what needs work. To be prepared, run through the lists in advance.

Consistency applies to match analysis—which should occur after easy games as well as tough games to establish a reliable approach to your team's evaluation process. Match analysis helps the team develop a consistency in how they view any opponent. We train, compete, and evaluate the same, regardless of the opponent. This reinforces the message that training mentality is about us being the best we can be.

The next step is to use the information gained to select a training topic. Make it clear which areas from the review will be the focus for the week, and organize your training to reflect this. If you have an upcoming match, choose topics relevant to the previous match in context of the upcoming match. Keep the team focused on the daily goals but also on the long-term objectives. This way, even in victory, important information is extracted from each match. As George Bernard Shaw said, "What we call results are only beginnings."

Work back from where you want to end. Perhaps your end goal is to qualify for state competition or to make the NCAAs. Create a calendar, work back from that end point by mapping out matches, time-off periods or days, and tournaments, then work down to a weekly rhythm. Working back from where you want to be ensures that you map out a plan to get you there. This doesn't mean you won't need to make adjustments or modifications, but it provides a framework to make the desired outcome more likely to happen.

Once you have a long-term plan in place, create smaller blocks of weekly and daily training sessions. For example, if we played Saturday, Sunday was an off day. In some instances, Sunday might include reserve training and light jogging or stretching for the starters. If Sunday was an off day, Monday might be a medium session. If Sunday was a light day, Monday was the off day. Tuesday included a hard workout, but Wednesday's workout was medium in intensity. Thursday was a medium session. Friday was a light practice leading into Saturday's match.

Some coaches like to schedule an off day the day before a game. If this is the case, Monday and Wednesday would be medium in intensity, Tuesday would be a hard practice, and Thursday would be light. Taking the day off before the game requires good leadership and an understanding of your team's ability to prepare and stay focused.

The commitment to have players stay on the same rhythm can go a step farther. Those who did not play or played minimally on Saturday performed some fitness after the match so they were on the same rhythm as those who saw the majority of action in the game. The next day they might play a small-sided match to keep their technical and tactical skills sharp. You might wonder how I dealt with the psychology of that situation. The key is to create an atmosphere, a culture, in which your players want and choose to do what's best for the team. The more often you have players choose the right thing, the better. Here our players wanted to do fitness activities because they knew it was in their own and the team's best interest. Committed players want to stay fit and be "played in." Our players learned they needed to be responsible to both their teammates and themselves. It's important for players to understand that these sessions show we care about their development and that they are assets to the team—if they weren't, we wouldn't care how they trained. Veteran players might choose to stay at the field to encourage reserve players doing their fitness work. Experienced players see this as part of team building. In fact, we often had to stop players who had played 90 minutes from running again with the reserve players. It was a great show of support and clear evidence of the leadership and mentality committed to the greater good of the team.

Many teams play more than one match per week, which alters the training rhythm. If both matches are difficult, you have to be careful not to overtrain. If one is hard and one is not, you can train through the easier game and taper into the harder one. Training through a match means treating it like a training session. This allows you to stay ahead of the game. When little time is available to prepare, focus most of your efforts on team organization and set pieces. When you take the field, all players should at least have a sense of the system of play, the general offensive and defensive strategies, and how to execute set pieces.

Consistency

One of the most important aspects of coaching is staying consistent. Players respond best when they know what is expected of them. Establishing consistent expectations from session to session in terms of player output is fundamental to creating this culture.

Work toward a consistent approach to giving feedback. Don't treat some players one way and other players another way. Apply standards evenly across the board. This does not mean you have to treat all players exactly the same—players are different and need to be approached as individuals. But the set of established standards should be the same for everyone. Certain demands are common to all players. For example, effort is not negotiable.

Consistency applies not only to setting standards for training but to the training time itself. Do your best to keep the designated time. Players will mentally and physically commit when a specified amount of time is honored. If possible, train for a set amount of time each session. With the U.S. women, we sought to finish field sessions in 90 minutes, which replicated how long they needed to focus during a match. By keeping the session shorter, we brought out the best in the players. They didn't feel the need to save themselves for a longer session because they knew how long we'd be out there. If they gave their all, and if we prepared and organized well, 90 minutes was enough time to do everything we needed to do.

Time also can be used as an incentive. Challenge your team by telling them that they'll train for only 90 minutes if they can get through everything (be sure it's possible to do so!). Reward players for exceptional intensity and focus. For instance, you might eliminate or reduce fitness training if the team meets your challenge to invest totally in the session for the whole 90 minutes. Always seek to reward rather than punish. Phrase your challenges accordingly. Punishment for lack of achievment is much less effective than rewarding for success. As you get closer to a match, consider reducing the length of training. Often the day before a game we'd train for only an hour, depending on the intensity of the other sessions that week and the potential intensity of the match ahead.

To instill familiarity and confidence in your players, have consistent water breaks. They'll know you care about them and are getting them what they need. Adequate water throughout training plays an important role in performance. You want your players fresh and ready to go at game time. If you end a session with players wanting more but having done what they need to, you have accomplished your training goal. This keeps players enthusiastic, eager for the next session. You'll be more successful if you inform players of the practice topic, what's expected of them, and how long the session will last.

Training Mentality

Champions don't just train—they invest in their development. One important aspect of player development is the quality of the training environment. Helping players learn to train pays huge dividends. Don't assume players know how to train or how to reach their potential. Our job as coaches is to impart and hold players accountable to the highest standard they can reach. We call it "training on your edge."

Training on the edge starts with focus and concentration, even during warm-up. Teach players to move past what's comfortable. Take the Coerver ball skill series, for example. Do you demand that players stretch themselves and their muscles to move faster, or are players allowed to simply go through the motions? One way to ensure focus is to ask a player to lead the team warm-up every so often. Unexpectedly having to orchestrate the warm-up raises a player's sense of preparedness and attentiveness. Players start spending time on their skills while waiting for training to start or at the end of a session. Developing a positive training mentality begins with players taking responsibility for their development.

A common error for both coaches and players is to train one way and then expect to play another way in the match. The way a team or player trains is often reflected in how the team or player plays in the game. Training mentality is about developing standards. Do your players enter every training session with the mindset that they want to be their best and help their teammates be their best? Challenge your players to train as if they are playing a match.

While most coaches won't have the level of players we had on the women's national team, you do have players who understand what it means to train hard. They become the building blocks of the foundation for building team-training mentality. Leadership within the women's national team has always been vital to creating training excellence. Bring in local high school, college, or professional players from time to time to show your players what it means to train or to demonstrate skills. Have these higher-level players train with your team or run a session. Having good players demonstrate their skills is a great way to add freshness and energy to your practice sessions.

Another way to demand intensity is to keep score. As soon as you introduce scoring, the intensity level rises. When you use scoring, the training mimics some of the excitement of a match. The pressure of winning or losing elevates the standard of play. Foster an environment that makes it permissible for players to win. These standards rival those needed to compete with the toughest opponents.

We began every national team training camp with a mentality session that allowed us to revisit a fundamental aspect of our success—our mentality. Mentality involves toughness, resolve, and commitment to do your part to ensure the success of the team. Along with the individual and small-sided competitions we played, we usually did fitness as well. The fitness test was as important psychologically as it was to give us information about our players' conditioning.

In the U.S. training camp, we often kept score in competitions and exercises. The veterans took each exercise or game seriously. They knew they were being evaluated every time they came into camp. They knew what they did mattered. The veterans knew every point and would dispute anything questionable because winning was on the line.

Identify what you're looking for when you see it. When players are not getting it right, it's usually not because they're unwilling but because they don't know what you want from them. Many players don't realize they can train harder or do the same exercise in a more realistic manner.

You can find keen mental focus in the smallest moments. As a coach, recognize that you can create an environment that rewards commitment. A consistent message is that every detail matters. Your approach to each aspect of the session reflects in how your players develop. I loved it when our captain pointed out that the players' mentality should include respect for the coaches.

"When coaches call you over, they want your attention. It shows them respect to jog over," said Carla Overbeck, former U.S. women's national team captain. "You're not chatting and wasting time. If you finish a five versus five game, you jog off for water. That's mentality."

Carla points out a very simple yet telling aspect of training that anyone can incorporate. Developing a consistent, focused training session starts in the smallest moments. Get your team in the habit of jogging on and off the field for everything. You might be surprised how much more you can get done in a shorter time. During a 90-minute game, you don't get to take a 5-minute water break. Train the habits you'll need for a 90-minute focus.

Leadership

Leadership is fundamental to the success of any team and is vital in helping the coach establish a positive training environment. Leadership emerges in many ways. Your challenge is to tap into it, foster it, and use it to construct the desired culture within the team.

Leadership is often determined when players are selected captain by their teammates or coaches. While captains are one source of leadership, other players also provide aspects of leadership in the way they train, unify players, or link the coach to the team. Make the most of leadership by putting players in positions that require them to step up and lead. For example, organize a session in which certain players have to pick teams that will compete in some drill or activity. First, this places players in your shoes and shows them it's not always easy to put together a group of players. Second, they take responsibility for the outcome and how well the players they selected play. When forming small-sided teams for a mini-competition, rotate players each competition. At the end of the session, record wins, losses, and ties. You can see who the common denominator is in the success of the small-sided team.

When organizing small-sided or full-field games, let your players sort out their lineups from time to time. This provides leadership moments within the team and encourages players to take responsibility. When players understand how to affect the outcome of a game, you have created on-field coaches. Remember that whatever you need, want, or expect in a match is best accomplished by introducing it in training.

The leadership of the national team has set an expectation, almost a culture, regarding fitness standards. National team players train out of respect for their teammates. They never want to let them down. Set the standards for your team. "When I think of our leadership, I think of Overbeck, Foudy, Lilly, Hamm, Chastain, Akers, Fawcett, Venturini," Tony DiCicco says. "All of them are very, very concerned with their fitness. When we do fitness, guess what? All the top players are at the top of the fitness ladder. If you are a young player coming on to our team, you won't see Mia Hamm down at the bottom of the fitness ladder. And fitness isn't getting fit for the season. Fitness is a life-long endeavor."

Just as players have different strengths on the field, they have different leadership qualities. Let them lead from their place of strength. Some may lead in one aspect of play. Maybe they have a long throw-in, are vocal from the bench, are organizers on the field, or work well with the reserves in practice. Perhaps they are leaders by example. Recognize the ways your players lead, then find ways to use their leadership during training sessions, in matches, and even off the field.

Work with your core players to set a level on which the team operates and lives, where commitment to each other manifests itself in how hard they prepare and train. This leads to great team chemistry and creates a positive training environment.

Team Chemistry

"Team before I" was our motto with the U.S. women's national team as we prepared for and ultimately won the 1999 Women's World Cup. Many players and coaches feel team chemistry is an illusive quality, a stroke of luck, that some teams have it and some don't. That's true to a degree, but both players and coaches *can* influence the dynamic of a team. They can affect team chemistry.

Doing so is an ongoing, active process. We invested in it every day. Good chemistry among teammates involves an attitude and atmosphere in which players and staff commit to the good of the team. Julie Foudy, captain of the U.S. national team, said, "If you don't make an effort to be a good teammate, you'll never make it on this team, even if you're the best player in the world." The message from our leadership was that if you want to play on this team, you have to make a contribution to the chemistry of this team. Young players get that message from the veterans.

Team chemistry is an energy that exists on and off the field. At the national team level, we placed a high value on cultivating good chemistry. When it came down to two players of equal ability, we would choose the one who blended best, who contributed to the chemistry of the team environment.

To work on enhancing chemistry on your own team, address and revisit this topic, plan sessions that seek to build cooperation not division, and set standards to which the team commits. We used a training session to build chemistry and commit to our mentality as a unit. It was a fitness session that required the unit to work together. Instead of testing an individual player's resolve, the session was meant to make players rely on each other. The outcome of the exercise was always positive. Teammates felt good about themselves and about each other's level of commitment to the team. Players should understand that every day they are responsible for making their environment positive.

Choosing the exercises for training and coaching within the session is an art. As a coach, do you reflect on how to handle players' mistakes and successes? Which moments do you choose to coach and educate players and which moments are allowed to fall by the wayside? Here's an opportunity for you to reinforce the standard of excellence you seek to establish. What you select to coach and how you coach it tells your players a lot about your expectations for each player and the team. How much, how little, and how you coach within a training session molds the team. Constantly evaluate to determine if what you're doing is producing the results you want.

Sometimes coaches are blessed with exceptionally talented players. Ironically, these same players can pose challenges for the coach. For instance, perhaps a player is a talented take-on artist, and his or her teammates are upset that he or she doesn't pass more often. Coaches often wonder what to do with such a player. How you react to these special players, who are willing to take on to make something happen, makes all the difference. These players are rare, and I feel protecting them serves them best in the long run. But how they are protected and encouraged affects both the team and the player. One solution is to be sure all players know what makes this player special. This way you do not single out a player, which goes against our philosophy of "team before I," but rather you highlight what the team does well and what this player does well. This conveys a sense from the coach to the players that each player needs to do what makes him or her special within the context of the team. Promote creativity and diversity on your team. In the end, teams with more players with unique qualities are harder to play against.

Defining Roles

You need to define your players' roles. Players should understand their contributions to the team and what makes them special. Knowing how each player serves the team is essential for that player and for team chemistry.

When we selected 20 players for the 1999 Women's World Cup roster, we were often asked if, in our view, these were the best 20 players in the country. Our answer was that although they were not necessarily the 20 best or most talented players, they formed the best composite of players we could find. We looked not only at soccer skills but at the ability to work together well with the team. We based our selections on players' abilities to understand and fulfill their roles. In some cases, that role meant coming off the bench—or sometimes *not* coming off it. On a World Cup roster, you often have three goalkeepers in case of injuries. The third goalkeeper must be of a caliber to help you win if called on, but he or she must also be willing to sit on the bench with only a small chance of stepping onto the field. It's a tough role to play and requires a special person with extreme commitment to the good of the team.

Use training to define player roles and rotations. For example, early in the season you want to show players that the lineup is up for grabs and players can compete for spots. You vary your lineups, looking for the best mix. When you prepare for a match late in the season, you might want to use the same lineup in training as you intend to use in the game. This tells players where they stand and how you might use them. Also, players who are not rotated into the starting lineup as often can recognize their roles.

When players understand their unique contributions, you're more likely to have players who come off the bench ready to perform their best. They are prepared when called on. I recommend regular conferences with your players to make sure that their roles are understood and comfortable.

The Four Pillars

As you organize training sessions, are you conscious of addressing the four pillars of the game—the technical, tactical, physical, and psychological? Each comes more or less into the foreground based on your team's strengths and weaknesses and where you are in the season. Sometimes the pillars can serve as a checklist to evaluate where your team is and plan accordingly. The more you can combine pillars into your exercises, the more efficient training can be.

Do you have your team jog for 10 minutes to warm up or do they use a ball? Be creative. See how effective you can be at disguising fitness or combining technical skill and tactical nuance. For example, work on bending balls in warm-up as a lead-in to final-third attacking play. If you want to revisit mentality and work on conditioning and individual tactics, such as attacking and defending in the final third, one-on-one training might accomplish this objective. Create a session that builds a theme from the warm-up into exercises that incorporate the theme in increasingly match-related conditions, ending with a match. This allows players to naturally move from simple executions with little pressure to putting it all together.

Whenever possible, tactical adjustments should be first played out in training. One important role of training is to work out the plan before competition. If you anticipate needing to make a change in your lineup, a system of play, or set piece, rehearse it first in training. Prepare your team for what they might experience in the match. If you introduce the changes during the match, players might take them for panicked adjustments rather than prepared maneuvers.

The psychological pillar is one of the most important and least attended of all the aspects of a soccer player. Elite athletes cite their emotions and mental state as the keys to their performance. Psychology is at least as important as technique, tactical nuances, or physical conditioning, and perhaps more so. Find ways during training to work on team and individual psychological skills. Although many coaches don't have access to a sports psychologist who can address psychological skills such as goal setting, imagery, visualization, and self-talk, you can make some headway by validating the importance of the psychological dimension.

For example, performance and confidence are extremely related. Learn to appreciate that what gives one player confidence might not work for another. Help players discover sources of confidence. Use training sessions to impart your confidence in a given player and your team. In some sessions, you want to build the confidence of a player or a unit. Sometimes with the women's national team, to get our attacking confidence up, we would play teams that we knew we could dominate, rather than play a men's team that would stretch us and force us to play in a different rhythm, although this would be effective for the technical or tactical pillars.

Fitness is always a test of psychological strength. "Mentally, it makes you tougher and stronger, knowing you can run past or run more than any team you face," says former U.S. national team captain Carla Overbeck. "Or maybe in the last few minutes when you are losing, your fitness is going to carry you and provide confidence, give you that extra edge or the winning goal." Conditioning builds psychological as well as physical strength. When you put what you're doing into context, your players see their training as positive and connected to a larger goal.

Players respond to their errors or successes based on how you respond to them in these instances. Players tend to be harder on themselves and have constant dialogue in their minds. Knowing each player as you do should guide you in how you instruct or compliment a player in order to help him or her take the comments constructively and translate it into positive self-talk.

The Role of Competition

Competition is a crucial ingredient in player development. The goal for training is to prepare the team to accomplish the defined goals. Games are about competition, so training should be too, if appropriate for the age group. Games are about performing at a quicker, more intense pace. They are about execution. Train those things. If games are more demanding physically and are faster and harder, then create that pace in training.

"I remember growing up, I wanted to win, but not at all costs," says Carla Overbeck. "You had friends on the team and you wanted everyone to like you. It was hard. It's part mentality and part process. Just knowing that it's okay if you beat this person because you are trying to make her better. When I got to school, I certainly did want to win, but I didn't win a one on one my entire freshman year. I had to learn, and I learned from the other players around me. When you see someone going after it in practice, it's contagious. When you see someone busting their hump, you want to do it too." "The great thing about our team is that it gets nasty at times, but we all understand that's what is making us better," said former national team midfielder Tisha Venturini. "Let's say I am going against Mia in one-on-ones. The harder we go, the more we help each other. If I am going 50 percent on defense, that doesn't make her any better. Sure, you can get angry. I get angry, but once the practice is over, that's it. It's healthy. It gets bad at times, but the personalities on the team won't let it carry off the field. Everyone understands that to be the best in the world this is how we have to train."

We did a lot of one-on-one work in training. In one-on-one training, there was only one winner, and we recorded wins, losses, and ties. We had small-sided games, heading duels, and fitness competitions. We were always looking for the players who factored into the margin of victory.

Instilling this type of mentality in training is at the core of establishing a training standard for your team. Teaching young women to compete might take time. I encountered this even with the women's national team. Girls tend to be more relational. To compete even in training with their friends feels threatening to what's most important to them. These tendencies are evolving over time with the wonderful role models we now have in women's soccer. But getting young women to be more competitive is a process you might need to work on.

Empowering Athletes

"A champion trains when no one is watching," said Carin Jennings Gabarra, 1991 world champion. One of the greatest gifts you can give players is the guidance and knowledge of how to train on their own. It's a phenomenal source of confidence for an individual player as well as a team.

Even motivated athletes need some guidance about what and how to train. I have found that many young people are willing to train on their own but lack good sense on how to go about it. Don't assume they know where you want them to be or how to get there. For example, in the collegiate game there's little time between early preseason and competition. If you haven't given players the tools they need to train on their own, your team will spend more time playing catch-up than on working as a cohesive unit. Teach players to train themselves. This is a wonderful off-season training topic. In training sessions, talk about how and what to train and the four pillars of the game. All programs can benefit when players take responsibility for their development away from the team. This allows you to focus on bringing the team together and preparing for competition.

Make it fun! Training should be enjoyable. Maybe not every day or every exercise brings the same excitement, but we should remember most players play because they love to play. It never hurts to make training more entertaining now and then. Know when to lighten up and when to bear down. Sense the mood of your team. Get input from your captains and leaders on the pulse of the team. Even with the women's national team, we had to make it fun. Soccer is first and foremost a game. Yes, you want to make the most of it and be the best you can be, but don't lose sight of the journey as you strive for your destination. If you enjoy the journey, your players will too.

CHAPTER 9

Conducting Innovative Training Sessions

Jeff Tipping

As coaches, we need to be inventive when incorporating exercises and drills into our training sessions. Creative and interesting activities help reinforce the game skills covered in training.

In this chapter, the first section is designed for players about 12 years old, who are coming into the "golden age of learning". Players younger than 12 have a difficult time learning the zonal concepts these exercises involve. The second section deals with counterattacking, the foremost method of scoring at advanced levels of play. The exercises are designed to encourage older players to transition rapidly from one part of the field to another.

When practicing zone defense with younger players, use markers so they know where their zones begin and end. Hard and fast rules such as "Never follow an opponent across the face of a fellow defender" might be necessary until your players are comfortable with this kind of defending. Some of the exercises can be used to teach young players or to warm up older players. Many players can be trained with these exercises.

Coaching counterattacking involves teaching a particular mentality almost as much as training physical movement. These exercises are free flowing, with few hard and fast rules. Try to structure exercises that make the opposing team throw many players forward; this leaves significant gaps in the backline that can be exploited with a sudden run or pass forward. Training counterattacking mentality is an important part of this series. Every player, from the goalkeeper to the striker, must defend with an aim to counterattack immediately after winning the ball.

Defending

These exercises are designed for players aged 9 to 12. You can also use them for senior players. They are meant to teach midfielders and fullbacks to defend as a block of eight and to train the following skills:

- **speed of approach**—pressuring the ball to prevent an opponent's forward movement;
- **angle of approach**—using the correct angle to make the opponent's play predictable; and
- **distance and angle of support**—forcing attackers to cover the player.

Shadow Defending From the Front

Set up four cones and place a ball five yards from each cone (figure 9.1). Players line up 10 yards from the cones. On the coach's whistle, the first line of defenders sprints to the cones with long strides. When they near the cones, they slow down (short strides), lower their center of gravity, and edge in sideways until they're about a yard away from the ball. When play-

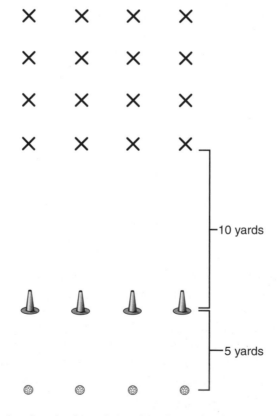

Figure 9.1 Setup for the shadow defending from the front.

ers have assumed the correct defensive stance relative to the ball (coaches sometimes use the term "close down the ball" to describe this maneuver), they return to their lines. The next player in each line then repeats the run to the ball (the ball represents an attacking player).

Angle of Pressure

The setup is the same as in shadow defending from the front, except the coach tells the player to show to right or left by moving at an angle after arriving at the cone (figure 9.2). As they leave their starting positions and run toward the cones and the ball, the pressuring players declare, "I've got ball."

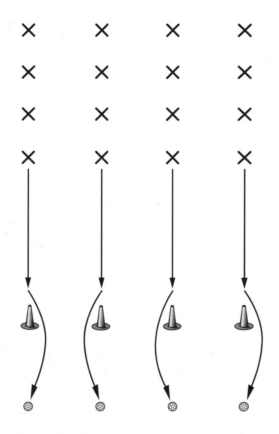

Figure 9.2 Setup for angle of pressure.

Four-Cone Drill

At the blow of a whistle, the first player in line runs to the first cone (figure 9.3). At a second whistle blow, the second player in line runs to the first line of cones, while the first player continues to the second cone. The drill continues with the next player in line running toward the first cone at each blow of the whistle. Players angle to the right at the first cone, left at the second cone, right at the third cone, and left at the fourth cone. After the fourth cone, players jog back to the end of the line.

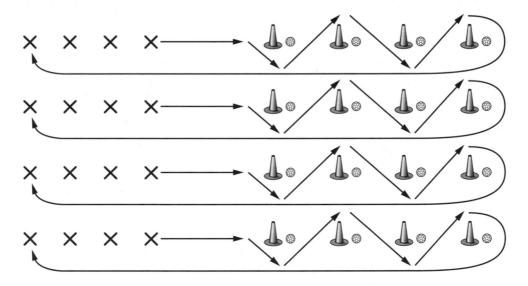

Figure 9.3   Setup for the four-cone drill.

Pressure and Cover

The setup is the same as for the four-cone drill. On the coach's whistle, the first two players in each line go together. The first player is the first defender; the second defender begins slightly behind. On the blow of the whistle, both players move toward the cone. Just before reaching the cone, the first defender declares, "I've got ball!" The second defender says, "Show right" or "Show left" to indicate how the first defender should approach to cover the second defender. The second defender adopts a 45-degree angle about three to four steps behind the first defender.

Midfield Zone Drill

We now activate the two players to alternately serve first as the pressurizing player, then as the covering player against the ball (which, again, simply represents an attacking player) (figure 9.4). Players alternate roles. The first player is the first defender on the first whistle, then the second defender on the second whistle, and so on.

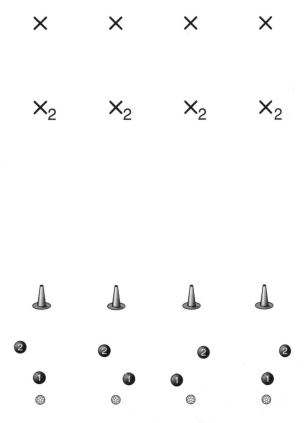

Figure 9.4 Setup for the pressure and cover exercises.

Defending As a Midfield Group

The four starting midfielders begin at the front of the four lines (figure 9.5a). With a second group of midfielders lined up behind them, a coach blows the whistle to signal when each of the four midfielders begin their approaches to ball 1. Each group of players first adjusts positions to defend as a midfield group at ball 1; group 2 follows when group 1 has completed its proper alignment. In succession, each midfield group is whistled to ball 2, ball 3, and finally, ball 4. Players focus on forming the correct alignment for each ball; make corrections if you observe incorrect positioning.

When the ball is in position 1 (left back third) (figure 9.5b), the left midfielder (11) pressures the ball to force inside by angling to the left of the ball; the center midfielder (6) covers at a 45-degree angle about five yards back; the other center midfielder (8) takes the same line as player 6 about eight yards away; and the right midfielder (7) takes the same line as players 6 and 8, then comes across until approximately in line with the far post.

When the ball is in position 2 (deep midfield), the left midfielder (11) covers at a 45-degree angle about eight yards back for the pressuring player (6); the center midfielder (6) pressures the ball; the other center midfielder (8) covers at a 45-degree angle about eight yards back for the pressuring player (6); and the right midfielder (7) takes the same line as 8 and 11.

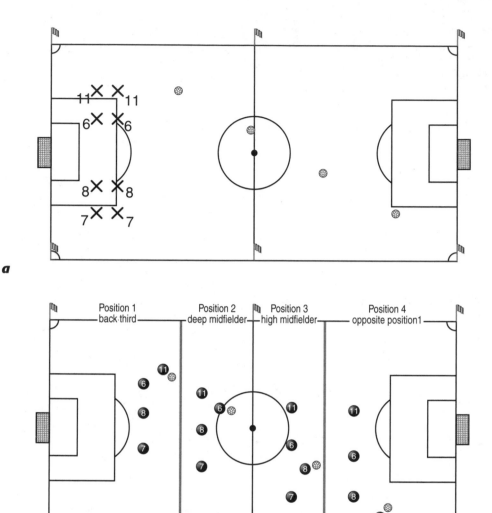

Figure 9.5 Defending as a midfielder: *(a)* initial setup; *(b)* player positions for the four ball positions.

When the ball is in position 3 (high midfield), the left midfielder (11) pinches in within the width of the box while taking the same line as 6; the center midfielder (6) covers at a 45-degree angle about eight yards back for the pressuring player; the other center midfielder (8) pressures the ball; and the right midfielder (7) covers at a 45-degree angle about eight yards back for player 8.

When the ball is in position 4, it is opposite to ball position 1. Again, the objective of the exercises is to ensure that each block of midfield players is properly aligned relative to the position of the ball on various sections of the field. Observe each group's actions and make alignment corrections as needed.

Defending As Two Blocks of Four, Backs and Midfielders

When coordinating the movements of backs and midfielders, remind the backline to keep 20 yards behind the midfielders and "mirror" the shape of the midfielders.

Now you'll coordinate the defensive alignment of the block of four defending midfielders with that of the four defensive backs. The starting positions for each group is the same as in figure 9.5a, except that the first line (7, 8, 6, 11) is the midfielder defenders and the second line (2, 4, 5, 3) acts as defending backs (figure 9.6). The backs and midfielders now move as a collective defending unit, maintaining about 20 yards between themselves. In every instance the midfielders' defensive alignment mirrors what has already been trained. Again, we're now concerned that the back four defenders are collectively properly positioned to cover their midfielder relative to the ball position on the field.

On a coach's whistle, the two lines move together. For ball position 1, the left midfielder (11) declares, "I've got ball!" The left midfielder (11) approaches the ball. When the left center midfielder (6) shouts, "Show inside" or "To the right," the left midfielder (11) angles the approach to force to the right. The players stop at the ball and move to the next ball on the coach's whistle. Check the position of all eight players. The distance of the backline from the midfield line gets closer in position a. but is about 20 yds. in the other positions and mirrors the shape of that group.

For ball position 2, the left center midfielder (6) declares, "I've got ball!" The left midfielder (11) and right center midfielder (8) form a triangle behind the left center midfielder (6).

In figures 9.6c and 9.6d we see the same shapes, but the players' roles are reversed. Note that the goalkeeper moves forward as the lines move

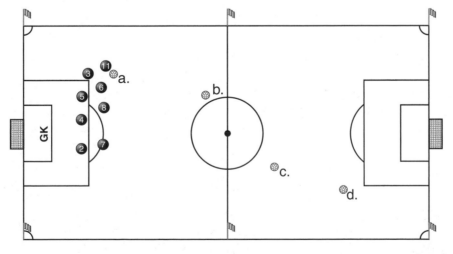

a

(continued)

Figure 9.6   Defending as two blocks of four: *(a)* ball in deep left position; *(b)* ball in deep midfield position; *(c)* ball in high midfield position; *(d)* ball in opposite position.

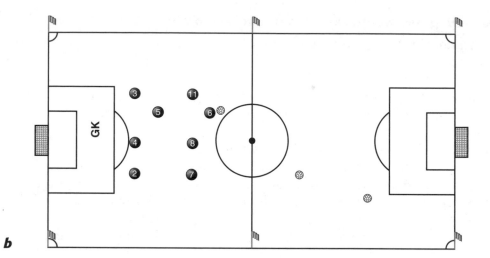

b

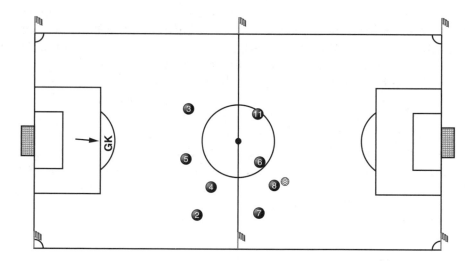

c

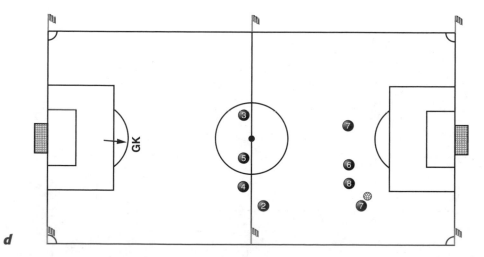

d

Figure 9.6 *(continued)*.

forward. After the team has gone through the sequence, players jog back to the beginning, and reserve players take a turn.

You might find that doing these exercises on a football field, with marked lines, helps your players maintain good spacing.

Counterattacking

As a tactical strategy, counterattacking is distinct from regular transitional play. As a pattern of play, fast transition is always encouraged. Counterattacking teams, however, build a whole attacking philosophy as the primary mode of attack.

Counterattacking is normally associated with low-pressure defending in which the opponent is invited to move forward with the ball, exposing the space behind them. The counterattacking team then seeks to win the ball and attack, at lightning speed, into that space before the opposing team can retreat into an organized defending unit.

Counterattacking is the number-one strategy for scoring goals at the international level, at which defenses are well organized and the opposition possesses advanced technique. International managers, ever mindful of the dangers of being counterattacked, must develop a system of play to answer the question, "What happens if we lose the ball now?"

Counterattacking teams choose this strategy for several reasons:

- **Superior opponent.** The counterattacking team protects the vital space at the top of the penalty box with large numbers, leaving only one or two forwards at the halfway line.
- **Inferior opponent.** If an inferior opponent clogs the vital space with large numbers, some teams play low pressure to draw out the inferior team, exposing space behind and counterattacking before the opponent can retreat.
- **Climate.** Teams that play in hot, humid conditions or at high altitude use a counterattack strategy to conserve energy.
- **Younger, fitter opponent.** Low pressure and counterattacking is sometimes employed by teams early in the season, in the 35+ age bracket, or when the opponent is younger.
- **Lead protection.** Teams protecting a lead "stay home" to protect vital space.
- **Man down.** When a player is ejected, many teams revert to low pressure and leave only one striker high (e.g., 4-4-1).
- **Fast striker.** Liverpool's use of Michael Owen, notable for his lightning speed, sometimes involves a strategy of low-pressure defending and counterattacking.

When devising a counterattacking strategy, train your team to work as a unit, demonstrate tremendous discipline, and recognize vital visual cues.

Consider where to begin defending. For most counterattacking teams, the center forwards begin defending inside the halfway circle.

You need to decide whether to show in or out. Under Craig Brown, the Scottish team split its two center forwards to invite opposition into the middle of the field (see figure 9.7). Bobby Clarke of the University of Notre Dame teaches his team to force flank players to go inside into the mass of midfielders (figure 9.8). This enables the defending team to win the ball and launch a counterattack from the middle of the field rather than from the outside where countering is less effective.

Players should know the disposition of the forwards when the ball goes past them. Counterattacking teams must have somebody in an advanced position to receive the pass for a counterattack to work. When playing with

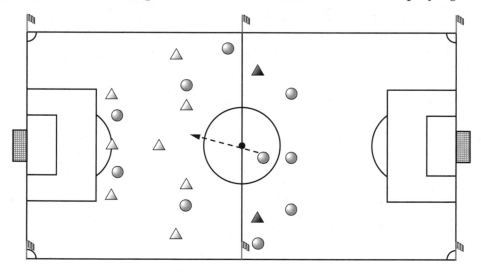

Figure 9.7 Showing in.

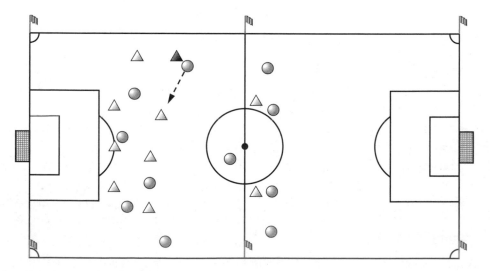

Figure 9.8 Forcing flanks in.

two center forwards, stagger them and use one for short passes and one for long passes (figure 9.9).

Players also need to recognize the moment of interception and transition. This is the critical cue to begin the counterattack. The interception and transition normally occurs after a tackle, after an interception of a pass, when the goalkeeper cuts off a cross or shot, or within a dead-ball situation such as a throw-in or free kick.

Recognize the quality of the first pass forward. The player must decide whether to pass the ball forward or run the ball. Running the ball takes longer but keeps possession secure and, if the opponent is really outnumbered, forces recognizable 2 v 1s in a very dangerous part of the field. If the dribble is not on, then the first attacker must decide whether to play the ball long and behind the defenders or in front of the defenders with a short pass that must be supported at once. This decision is based largely on the visual cue of defensive depth (figure 9.10). If the backline is square, the ball can be played into the space behind. If there is depth, the ball may need to be played to the feet of the attacker and quickly supported by midfielders.

Consider changing the point of attack. Keep the counterattack going at speed. Defenders will react to the counter by dropping. More sophisticated

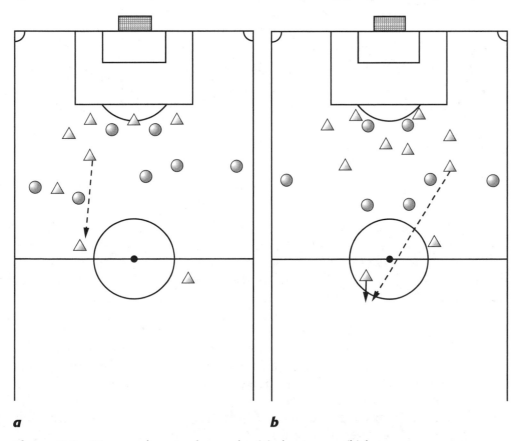

a   *b*

Figure 9.9   Staggered center forwards: *(a)* short pass; *(b)* long pass.

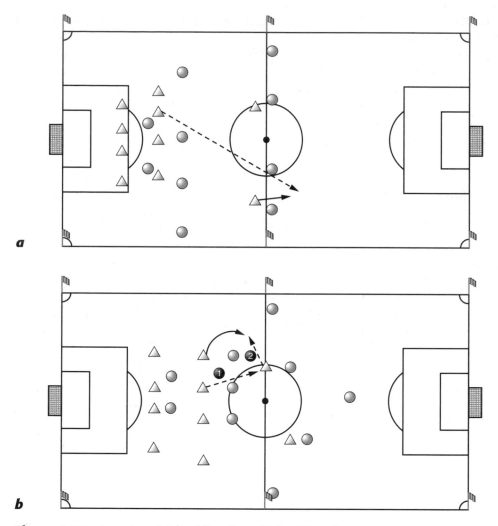

Figure 9.10 Counter: *(a)* backline flat; *(b)* backline deep.

teams will edge toward the ball to slow down the counter. As a defender does this, the first attacker keeps driving forward, looks across, and, if necessary, switches play to a player on the other side of the field to force the defenders to shift again. When this is done quickly, defenders frequently get caught with a ball behind them. They are outflanked and can't prevent the attacker from breaking in on the goal.

Look for the one on one. Players who are one on one with the goalkeeper should drive at one of the posts, forcing the goalkeeper to move. Goalkeepers will try to intersect the V formed between the ball and the two posts. By making the goalkeeper move laterally, the first attacker can slip the ball under the keeper's body as the keeper protects near the post or can clip the ball over the keeper's legs. Another alternative is to dribble around after forcing the goalkeeper to go around with a fake move or shot. A stationed goalkeeper adopting a low crouch can frequently be nutmegged.

Transition Mentality

Four attackers play against two defenders in one half of the field. The defending players' teammates stand in the other half of the field. The attackers begin with possession of the ball. They can score a goal by splitting the two defenders (although they are limited to two touches). When the defenders win the ball, they play the ball across the half-line to the two other defenders. The attacking team is not allowed over the half-line until the ball crosses over. When the ball goes over the half-line, two former attackers can go across to begin defending (figure 9.11). A ball out of play goes to the defending team.

To avoid being split with one pass, defenders stay close together. They should try to read the attackers' mistakes, such as a bad first touch, and spring forward, together, to intercept the ball. Defenders might have to pass the ball sideways to break the pressure before playing forward.

To vary the drill, increase or decrease the number of defenders or the numbers of touches allowed.

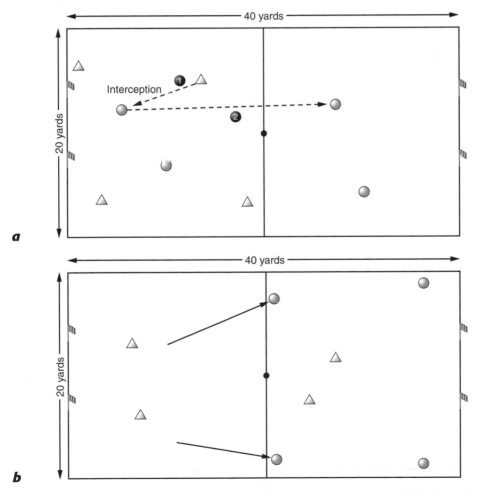

Figure 9.11   Transition mentality: (a) the defender intercepts the ball; (b) defenders retreat over the half-line, followed by attackers.

4 v 4

In this exercise, the tactic for the defending team is to remain extremely compact around its goal and invite the attacking team "into" its lair. Defending with the compact three while leaving one player up high is the alignment in this 4 v 4 training game.

When the attacking team loses the ball, they immediately retreat and defend with three players. The ideal for defenders is to form a defensive triangle. Win the ball and counter to the center forward. Run the ball forward at speed. If there's space behind the last defender, play the ball into that space. If space behind is not available, play to the feet of the center forward and sprint to support the pass (figure 9.12a). If the countering player runs (dribbles) the ball, the center forward bends away to create a two on one against the defenders (figure 9.12b).

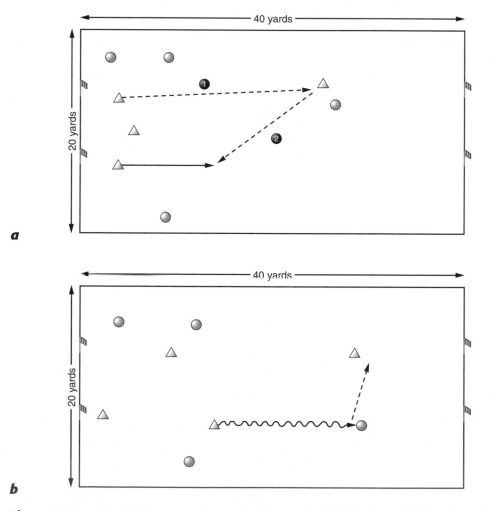

Figure 9.12 4 v 4: *(a)* pass to the center forward; *(b)* dribble upfield.

9 v 8

Set goals 78 yards apart. Use the halfway line as the top of the second penalty box. Use cones to mark a line 10 yards inside the defending half. The defending unit of backs and midfielders get into a 4-4, 3-4, or 3-5 plus goalkeeper alignment and play against an attacking unit of midfield and center forwards in a specified formation, such as the 5-2. These players are inside the line of cones. One center forward marked by one defender are on the other side of the line of cones and aren't allowed inside the line.

The coach begins by passing the ball to the attacking midfielder and center forward. The defensive unit's objective is to prevent attackers from scoring, win the ball, and counterattack off of the center forward to score. When the defending team wins the ball, they play the ball to the center forward before being allowed over the line of cones to attack the goal. Players look for one-two passes or three-man combinations off the center forward to get over the line (figure 9.13).

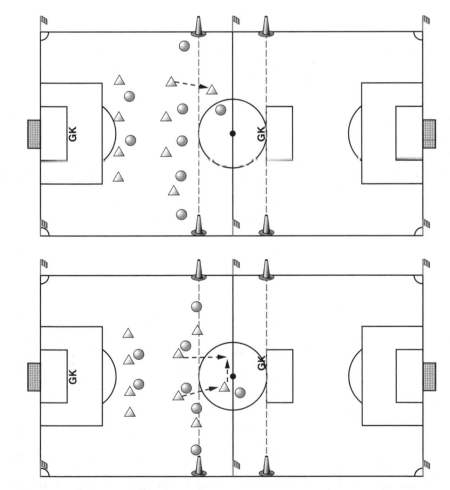

Figure 9.13   9 v 8: (a) playing to short center forward; (b) three-player combination.

For more advanced players, extend the field to full length. Add a second center forward and a third defender. Instruct the third defender to alternate playing flat or deep. The counterattacking team is encouraged to play the ball into the feet if the third defender is deep or into space if the third defender is flat (figure 9.14).

The two center forwards try to stagger their positions. The deep center forward mirrors the ball by staying in a vertical line with the ball. The high center forward tries to be diagonally opposite in relation to the ball position to provide an angled pass from teammates.

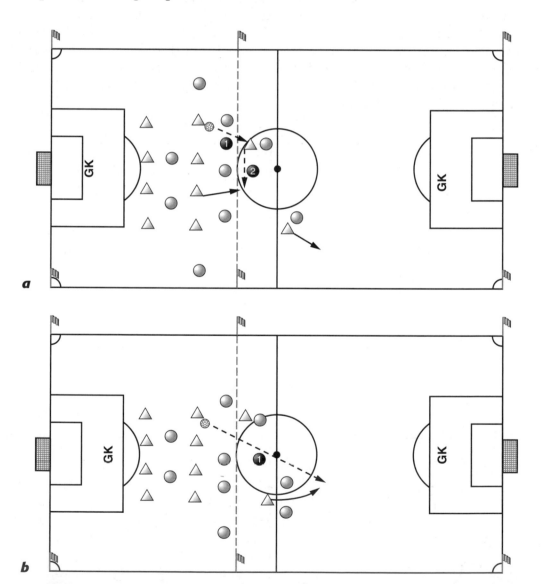

Figure 9.14 Advanced 10 v 9: (a) counter versus deep defender; (b) counter versus flat defender.

Final Game- 11 v 11

Counterattack team drops to halfway line when opposition gains possession of ball. They will look to counterattack when an interception occurs (figure 9.15).

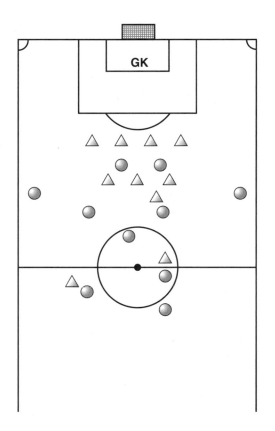

Figure 9.15   11 v 11: counterattack upon interception.

Summary

When designing innovative training sessions, use a logical progression. The two sessions presented in this chapter demand that you dissect play and decide what aspects need to be emphasized during each phase of the training session. As your players master each phase, increase the difficulty. You might initially place restrictions on play and then lift the restrictions as your players progress. As your players demonstrate mastery of the skills in training, their team play will elevate during matches, and you'll know your sessions have been a success.

CHAPTER 10

Teaching Players to Think Creatively

Barry Gorman

How do you get players to think? At first, I thought this was a ridiculous question to ask any soccer player or coach. Why must coaches get players to think? Players think; how could they not? After all, don't we consider soccer a game for thinkers and executioners? In a world where coaches of other sports are given more timeouts and greater control over plays, soccer stands alone as a player's game. Once they kick off, players have to make their own decisions, drawing on their practice and previous game knowledge.

On reflection, however, I recognized that many players merely respond or react to game scenarios, especially in the United States, where players are not exposed to the game to the same extent as their "football" counterparts around the globe. Only when the discussion in the pub, playground, or classroom is of last night's soccer game and not "Did you see that triple play in the third inning last night?" will I believe that our players see the game in their mind's eye.

Are we doing a poor job of getting players to think for themselves? I'm reminded of an old soccer story. A young player in his senior team debut is getting a lot of unrequested advice from spectators and coaches alike. The first time the young lad gets a pass, the nonplaying participants shout, "Pass it!" The next time, they say, "Dribble the ball!" The third time, he hears, "Shoot it before you lose it!" Over the course of the game, the young man is trapped in the corner, surrounded by mean, menacing defenders bent on destroying his career before it even begins. With the situation desperate, the young forward puts his foot on the ball and calls timeout. When he doesn't hear any advice, he turns expectantly to the quiet onlookers and asks, "What should I do now?"

"Improvise," they respond.

Are "footballers" made or born? This question is often asked when the game and spectators cry out for the next Pele, Best, Cryuff, Zidane, Ronaldo, or Henry. Those players could *improvise,* but was it a natural reaction or the result of endless hours spent on the practice pitch? Or was it an environmentally suitable upbringing honed by hours of street soccer? With street soccer dying a slow death in a world of home computers and video games, the so-called soccer experts predict a future void of special game-day, crowd-appealing superstars.

Creating the Environment

As coaching educators, we know we must re-create gamelike situations in the training environment or face the extinction of the player who "thinks with his feet." Yet many of today's coaches fail to formulate a practice atmosphere that elicits fun, excitement, creativity, and learning. How then can we motivate players to live, sleep, eat, drink, and think the game?

If the game is a simple one, surely the answer should be elementary and forthcoming. To get coaches to invigorate practices and create mentally stimulating learning environments is an ongoing challenge that faces all soccer educators today.

If they want to encourage players to think, coaches must include three elements in their practices. First, practices should be gamelike and as much fun as possible. Second, practices should include specific match obstacles that every player must circumvent. Third, practices should flow to allow players to express themselves as they make game-deciding decisions.

Soccer is a simple game played with the mind, body, and spirit. Often the enthusiasm, effort, and energy generated does not complement the intellectual thought process. Unfortunately, rote learning often replaces creativity, flair, and improvisation. Together, coaches and players must maintain a fine balance if they are to develop and nurture the future stars needed to entertain and produce results in a sport where player performance is increasingly under public and media scrutiny.

The task of implementing theory into practice falls on the coach. From presession planning to postpractice debriefing, the coach must plan for every eventuality but also allow for freedom of expression and moments of brilliance. The coach must think of him- or herself as "Coach OOI"—organizer, observer, and instructor. Unlike Agent 007, coach OOI is licensed to teach.

The coaching session must be an organizational gem, using all human and material resources to promote optimal learning within the time allotted. The coach must be observant and note successes and failures while recognizing potential solutions to improve personal performances and enhance team production. The coach must teach while allowing creativity, flair, and genius to shine through.

Warm-Up

The typical practice begins with the warm-up. Right from the start, the coach must ensure that the session is realistic, efficient, and purposeful. The session should be realistic in that it's gamelike or game related. It's efficient in that it's meaningful, time sensitive, technically and tactically connected to the previous match as well as the match to come. It's purposeful in that the result is productively preplanned rather than haphazard, unrelated, and meaningless.

Great teams dismantle their opponents in a premeditated fashion. Coaches must prepare their teams for the task at hand while getting players to think about their roles in the game plan. The warm-up sets the tone for the practice session, so let's examine what should occur while players are warming up.

The warm-up should be energetic and directly related to the theme of the practice. It should include stretching, movement, and individual ball contact. During warm-up, players should reproduce movements and skills they enjoy and like to do in the match itself. The warm-up should be challenging because players must be encouraged to start thinking from the moment practice begins to the instant it ends. Obviously, we want—no, demand—that players think from first instruction until last whistle.

Often players amble through preset routines that produce repetitive reactions requiring little to no thought. These practices don't do much to encourage players to see the game in their mind's eye. Cerebral players capable of determining the outcome of matches with moments of pure premeditated soccer skill executed with practiced perfection need thought-provoking practice sessions to stimulate their creative genius. Because the game belongs to the players, and players make decisions on and off the ball, players must be taught to express their creative ideas in combination with teammates. Movement patterns must be seen as logical, preplanned moves expressed with aplomb, flair, and skill.

Such warm-ups encourage players to think.

Group Combinations

Mark an area 40 × 30 yards. Divide a squad of 16 players into two equal teams. Goalies warm up separately. Members on one team are given a ball and asked to play wall passes, takeovers, double passes, and overlaps with a member of the other team (figure 10.1). Members of the other team move and seek out opportunities to combine with a player in possession of a ball. The flurry of movement symbolizes the hustle and bustle of game play, and the player with the ball pinpoints the player with whom he or she is going to combine and make it happen despite others trying to create other combinations in the same area.

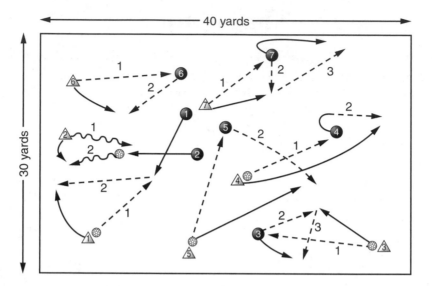

Figure 10.1 Group combination warm-up.

At first, the players in possession are told to perform the same skill, but as time progresses, they are encouraged to decide on their own combination and what's required to complete it successfully.

Circle Combinations

Divide a 16-player squad into two equal teams. Both teams form circles. Initially, one player from each team is in the middle of the circle with a ball. This player seeks out a teammate with whom to combine. The coach sets a series of exchange moves in motion (figure 10.2). Players on the outside of the circle are on their toes and thinking ahead to complete the combination and avoid running into players doing similar tasks.

For the three-man combination, player 1 plays to player 2 and runs to replace player 3. Player 2 plays a through ball for player 3 to move on to.

For the four-man combination, player 1 passes to player 2 to play a first-time ball to player 3. Player 3 lays the ball off to player 4, who runs to support player 3 as he/she receives the long pass from player 2. All players need to be ready to receive, lay off, and support. They must think ahead. In this example, four players are involved in the movement. Every player must replace the player on the circle to whom they pass.

For the five-man combination, as player 1 passes to player 2, players 3 and 4 overlap. Player 2 passes back to player 1, who lays the ball off to player 3. Player 3 passes across the circle to player 5, who in turn lays the ball off to player 4, who has continued his run. Five players are involved in this move. Once a sequence has been completed, the initial pass from the center and back triggers another overlapping movement.

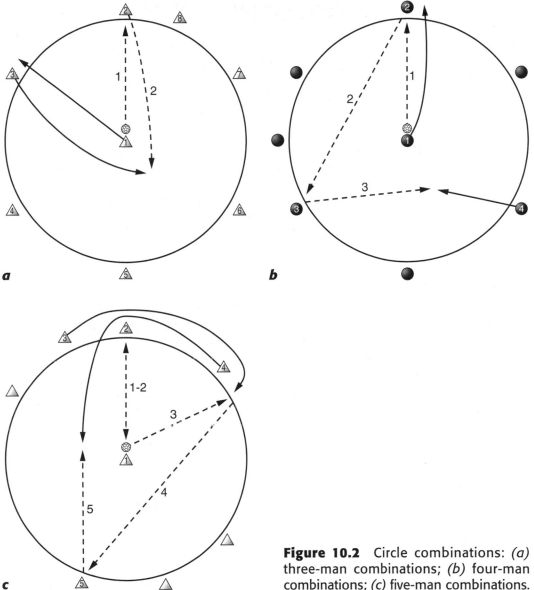

Figure 10.2 Circle combinations: *(a)* three-man combinations; *(b)* four-man combinations; *(c)* five-man combinations.

Once players master combinations, the two teams form a larger circle and complete three-man, four-man, or five-man combinations at the same time in the same area.

Again, the movement of the teams simulates gamelike conditions. Players are asked to improvise and elaborate as they master basic patterns and develop understanding with one another. Players are asked to visualize the patterns that might occur in a game. Functionally, they should be creating possible moves within the context of their roles in the team game plan.

Match-Related Phase

From the warm-up, the session moves smoothly into the developmental stage of the practice without unnecessary interruptions. This stage is the conduit, appreciated by all, where teaching and learning occurs because the environment created by the coaching staff is conducive to it. The coach creates an environment that clearly demonstrates what he or she wants players to get out of the session. The exercises challenge the players while promoting thought-provoking self-evaluation. Learning, therefore, can be cooperative, with players allowed to give their input in an appropriate manner, time, and place.

The following exercise demonstrates a possible thought-provoking passing progression with the goal of penetrating. In a competitive playing environment, players are asked to perform at match pace and under match conditions to recreate game circumstances.

Keep Away and Penetrate (9 v 9)

Two teams of nine play against each other on half a field (figure 10.3). The objective is to get through the cones under control, using combination plays, and then deliver telling crosses into dangerous areas in front of the goal.

Player 1 passes to the forward, player 2. Player 2 lays the ball off to player 3, who plays a through ball for an overlapping flank player, player 4, to get between the cones to deliver an early cross to either the forward (5) or opposite flank player (6), making penetrating runs in the penalty area.

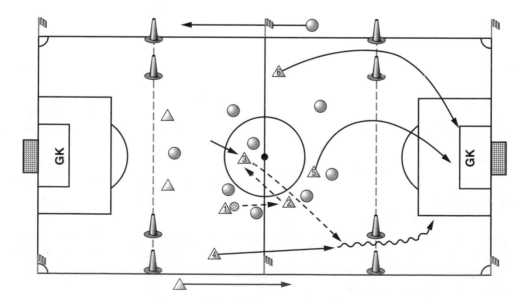

Figure 10.3 Keep away and penetrate.

Match Play

The concluding activity in any practice session is, of course, match play. In this phase, players and coaches can see if what they practiced does, in fact, work under game circumstances without coaching stoppages and directions.

Often, however, coaches and players lose the plot when it comes to the ability to think clearly under match conditions. Thus, if we want to encourage players to think, this stage of practice has important feedback value. We want individual players and the team as a whole to assess their abilities. Remember that players are allowed to ad lib within the confines of the theme of the practice. Otherwise, they tend to lose focus and regurgitate what the coach drills into them.

Certainly, we want our players to think and be proactive while applying what we've been working on in practice. Together, coach and players try to create a stylish ball club. However, reality is in preparation for the upcoming fixture. Better-trained athletes and players who are taught to think for themselves can assert their brand of soccer regardless of the opposition's intentions.

For example, imagine that the next opponent plays on a particularly narrow field and in a direct, aggressive manner. How can you get your players to handle this type of offense in this environment without sacrificing their natural tendencies? By manipulating numbers, time, and space, you can realistically create a match environment that your players can expect for the next game.

In the example shown in figure 10.4, the coach and players work on breaking pressure by practicing a flank double pass to free a wide player

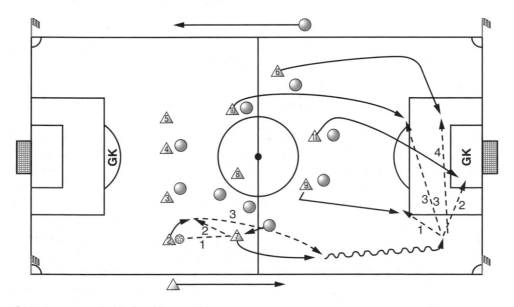

Figure 10.4   Flank double pass.

to deliver a penetrating through ball. The sequence begins with player 2 playing a short, soft pass outside to encourage player 7 to come back for the ball and tease player 7's defender into trying a tackle. Player 7 quickly plays the ball back inside to player 2 and spins to run behind the defender. Player 2 plays a through ball to player 7, who proceeds to dribble to the opponent's endline.

At this point, player 7 has several options if his teammates make intelligent runs off the ball, shake their markers, and arrive in dangerous attacking spaces to receive a killer pass from player 7. The forward (9) checks back and looks to drop in behind player 7 for a laid back pass—option 1—at an acute angle from which he or she can shoot to score. After fading away during the initial movement between players 2 and 7 to get behind his marker, the other forward (11) times his or her run for a possible hard-driven ball—option 2—played toward the near post. Meanwhile, the central midfielder (10) arrives late in the penalty box about 16 yards from the goal as a possibility for getting on the end of a pass pulled back—option 3. The wide midfielder (6) arrives fast and late at the back post for the ball that player 7 might chip over and behind the goalie—option 4.

Obviously, any time you can get your players to get into dangerous positions and have teammates arriving free to facilitate four penetrating passing options, a lot of intelligent combinations have to take place on and off the ball. If each player, individually, doesn't see the possibilities in his or her "mind's eye" and the attacking unit, collectively, doesn't see the options in their minds, nothing will happen. As coach, you're the coordinator and architect of such movements. Your observations have to be all encompassing to orchestrate such precision passing and calculated runs to bring about predetermined movements that result in clinical finishing. That's a lot of soccer to conceive, plan, and present. Now, of course, the simple matter is to get the players to execute and score. Isn't that the beautiful goal of any master coach working with outstanding talent?

Summary

The kind of learning and improvement discussed in this chapter often takes seasons and years to bear fruit. Slowly but surely, soccer coaches have come to realize that working harder, faster, and longer hours does not necessarily bring results. Today's coach and player must appreciate the need to work smarter and more efficiently while continuing to think. Much like the youngster who plays the game on the street or sandlot, it begins with seeing combinations, movements, and plays in your mind's eye. Spectacular moves and video highlight goals are fashioned in such childhood dream games years before the next superstar's emergence on soccer's world stage.

Getting players to think is and always will be the same as getting the horse to the drinking trough. You can't force it to drink. There are three types of players: those who make things happen, those who see what happens, and those who ask what happened. Players who want to make things happen will flourish in the right environment, especially if they're encouraged to think and combine with teammates. Coach OOI will know when and where to apply the right amount of fertilizer.

Are great players born or bred? The debate will continue as long as there are soccer matches worth watching. Do you coach soccer or coach players? The thinking coach knows the answer, and his or her players will realize what kind of player each is likely to become. You had better believe that players have to think. If you want to be a coach of soccer and a coach of players, you better get your charges to think from start to finish. For sure as not shooting, one of those players won't get to the right place at the right time.

One last thought as a reminder to us all that coaching is an ongoing labor of love. Lest we forget, let the following old coaching tale put it all in perspective.

During a particularly tight, exciting, league-deciding game, the coach, who is completely consumed with what's not happening on the field, mumbles to his bench for a certain reserve striker to get ready to sub in. Without looking around, the coach utters complex, incoherent instructions to the eager substitute. Unfortunately, the wrong substitute has answered the coach's call to action in an effort to save the team in the waning moments of this important game. Inexplicably, the wrong substitute enters the game and takes out the wrong starter. Furthermore, the sub proceeds to play in the wrong position and ends up in the wrong place at the wrong time to score the winning goal in the dying seconds of the championship clincher. Without missing a beat, the coach turns to the players on the bench and announces, "Now that's coaching!"

Enjoy the game while teaching your players to think. If you don't, you're leaving the outcome of games to chance.

CHAPTER 11

Training for High-Level Soccer Fitness

Ron McEachen

We can define soccer fitness as the body's and mind's ability to perform desired tasks demanded by the sport at an optimal level. In the past, players prepared for a season by doing some running, but the game's fitness demands have changed over the years. The speed of the game is much faster, so fitness training demands have increased. Many experts consider fitness to be the key element in preparing a team to compete at a high level. Fitness training is now a year-round process, and players who wish to compete must accept the responsibility of maintaining this critical component.

I want to share an important fitness lesson I learned during six memorable weeks in Europe. It was the spring of 1982. I had just arrived from Sweden, where I had spent three weeks training and observing Malmo FF and IFC Goteborg, coached respectively by Roy Hodgson (former Switzerland national team coach) and Sven Goran Ericsson (current England national team coach). I was able to train with Goteborg in their successful run to the UEFA title. It was a revelation to see how they prepared physically and how they tapered training leading up to the big match.

I spent my next three weeks with the Southampton (England) Football Club and Steve Mills, my former teammate on the Miami Toros. My fitness level was good, and I was invited to train with the team that included England national team players Alan Ball, Mick Shannon, and Kevin Keegan. It was marvelous to participate in their training. At the end of training, we assembled to finish with some shuttle runs. We divided into groups of three and spread cones every seven yards across the field.

---

* Written with contributions from Denise Smith (Skidmore College).

Keegan stood alone at the end of the group. We were doing four sets with a short rest between each set. We began the sprints, and Kevin did all three runs and ended up winning the first round. He also won the next three rounds as players worked their hardest to defeat him. I knew then why he was the European Footballer of the Year and one of the greatest forwards ever to play the game. He worked harder than anyone else. That weekend he was the hardest worker and the fittest player on the field. While others tired, he seemed to gain strength. It was no accident that he scored the goal to win the game against their division one rival.

These visits helped shape my philosophy on player fitness. At first I knew little of the concepts of interval training or how the overload principle applied to training, but my teams at Middlebury, Vermont, and Skidmore were rarely beaten because of lack of fitness. In fact, we won several games because we were more physically fit than our opponents. I knew that this was a huge psychological advantage to our players, and we played it to the max. We prided ourselves on working harder in training and translating it onto the playing field. It continues to work to this day with an even more refined approach.

Functional Physical Demands

Soccer is a dynamic game of contact and movement played over a period of 90-plus minutes. Play consists of a series of individual and group duals over the entire field. Players run up to nine miles, do upward of 200 sprints of varying distances, kick the ball 75 to 100 times, and jump to head the ball as many as 100 times. It's a physical game in which players make full-speed contact with each other as often as 50 times a game. Thus, it's critical to understand the fitness needs of players and structure training to meet the demands of the game, especially in regard to the specific responsibilities of each position. When looking at the fitness of the team and individuals, define the activity surrounding each position and decide how to accomplish the task of getting each player to successfully compete at an optimal level.

Goalkeepers must be able to jump to win balls in the air, take a hit by opposing players, dive to either side as well as forward and backward instantaneously, kick balls well beyond midfield, move from side to side as the ball bobbles around the penalty area, sprint out to thwart an onrushing forward, and sprint to corral a ball played over the top of the defense.

Backs must time their jumps to head a ball sailing from 70 yards away, make short and long sprints to mark and close down players and assist in attack, run backward at speed to defend an attacking forward, twist and turn as the forward tries to deceive the back into making a mistake, tackle with ferocity and technical expertise, kick 60-yard diagonal balls to breaking players, and slide while running at full speed to tackle an opposing forward.

Midfielders must run from their penalty area to the opponent's penalty area several times a game, spin and turn on a dime, fake and feint opponents while changing speed, sprint to receive balls and win tackles, hold the ball while being kicked and pressured by an opponent, strike the ball in excess of 100 times, and win heading duals.

Forwards must have great acceleration and quickness, the ability to feint and fake opponents while maintaining possession of the ball, change pace with and without the ball, head while challenged by an opponent, shield the ball under extreme pressure of an opponent, kick the ball with power and accuracy, react to any changes of the ball while in and around the penalty area, and pressure and tackle backs who try to play out of the back.

Components of Fitness

Match demands can be met through training for the major fitness components of power, muscular strength and endurance, speed, quickness, acceleration, mobility, flexibility, agility, balance, coordination, and aerobic and anaerobic cardiorespiratory capacity.

Power is the combination of strength and speed. It's essential for acceleration, explosion, quickness, and reaction. Power is essential for the modern soccer player. One must be ready to lift weights, run circuits, perform plyometrics, and do the interval training necessary to enhance this fitness component.

Strength is the amount of force used by a muscle or group of muscles to produce a maximum effort. Muscular endurance allows an athlete to compete at an optimal level for a long time. Strength and muscular endurance are becoming more and more important in realizing peak performance.

Speed has been called the single greatest factor in sport performance. The game of soccer is getting faster. Although speed can be improved through training, it's mainly a factor of the types of muscle fibers inherited. Fast-twitch fibers are used in anaerobic training, and slow-twitch fibers are used in aerobic training. Although some animal studies have shown a marked increase in changing slow-twitch fibers to fast-twitch, not much success has been seen in humans. Exercises such as bounding; running while hitting the heels to the gluteus maximus; running while taking short, quick steps; running with knees up, touching the hands; and running with long strides assist in improving speed. Other techniques to improve speed are pulling a weighted sled; using a harness or tube; running uphill or downhill; putting light weights in the shoes or on the ankles; and running stadium stairs.

While playing with the Toros, I had the pleasure of training with Steve David, the league scoring leader the previous season. We stayed after training and ran sprints using the markings of the field, alternating jogging and sprinting each line two to three times around the entire field. He was the fastest player I ever competed against, and this training aided in his ability to do short sprints as well as longer sprints. Several years later, I was told that he represented his country in the 4 × 100 relay.

Speed endurance is the key to meeting the demands of pace for an entire match. Interval training is critical in attaining the fitness level required. Sprints of 10 to 80 yards with 8 to 15 repetitions and decreasing rest periods are recommended to replicate match conditions. These sprints can be done with a ball to more closely mirror game conditions. Other methods of improving speed endurance are the Carolina shuttle run (five cones are set at five-yard intervals and players run 10 timed sets), stationary cycling, downhill running of 50 meters with a slope of less than 7 percent, and treadmill sprinting to increase rate and length of stride.

Agility is the body's ability to move and react quickly in difficult situations. Efficiency and coordination make these tasks look effortless. Agility is a key factor in reaching the top level of play. Agile athletes have a definite edge in decreasing the risk of injury because agility allows athletes to instantly adjust their bodies to changes that arise in a game. Agility can be tested with dot drills, ladder drills, and various cone configurations.

Coordination refers to how efficiently muscles work together. Coordination is vital to success in soccer. A player who lacks coordination often fails because of his inability to recover and maintain proper body position. One need only watch a player to understand that he either does or doesn't have total command of his body in all match situations.

Balance is critical to every fundamental technique of the game. It's important for athletes to be able to control their bodies during competition. Players who get knocked off the ball or land on the ground need to improve their footwork and the strength of their hamstrings and quadriceps to enhance their balance. The basic stance is weight low with feet shoulder-width apart; this basic stance is important to achieving good balance during play. Balance is the key to kicking a ball, jumping to head the ball, tackling an opponent, shooting on goal, or making a successful pass. Exercises to improve balance include squats, lunges, leg presses, stands on one leg, stands on one leg while striking a ball, hops forward and sideways, jumps into the air while making contact with an opponent and landing low on two feet, hops over cones, and alternate leg hops. Plyoballs can also be used. The true test is if a player can maintain a good base of support in all situations while competing.

Flexibility is the ability to move the joints freely and easily through different ranges of motion as demanded by the game. Good flexibility aids in the efficiency of all movement. It helps increase speed, enhances coordination, develops power, decreases soreness, eliminates lactic acid, and enhances performance in all endurance and power sports.

It's important to warm up the muscles and joints before embarking on an intense stretching program. Before stretching, do some light jogging. Low-intensity stretching aids in the recovery of damaged muscle tissue, aids in breaking down scar tissue, and quickens recovery from injury. A static stretch is held in place for 20 to 30 seconds with a 10-second rest between stretches. Static stretching is successful because of little stress on the muscles and joints. Ballistic stretches require a bouncing movement. This type of stretching is detrimental when done without a good warm-up. The muscle tends to contract because of the stress initiated by the bouncing, and the muscle doesn't lengthen. Proprioceptive nueromuscular facilitation (PNF) has been found to have good results. PNF begins with a 6- to 10-second isometric stretch while a partner holds the muscle at full range of motion. The stretcher works against the partner's resistance. After a short rest, the stretcher performs a static stretch of 15 to 30 seconds.

Fine-Tuning the Cardiorespiratory System

Let's move to the cardiorespiratory system and aerobic and anaerobic training as they relate to soccer. The cardiorespiratory system allows the body to work at levels of high intensity over long periods of time. The body's ability to use the greatest amount of oxygen during a stressful exercise is referred to as maximum oxygen uptake ($\dot{V}O_2$max). It is one of the best ways to determine cardiorespiratory fitness. A 1.5-mile run to measure $\dot{V}O_2$max, devised by Dr. Kenneth Cooper, is a great test to measure cardiorespiratory fitness. A 20-year-old male who runs the 1.5 mile in under nine minutes has a $\dot{V}O_2$max of 62 and is considered to have a very high level of fitness. The average female has a 15 to 20 percent lower $\dot{V}O_2$max than males because of differences in body size.

Aerobic training refers to working with oxygen; anaerobic training emphasizes metabolism without oxygen to supply energy. The demands of soccer dictate that we spend more time training the anaerobic side than we have in the past, but it's important to understand that the two systems work together simultaneously. The modern game uses about 40 percent anaerobic fitness and 60 percent aerobic fitness. Many experts predict this fitness mix increasing to 50-50 because of higher anaerobic demands inherent in the game.

Anaerobic training refers to all-out activity lasting less than two minutes and includes activities such as sprinting and jumping, which are so critical to the game of soccer. Anaerobic training produces a substance called lactic acid, which causes muscle fatigue. The fittest players can put off this buildup of lactic acid longer and sustain optimal performance levels. Lactic acid is produced when glycogen is used without the presence of oxygen. Anaerobic training should be included in practice. In a 90-minute training session, devote at least 36 minutes of maximal 2-minute bouts of exercise. This can be done through well-planned training sessions that can include methods such as plyometrics, circuit training, weight training, and interval training.

Aerobic training is low to moderate intensity for endurance and consists of distance runs with an introduction of Fartlek training. Fartlek training includes gradual sprinting activities while running and allows the body to become more accustomed to anaerobic training. Aerobic training allows the player to work longer anaerobically when competing at top levels. Aerobic training is the basis for all training and allows a player to continue to improve fitness levels and progress to anaerobic training.

Fortunately, the aerobic and anaerobic systems work together. The aerobic system prevents the buildup of lactic acid and allows the body to prepare for other high-intensity bursts of activity. The right balance needs to be struck; too much aerobic training will develop slow-twitch muscle fibers and negate quickness, lessen skill improvement, and affect overall performance. To train effectively and build cardiovascular endurance, players must train at an intensity of at least 70 percent of their maximum heart rate. Maximum heart rate can be estimated by subtracting age from 220 then multiplying the result by 0.80. For example, for a 20-year-old player, we would figure $220 - 20 = 200 \times 0.80 = 160$ beats per minute. Players need to exercise for at least 30 minutes three to four times a week to maintain fitness levels.

Building Muscular Endurance

Muscular endurance is the ability to perform continuous muscular movements over a period of time. The ability to perform at regular intervals is the demand of modern soccer. Muscular endurance needs to be trained appropriately with weight training (using high repetitions and low resistance), plyometrics, intervals, and circuits.

Circuit Training

Circuit training combines strength, muscular and cardiorespiratory endurance, skill, and all the components of fitness in a series of stations in which players perform various activities. Establish stations at which players perform timed tasks specific to the needs of the team. Stations are timed with an equal rest period between stations. Stations often are set up so players switch from a physical activity to a tactical one. A typical circuit has 10 to 20 stations. Players spend about one minute at each station. Brazilian teams initiated this training method in the 1970s; they have since maintained it as an integral part of their development.

Plyometrics Training

Plyometrics were credited for the Eastern European domination in track and field several years ago. Back then, plyometrics were known as the jump-training program. Plyometrics exercises allow the muscle to reach maximum strength as quickly as possible. Plyometrics should be done more frequently during the buildup to the season and slowed down in season. The best way to understand how plyometrics work is to think about how a moving player plants his foot before jumping to head or catch a ball. The planting phase is the shortening or *concentric* phase; the jumping initiates an immediate lengthening or *eccentric* phase. Plyometrics training was introduced to other sports to improve speed and strength and produce power. Players develop the ability to get off the mark more quickly, improve speed, and change directions quickly. A good plyometrics program can help an elite athlete improve explosiveness, reaction time, and speed.

Another component of plyometrics is a program of ballistic and static stretching. It's best to begin with the static stretch and then progress to controlled ballistic stretching before performing plyometrics exercises. This sequence may reduce the risk of injury and prepare the body for the demands of training. Plyometrics are anaerobic exercises. Full recovery is necessary to derive full benefit. Plyometrics can and should be used with other training systems. Plyometrics training aids the performance of weight training and anaerobic training and vice versa.

Examples of plyometrics exercises are jumps in place, hops and jumps over lines and cones, depth jumps using boxes of various heights, long jumps, bounds, runs and hops up and down stairs or bleachers, and medicine ball throws that develop the upper body. All these exercises can be used to mimic soccer movement to effectively build a training base. Progress slowly to minimize risk of injury and maximize improvement. Allow 48 to 72 hours for recovery between sessions.

Interval Training

Interval training is thought to be the best method for improving anaerobic capacity. This kind of training consists of an intense series of work done within time restrictions. Interval length is determined by the athlete's fitness level. A sound six- to eight-week program of aerobic exercise, three to four days a week for 30 minutes, is highly recommended before engaging in interval training. Activities such as running, swimming, and cycling are sufficient forms of aerobic exercise. I ask my players to incorporate a series of sprints (50 to 75 percent of $\dot{V}O_2$max) of various distances (5 to 75 yards) into their runs before they arrive at preseason camp. I ask them to increase the number of sprints as they increase the distance, but not to reduce the sprinting speed. This is a form of Fartlek training and prepares players well to meet the demands of interval training. If this isn't done, players will not recover as well during interval training and will be more susceptible to injury.

The work-to-rest ratio is critical to the success of interval training. The duration of the work and the level of fitness of the player are critical factors. In the early stages of interval training, it might be best to have a rest ratio of 3:1 or 4:1. The interval ratio needs to be adjusted as players check pulse rates and determine that they're working at 60 to 70 percent of their maximum heart rates. The rest ratio decreases to 1:1 as high levels of fitness are reached. Occasionally, a ratio of 1:2 is used to push certain athletes to new limits of anaerobic fitness. One to two weeks before the first match, the work ratio should decrease to 2:1 or 3:1. During the season, reduce the ratio to 3:1 or 4:1 to maintain fitness and familiarity. A maximum of three alternate days a week should be sufficient in attaining this fitness level.

An example of interval training in soccer would be one-on-one and two-on-two competitions during preseason. This could be done in groups of four and eight players, respectively. The one-on-one keep-away competition uses a field 15 $\times$ 25 yards with players at either end. The first two players compete for 30 to 90 seconds. As soon as they finish, the other two players immediately start passing the ball. We normally do 5 to 10 sets at 60 seconds, depending on where we are on the fitness chart. Don't forget the warm-up and cool-down, and allow time to stretch after each phase.

Weight Training

Weight training, also known as strength training, has become more influential in soccer training programs. A player who isn't doing some type of lifting program often doesn't make the grade. The psychological advantage of knowing that you have increased strength and power, decreased the chance of injury, and improved performance is huge. Strength is often the difference in matches when everything else is equal.

For example, consider a very technical French player who played for me at Vermont. He was quite fast but lacked something to put him at a higher level. We sold him on the idea of a weight-training program, and he began the transition from a good player to a top player. By the end of his senior year, he had no peer in the league. He went home and became a starter on a third-division French professional team. I should mention that we like to make such training a team-bonding experience as all players support and push each other in the weight room.

Many players set performance goals yet forget to do the same with fitness goals. Set short- and long-term goals for the weight-training program and keep a log of training performance and improvement. We try to set realistic goals and keep the emphasis on endurance and speed. Our emphasis is on working all the muscle groups three to four times a week with two to three sets of lifting 50 to 60 percent of the player's maximal lift.

Most players use free weights, which allow them to go through the entire range of motion and closely replicate soccer action. When players are looking to develop strength and power, we recommend that they use free weights, Cybex, or Nautilus machines.

Our players use an effective system called "pyramiding" to increase strength and power. For example, a player lifts 100 pounds for 10 reps, 125 pounds for 8 reps, 150 pounds for 6 reps, 170 pounds for 4 reps, 190 pounds for 2 reps, and 200 pounds for 1 rep. The player rests a minimum of two minutes between each set and then moves back down the pyramid. This type of program applies the overload principle—to achieve success, you must overload the muscles with increased stress by changing weight, repetitions, sets, rest, and number of workouts.

Many players begin training on machines such as Universal, Nautilus, Cybex, Fitron, or Hydra Fitness. The advantages of machines are safety and ease of work, but machines also have disadvantages. They are expensive, offer limited exercises and little specific sport movement, and might be limited to eccentric contraction. Free weights offer more options, can copy the movement desired, and require concentric and eccentric contraction, but they are also more dangerous, require a spotter, and demand proper technique for maximum results.

Children and young teens must be very careful not to endanger themselves by pushing beyond reasonable limits. Informed adults should closely monitor their workouts. Many problems arise when parents push their children into unrealistic situations. Injuries have been caused by improper technique, lengthy sessions, and using excess weight. Experts recommend light weights with ample repetitions.

It's also important to note some gender differences that relate to training. Women train similarly to men, can do anything men can, and are closing the gap in every fitness category. On average, men have up to 50 percent more upper-body strength and up to 30 percent more lower-body strength than women. This may decrease as the demands of the women's game come closer to those of the men's game.

Testosterone is responsible for the differences in muscle mass and strength between men and women. Women can attain gains in strength at least equal to men. Women have less muscle definition than men because of lower levels of testosterone and higher levels of body fat (10 to 14 percent in women versus 4 to 10 percent in men). It's important for athletic women to maintain their natural weight and body-fat levels. The loss of too much weight can lead to irregular or no menstrual cycles (amenorrhea). This affects the estrogen level and can lead to stress fractures. Athletes who experience amenorrhea must increase calcium intake, decrease training, and increase body weight and fat to 10 percent. Interestingly, women retain higher fat levels even when they train similarly to men. $\dot{V}O_2$max levels are 15 to 20 percent lower in women.

Periodization

When speaking of training programs, periodization immediately comes to mind. Periodization is a year-round training regimen that reduces the risk of overtraining and staleness. It implements the three principles of training:

- The overload principle: increasing demands on cardiovascular or muscular systems by increasing repetitions, intensity, and time during training.

- The progression principle: beginning slowly and working to a high level of intensity.
- The principle of regularity: training three to four times a week throughout the year.

Periodization is widely used by coaches in all sports to more effectively and efficiently train the cardiorespiratory system. The process generally includes weight training. Periodization prepares players to perform at optimal levels.

A three- to six-month phase that begins in the preseason and goes through the regular competitive season makes up the first phase. The focus during this period is to train the athlete to peak around the championship weekend. This period uses tapering—gradually decreasing work and intensity—and achieves optimal performances as the season winds down. This phase includes shorter training times, lower intensity training, small-sided games with different fitness restrictions and stipulations, individual work days, less time watching videos or attending chalk talks, and occasional days for fun or free time.

After the competitive period, there is a two- to four-week transition period in which the athlete relaxes physically and mentally. He or she continues to train, but only at half the intensity of the competitive stage. Ideally, athletes perform three to four sessions per week and try other activities such as swimming, biking, or tennis. An athlete can lose up to four percent of his or her fitness by not training for a week and see decreases in speed, quickness, and endurance.

During the four- to eight-month preparation period, athletes train to achieve general fitness, improve technique, and master tactical skills for the upcoming competitive season. This period is the base on which the competitive season is built. The work done during this period allows the athlete to progress through the more rigorous specificity of training and the requirements to compete successfully.

Nutrition

Good nutrition is the foundation for physical performance and one of the most important variables in attaining a high level of fitness. Food fuels our systems and forms new tissue. The first Mr. Olympia was quoted as saying muscle building was 10 percent hard work and 90 percent nutrition. Many experts note that professional male soccer players must consume 3,000 to 3,600 calories to meet the energy demands of the sport. Upper-level female players might need up to 2,500 calories. The recommended ratio is 60 to 75 percent carbohydrates, 15 to 20 percent protein, and 15 to 20 percent fat sources. In addition, sufficient sources of water, vitamins, and minerals must be part of the everyday diet.

Carbohydrates are an important source of energy for aerobic exercise. They also provide the fuel used during intense anaerobic exercise. Athletes with diets high in carbohydrates perform significantly better than those with low-carb diets during the late stages of competition. Players who consume lower levels of carbohydrate have lower glycogen levels and become stale and unable to perform. Because most goals are scored in the final 30 minutes, it's important to eat intelligently to prolong optimal performance.

Increasing carbohydrate intake to 75 to 85 percent a few days before competition has been shown to improve performance. In *Soccer Journal* (May 2002), Dr. Donald Kirkendall related the importance of taking a six- to eight-percent carbohydrate drink just before competition and at halftime to enhance performance. A recent University of Texas study by Dr. John Ivy found that a carbohydrate–protein drink with a 4:1 ratio enhanced performance more than a carbohydrate-only drink. The carbohydrate–protein drink replenished energy, electrolytes (potassium, sodium, and chlorine), and fluids; reduced muscle damage after competition; and increased endurance at the next workout. This has great implications for teams that play back-to-back matches within a 24-hour period. It takes a minimum of 20 hours to restore glycogen stores, so it's critical to begin ingesting carbohydrates and protein as soon as competition is over to optimize recovery.

Carbohydrate loading, which increases glycogen reserves, is a method intended to improve performance on game day. One method is a six-day program in which players consume 50 percent of calories as carbohydrates for the first three days and 70 percent the last three days. A 90-minute workout decreases in intensity each day leading up to competition. Precompetition meals should be eaten three to four hours before the game and should contain protein to prevent large swings in insulin or glucose. A typical meal might include eggs, a turkey or chicken sandwich, yogurt or low-fat milk, juice, fruit, whole wheat bread, and jelly.

Protein should make up 15 to 20 percent of a player's diet. Protein is important for building and repairing muscle tissue. Children and teens need more protein than adults do. Recent evidence has shown that protein is more important in extended exercise and recovery than previously thought. Good sources of protein include eggs, fish, lean beef, and poultry.

Fat (saturated and unsaturated) is essential as a major source of stored energy. Players should have at least 15 percent fat in their daily diet. As glycogen supplies dwindle during prolonged exercise, more energy is produced through fat metabolism. Fat plays a key role in muscular development and acts as a cushion to protect internal organs.

Saturated fats often come from animal products, dairy, oils, cakes, pies, and cookies purchased in stores. Unsaturated fats, such as various nuts, olive and safflower oil, and some plants, offer a safer alternative to saturated fat calories. For better health, the majority of fat should come from unsaturated sources rather than saturated sources. Athletes should not consume fatty foods within four hours of competition because they take longer to digest.

Water is the most important fluid we put into our systems. It accounts for 40 to 60 percent of our body mass. Hydration is an everyday function that's critical for optimal performance. Most people should drink five to six glasses of water (12 to 16 ounces each) to maintain fluid balance, and athletes who lose fluids through sweat should consume more water. Sport drinks are also fine sources of fluids, but stay away from caffeinated drinks and alcohol because they're diuretics and can cause dehydration. Players need to drink water throughout training and games because fluid is lost through sweating and urination. Dehydration of 1 to 2 percent of body weight has been shown to decrease performance significantly, especially as the game enters the late stages. Players can assess their hydration levels by checking the color of their urine. If it's clear, they're ready to play. If it's yellow, they haven't hydrated sufficiently and probably won't play their best.

Supplements have become a multibillion-dollar industry. The quest for a magic potion to increase size, strength, speed, and performance without negative side effects continues. Many athletes use protein supplements to enhance performance and have had some positive results. Caffeine (two and a half cups of coffee consumed an hour before training) is another substance shown to extend endurance and reportedly leaves some athletes feeling that they could easily complete training. Many athletes have used other substances such as anabolic steroids, DHEA, creatine, human growth hormone, androstenedione, ephedrine, and amphetamines, but each of these substances has long-term negative health consequences. Unfortunately, many elite athletes are willing to sacrifice long-term health for short-term gains in performance.

A real problem is the evidence that younger, less mature athletes are testing these substances and experiencing severe side effects, including increased blood pressure, internal organ stress, antisocial behavior, and addiction. Most experts suggest good nutritional habits and vigorous exercise to achieve maximum performance. Every letter or e-mail I send to players makes it very clear that there are no shortcuts to success. Only dedication and hard work get us where we want to be.

Handling Injuries

Injuries can make or break a season. We've breezed through seasons injury-free, and we've suffered through seasons in which key players were lost for critical games. The key to an injury-free season is maintaining physical condition year-round. Weight training and flexibility work help decrease the risk of injury.

The most common soccer injuries are sprains, strains, and bruises. For more severe injuries, immediate professional treatment and rehabilitation are required along with rest, ice, compression, and elevation (RICE). Anti-inflamatory drugs such as aspirin might be prescribed to aid in recovery.

Training can promote injuries if the coach is not aware of proper training methods, such as periodization. Stretching before and after every session eliminates or reduces soreness and prepares athletes for the next day of training.

Sometimes coaches must adopt the concept of "less is more" and taper training intensity to suit the needs of the team. Athlete recovery is basic to everything we do in training. Allow athletes time to relax, refuel, and regenerate. The day after a match is very important in the recovery process, yet most coaches give the day off. A light workout and stretching routine complement the previous day's work and pay great dividends for a short amount of time.

Nothing is worse than an overtrained team. They tend to struggle physically and mentally. They often find it difficult to prepare and sustain effort during competition. I witnessed firsthand a classic case of overtraining the year I spent with the New England Revolution. We spent so much time running that the other league teams joked that we were a cross-country team. The running caused mental and physical staleness that permeated every crack and crevice in the team, inhibiting the players' approach to training and competition.

Testing

Finally, we should discuss testing policies and procedures for measuring players' fitness levels.

We need to be flexible in our demands that players achieve certain times and repetitions on these measurement tests. I've heard of coaches withholding players from games until they completed a required distance or time. We all have our strengths and weaknesses, and even your best players might not be so great at the distance run. If they don't make the grade, I suggest adjusting your required test scores rather than adjusting your roster.

The tests measure agility, vertical jump, speed, endurance, $\dot{V}O_2$max, body fat, and flexibility. Tests to determine aerobic fitness include the Cooper test, in which players are asked to run 12 minutes and finish a certain number of laps, and another form of Cooper test, in which players run 1.5 miles. The Beep test, which consists of 20-meter runs with decreasing time intervals, demonstrates aerobic fitness as well.

The skinfold test determines body composition. Anaerobic training consists of shuttle runs, such as the Ajax test in which players run from one cone to another cone 10 yards away, back and forth, five times in about 10 seconds.

Several good testing procedures for heading, sprinting, individual competitions, and shooting can be found in Anson Dorrance's book *Training Soccer Champions* (JTC SportsInc., 1996).

IV

Technical and Tactical Insights for Competitive Success

CHAPTER 12

Controlling the Ball

Steve Sampson

Ball control is the foundation on which individual players can make a difference in the outcome of a game. Ball handling is also the element of the game that's most appealing to spectators. The most gifted soccer players are remembered for their exceptional skill under pressure. Pele, Eusebio, Maradona, George Best, Puskas, Zidane, Ronaldo, Roberto Carlos, Beckham, and Figo are just a few who have made fans stand on their feet in appreciation of their dazzling skills with the ball.

Many believe skill is not developed but inherent. I don't believe that a player is born with great skill. I do believe, however, that comfort with the ball is enhanced and developed at a much faster rate within some environments. Great soccer players reflect the environments they grew up in, the influences around them, the quality of coaching, and the level of competition provided in their developmental years.

Early Skill Development

It's well known that developing countries or countries in which most children continue to play unstructured soccer in the streets or on beaches tend to develop the most gifted soccer players. This is because these children are allowed to experiment, take risks, and be creative without outside influences.

Additionally, parents who have played the game have a great influence on the development of skillful players. Their ability to play with their children, interact with them about the game, and instill a passion are just some of the ingredients that go into forming skillful players. More soccer players in the United States are beginning to enjoy this kind of interaction. More U.S adults have played the game at some level and can teach their children. This has had a dramatic influence on the U.S. national teams and on Major League Soccer. As more Americans play the game at increasingly higher levels, we'll witness an overwhelming effect on future generations of elite soccer players in the United States.

Children who see soccer extensively on television and have an opportunity to watch their local professional teams in person have an advantage in skill development. Children who watch seasoned professional players tend to experiment and imitate the moves they see. This is no different than the kids in the United States who imitate Michael Jordan or Kobe Bryant when they play basketball. These players learned to coach themselves without the guidance of parents or coaches. There are no referees, just players deciding for themselves who was fouled and who scored. Young players play alongside older players to gain experience. If they don't survive, then they just don't play. Older players taunt the rookies, providing acceptance only after the rookies prove themselves. If they prove themselves, their future is bright.

American soccer players are watching more high-level soccer on television than ever before, which is a big positive. However, they typically train only two to three times a week with their club teams and five times a week with their high school teams. Compared to the rest of the world, this is not enough time to develop sound ball control. In the absence of abundant training opportunities, the typical United States player must work very hard on his or her own to master the skills of the game. When players are fortunate and disciplined enough to arrive at an elite or professional level, their personal commitment to work on the skills of the game will continue to pay off.

Technical Training for Pros

Once a player begins to play professionally, it's difficult to dramatically change technical ability, but it's not impossible. Constant repetition under varying conditions is the key to improving ball control, even as a professional. The best players in the world find time outside the normal training sessions to work on their skills.

I remember watching F.C. Barcelona train the day after the magical Champions League final between Manchester United and Bayern Munich in 1999 in Barcelona. Rivaldo, who was playing for Barcelona at the time, was working on playing balls over distance (40 to 60 yards), alternating his feet. He would ask a teammate to receive the driven balls first in a standing position and then on the run. Rivaldo would hit 20 balls to his teammates. If one was not perfect, he would start all over again.

Rivaldo's exercise (figure 12.1) started in the middle of the center circle. Two players stood on the touchline near the penalty area, one on each side of the field. Rivaldo drove a stationary ball with his right foot (1) to the teammate on the left side of the field, then used his left foot (2) to kick a ball to a teammate on the right side of the field. Each ball had to hit between the chest and foot of the receiver. If the ball did not hit the target, or if the ball was too lofted, Rivaldo would start over again.

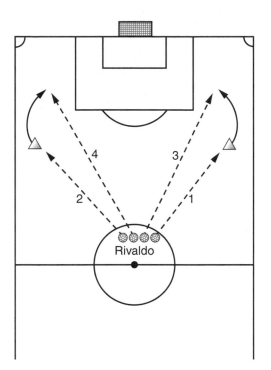

Figure 12.1   Rivaldo's technical session.

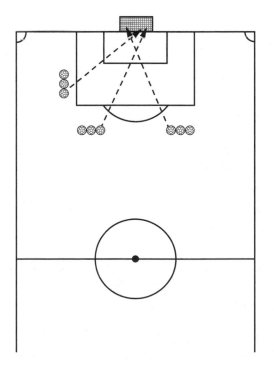

Figure 12.2   Beckham's free-kick drill.

After hitting 10 perfect balls to the left and 10 perfect balls to the right, Rivaldo would progress to hitting a moving ball to a moving target (3 and 4). The same teammates would run down the flanks until they were between the penalty area and the touchline. If the ball arrived too early or too late, or if the ball was lofted, Rivaldo would start all over again. He would repeat the exercise until he hit 20 perfect balls.

Rivaldo spent another 45 minutes working on driven balls after a full two-hour practice with F.C. Barcelona. Rivaldo grew up in Brazil, a soccer-passionate country. He developed into a skilled player during his youth. But it was his dedication to perfecting his game even as a professional that made him one of the best players in the world.

On a separate occasion, while researching the academy program in England, I had the pleasure of observing the training of Manchester United (figure 12.2). At the end of the training session, David Beckham took a bag of balls and picked a spot just outside the penalty area to practice free kicks. The equipment manager set up a portable wall 8 to 10 yards away from the ball and stepped back to watch Beckham do his magic. It was a simple exercise of placing the ball in the corner of the goal from varying angles and varying distances over or around the portable wall. Beckham would not move the angle or distance of the ball until he hit three perfectly placed balls into the back of the net. He used eight different angles without a goalkeeper and then progressed to performing the same series of kicks with a goalkeeper. Again, he would not move the angle or distance until he hit three perfectly placed balls into the back of the net.

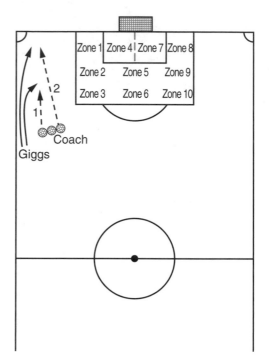

Figure 12.3 Giggs' crossing exercise.

During that same training session with Manchester United, Ryan Giggs was asked to perform a technical, physical exercise to work on his crossing from the left side of the field (figure 12.3). The penalty area was divided into the near-deep 18 (zone 1), the near-middle 18 (zone 2), the near-far 18 (zone 3), the middle 18 (zone 5), the middle-far 18 (zone 6), the far-near 18 (zone 8), the far-middle 18 (zone 9), and the far-far 18 (zone 10). It seems complicated, but it really isn't. The goal box was divided into near (zone 4) and far (zone 7).

The coach stood with 10 balls about 40 yards from the goal line and 15 yards inside the touchline. Ryan Giggs started the exercise on the touchline aligned with the coach. At the coach's word, Giggs sprinted down the touchline. The coach played a ball into the space between the touchline and the penalty area and told Giggs to cross the ball into a designated area of the penalty area. Each designated area was used in the exercise. After each cross, Giggs was allowed to walk or jog back to his position.

It was an exhausting exercise that should only be done with at least two days remaining before a match. Remarkably, Giggs performed each cross with incredible accuracy. Even more remarkable was his ability to focus and perform each cross with great precision—even at the end of the exercise, when he was physically exhausted.

Giggs' crossing exercise is effective only if the player receiving the cross has run to get inside the defender and is able to shoot the ball on target. The timing and precision of the cross, the timing of the supporting run, and the precision of the shot are all skills that must be trained constantly.

The precision passing exercise shown in figure 12.4 incorporates all the elements of precision passing, supporting run timing, and goal finishes. Players 1, 2, and 5 have six balls each. Player 2 plays the ball (pass 1) to player 4 for a wall pass (pass 2) to shoot at goal. Player 2 then immediately runs around player 5. Player 1 simultaneously plays a ball into space (pass

3) for player 3, who is running down the touchline (figure 12.4a). Player 3 crosses the ball (pass 4) to player 1, who runs into the box. Player 1 then plays a ball to player 2 down the touchline (pass 5), who crosses the ball to players 3 and 1 (pass 6), who finish on goal (figure 12.4b).

Once all six balls have been played, the exercise can be reversed to produce the same runs from the opposite side of the field.

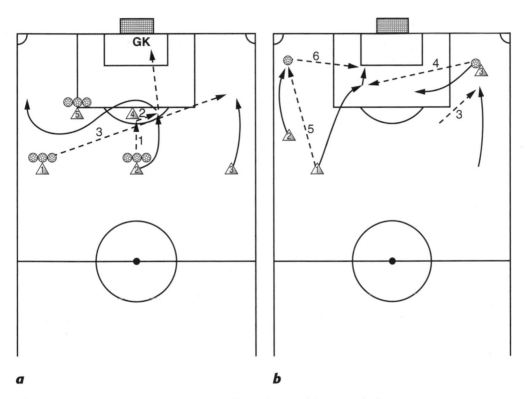

a   *b*

Figure 12.4   Precision passing: *(a)* first phase; *(b)* second phase.

Three of the four exercises presented in this chapter were performed without the pressure of an opponent to put the emphasis on repetition and accuracy. The natural progression for each of the exercises is to incorporate defenders who provide pressure to make the exercises more gamelike.

CHAPTER 13

Scoring Tactics of Strikers

Jim Lennox

The most important function of the striker is to score goals. A striker who can consistently score goals is the most important player in the game. Through superior physical and psychological play, some strikers have a unique ability to score. Such players, from the beginning of their playing careers, have been able to produce goals. It's rare for an older player to suddenly become a scorer. A logical extension might be that goal scorers are "naturals" and that coaching can have little effect on their goal-scoring abilities. To an extent this might be true; however, good coaching can usually improve even natural goal scorers.

Goal scorers can be broadly categorized into two types. The first type is the player who scores by getting on the end of passes. This player has a knack for leaving spaces alive, then exploding into that space to get there the instant the ball arrives to finish a cross or get on the end of a through pass. Often these players possess powerful shooting abilities and can strike from a distance. Players in this category are often fast, powerful runners who possess size and great anaerobic capacity.

The second type is the goal scorer who is an initiating, improvisational player, who prefers to receive passes at the feet and then, through elusive dribbling and exciting use of combination play, makes space to score. This player plays the ball past the goalkeeper by slotting it around the keeper, using a toe poke, even chipping the keeper on occasion.

The coach must be aware of the physical, technical, and psychological playing characteristics that each striker possesses. The coach must then design training sessions to match the specific characteristics of the striker and add to the ways in which the striker aids team tactics and functions. A striker who is a fast runner and wants balls in space to launch counters or vertically stretch the opponent's collective defending action must be taught where to run, how to time runs, and how to receive balls in space. A striker who is a technical player and prefers balls at his feet needs to be trained to show toward the midfield to become part of the tactical buildup or how to combine with other attackers to achieve breakthroughs.

All strikers need a constant daily regimen of finishing. Finishing may be striking a long shot, bending the ball around a keeper, dribbling past the keeper, heading, and so on. This training may take the form of pure technical training without opposition, but the coach must design training that replicates what the player will experience in the real game as closely as possible.

Although scoring goals is the ultimate function of strikers, strikers must perform other tactical tasks as part of the team. In today's game, the instant possession is won a possible chronology of a striker's tactics would be mounting the counterattack, becoming part of the tactical buildup or playing as a target for direct play, and playing in the final third and finishing.

Counterattacking

Countering is a mentality. It is an extension of collective defending in which the players, as a team, become compressed vertically during the opponent's possession. Imagine the entire team becoming a spring being compressed backward, becoming more and more loaded the closer the opponent approaches the goal. At the instant the defending team wins possession, the spring explodes forward as the counterattack is launched.

The striker's role in the counterattack begins with a starting position that maximizes his or her tactical options. At least one striker's starting position during the opponent's attack is as central and advanced as possible. The striker should always adopt this central, advanced position. If the team can't defend with 10 players behind the ball, they will not be able to defend with 11. By leaving one striker high and central, he or she can occupy two opponents. This position puts the striker in the optimal starting position to counter.

The two optimal times to counter are when the defending team cuts out a pass or when the defending team wins a ball in a tackle or 50-50 ball. In both cases, the defending team gets the ball unpressured and can play the ball forward through any angle. In both instances, the defenders catch the opponent in an attacking shape and mentality—the ideal moment to launch the counterattack.

The striker positioned high and central allows the player launching the counter to play the ball to one of three spaces (figure 13.1). A ball may be played over attacker 1 and defender 1 into space A. Space A is available if the ball's flight time is short or if the opponent's goalkeeper is not far enough off his or her line. A ball may be played to space B when the striker must run forward diagonally. The ball is played into the space beside striker 1 and away from defender 1. This is often the best option because central cover-

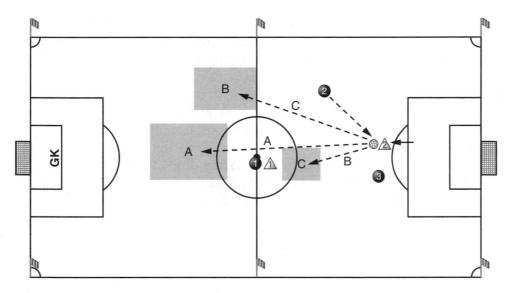

Figure 13.1   Counterattack passes to the striker.

ing systems and proper goalkeeper positioning precludes simply whacking the ball over the top. A third option is for the striker to show back toward the teammate who won possession. Midfield teammates who break out into space C with the vertical ball to the striker's feet will connect with the striker and continue the counter.

Figure 13.2 shows a sample progression to teach countering and the striker's specific functions. Defender 1 marks striker 1. Attacker 2 dribbles the ball toward the goal. A ground pass is made to attacker 3 that defender 2 cuts out. At this stage, the dribble and pass by attacker 2 to attacker 3 are

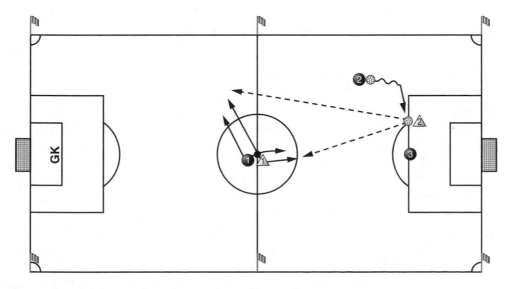

Figure 13.2   Countering progression with a striker.

shadow play, not live. The purpose is for the striker to identify the precise instant when defender 2 cuts out the pass and can play the ball forward. That microsecond when defender 2 can play the ball forward is striker 1's cue to explode and get on the end of attacker 2's pass.

Figure 13.3 progresses to two strikers, striker 1 and striker 2, who are marked by defender 1 and defender 2. A fourth defender is added as a midfield player. From the same shadow format, both strikers look for the cue that tells them when to run. Their acceleration into a specific space tells defender 3 where to play the ball. When defender 3 cuts out the pass, striker 1 sprints as midfielder 4 breaks out from his or her former defending job to connect with defender 2 and play the ball forward.

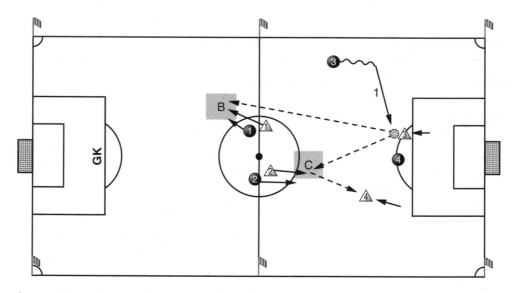

Figure 13.3   Countering progression with two strikers.

According to the needs of the players, the coach monitors the marking roles of attackers 1 and 2. In the learning stages, defenders 1 and 2 are shadow defenders, not live. The coach can manipulate this variable by asking both defenders to shadow, having one shadow and the other play live, having both play live, or adding a third defender. The coach makes these decisions based on the players' needs. As strikers become more skilled with their tactical options and are able to identify when to run, the coach must make the exercise more gamelike.

The exercise shown in figure 13.4 uses the same format as the countering progression with two strikers, except a fifth defender is added. Defender 5 is in a reasonable position to begin sprinting forward to become another option for the counter the instant defender 3 cuts out the pass. Defender 3 cuts out attacker 3's pass. Defender 1 sprints forward, and defender 2 shows back to defender 3. Defender 3 can play the long ball to defender 1 or play

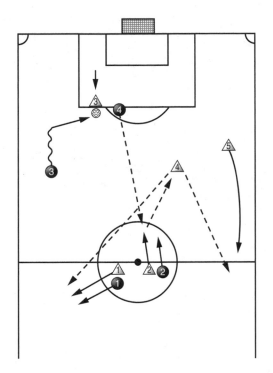

Figure 13.4   Countering progression with a fifth defender.

the short ball to defender 2, who plays it back for defender 4 to play either long to defender 1 or wide to defender 5.

The next progression is shown in figure 13.5. Mark a zone 30 to 40 yards from the goal, depending on your players' abilities. Play three attackers versus five defenders in the marked zone. At the halfway line, the coach can organize any number situation based on where the strikers are in the learning process—1 v 1 or even 2 v 1 with shadow defenders early in the learning process, progressing to 2 v 3 with live defenders as the exercise becomes more gamelike. The situation in the back third—three attackers versus five defenders—should provide opportunities to counter when the defenders win the ball. The coach can use any number that results in the defenders' winning the ball with the opportunity to counter. The 3 v 5 in the back third should be a live game. One option is for the coach or an assistant to start play with balls played to either the defense or the attacking team, then let play happen realistically. Of course the emphasis is on the first ball out of the defense to the attackers.

Figure 13.6 shows further progression toward the real game. Add a block of midfield players in the middle one-third. Again, the coach can manipulate the numbers to achieve the desired outcome, perhaps beginning with 1 v 1 in the midfield. To really make the exercise easy in the early stages, have two defenders and only one attacker. That leaves easy options when the counter is possible. Gradually include more players until the midfield

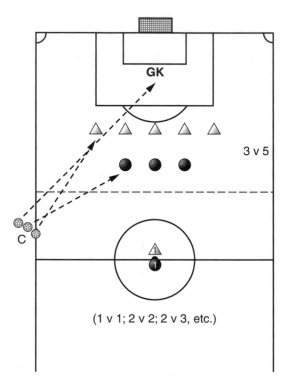

Figure 13.5 3 v 5 with strikers.

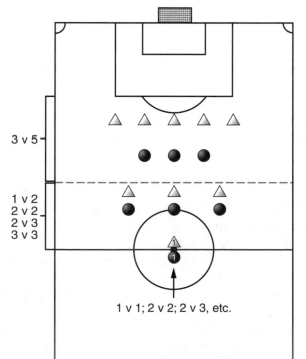

Figure 13.6 Countering progression with midfield players.

block is 3 v 3. Initially, the 3 v 3 is restricted to the middle third. The play in the middle third can progress to allowing one attacking midfield player to enter the back third, then two, with the manipulations up to the coach. The strikers at the top are always looking for that instant when possession is won and the counterattack is on.

Direct Attacking

When possession is won and the counter is not on, the attacking team implements its style of attack. A team that features a direct style will play vertical balls to put as many defenders out of the game as possible, often with the secondary task of forcing the opponent's defending block to turn and run toward its own goal.

Strikers playing in a direct style of attack usually perform two functions. They make diagonal runs to receive long vertical balls played through and over the top of the defense, and they play a relatively stationary role to receive and hold long passes or head balls to teammates.

Figure 13.7 shows a setup similar to a counterattack exercise, except that the coach serves a high ball into the marked area so that a defending player has time to close the player receiving the ball and force the defenders to keep possession until pressure is broken and the direct ball can be played. Figure 13.7 shows 3 v 5, but the coach can manipulate the numbers to get the required outcome. In the past, we have started with 2 v 2 (two strikers and two markers) at the halfway line. The numbers at the halfway line reflect the playing experience of the strikers. In the learning stages, you might want to begin with two strikers and one defender, whereas better skilled, experienced strikers play 2 v 3 or 2 v 4.

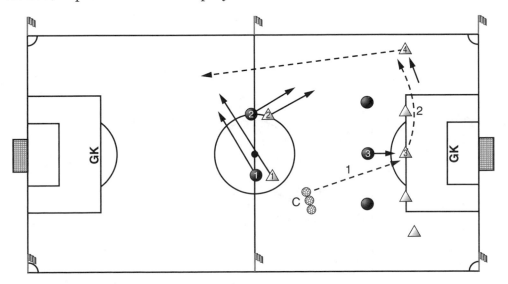

Figure 13.7   Direct attack setup.

The coach must be aware of the physical parameters of the strikers. For example, striker 1 is a fast runner and striker 2 is a great technician, though not as fast. To exploit striker 1's speed, striker 2 always shows toward the player in possession, whereas striker 1 tries to involve attacker 1 in a long footrace to the ball, exploiting striker 1's speed and possibly isolating striker 1 in a one-on-one duel. A high ball toward defender 3, which allows attacker 3 to close, initiates the exercise. Defender 3 plays a ball wide to defender 4, who then plays the long direct ball past midfield and into space for striker 1 to run into and receive.

Against good marking, the striker needs to slightly adjust the angle of his or her run to receive the pass one step in advance of the ball so the defender will have no path to the ball (figure 13.8). A general concept for playing this or most any pass is to play the ball to a space where the defender can't be first.

Exercises for the stationary striker are similar to figure 13.7 with the addition of a midfield group that runs to support the striker as he or she receives a direct ball or sprints beyond the striker to get on the end of a flicked header. Balls to a tall striker can be played high; balls to a shorter striker might have to be clipped into the space short of the striker. If focusing on technique, the coach may condition the exercise by allowing the striker first contact, then the exercise is live. Defenders can be asked to shadow, defend, or be live.

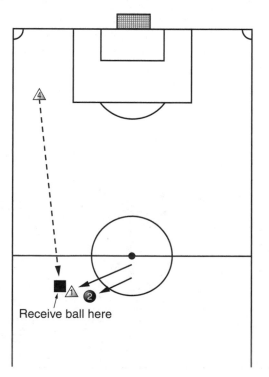

Receive ball here

Figure 13.8 Striker slightly adjusts the angle of his or her run to receive the pass one step ahead of the ball.

Indirect Attacking

In addition to operating as a striker in a direct style of attack, the striker might be asked to become part of the tactical buildup. This usually means showing back toward defenders and midfield players and acting as a wall as they play the ball into the striker's feet and run off it. The striker who shows back for a pass will be marked by a defender who is then pulled out of his/her connection with teammate defenders. Other attacking players can exploit the gap that is created. The striker who shows correctly also creates a numerical advantage in the midfield.

It's important that strikers who show (check back, withdraw, and so on) for passes run at angles. A striker who checks at an angle has vision of his marker, interposes his body between the marker and the ball, and creates space where the ball can be played or other attackers can run. Figure 13.9 illustrates a striker checking for a pass from midfield player 2. Midfielder 2 plays the ball into the space in front of the foot away from the marker. Striker 1 tells midfielder 2 where he or she wants the ball by the way in which he or she runs.

If the midfielder sees space behind the withdrawing striker, he or she sprints vertically, telling the striker to play the ball first into defender 2's path (figure 13.10). If defender 2 stands or moves laterally, he or she is saying the defenders are organized and compressed behind the strikers,

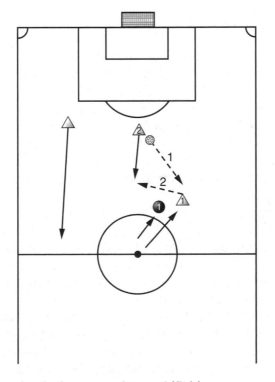

Figure 13.9   Striker checks for a pass from midfield.

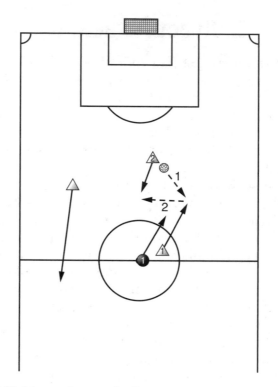

Figure 13.10 Midfielder sprints vertically.

so play it back. Thus, the attackers keep possession and are still facing the opponent's goal.

The exercise shown in figure 13.11 is for players in the learning stages. Three defenders against two strikers, and four midfielders play against three midfield defenders. The numbers are organized to give the midfield attackers the opportunity to play many vertical balls into the feet of checking strikers. The coach decides what aspects of the striker's play need to be trained. Showing on time, running at angles, playing balls back one time to ensure possession, being a wall for dribbling midfielders, using decoy running to make space for the striking partner are a few of the striker's tactical choices to be trained.

The exercise shown in figure 13.12 is a logical progression from the previous exercise. In this exercise, 10 attackers arranged in a 4-4-2 framework play against eight defenders. Defenders can be arranged to play three in the back, two markers and a sweeper, four zonally or man to man in the midfield—the coach decides. Likewise, the coach arranges the team into its preferred attacking framework.

With the emphasis on the strikers' play, a coach stands close to them, coaching during play or stopping play to make cogent coaching points. By manipulating variables, the coach can bring out different aspects of play from the strikers. With the focus on strikers becoming part of the tactical

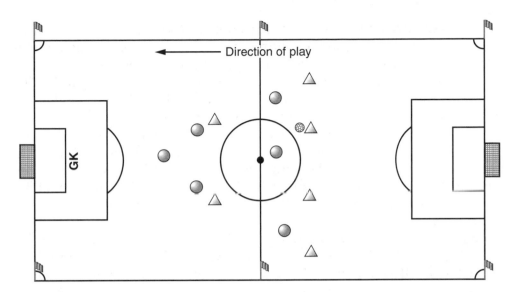

Figure 13.11 Early exercise for strikers.

buildup, the coach emphasizes the tactics of the strikers as they show back toward the back and midfield teammates in possession.

During the build-up phase, a withdrawing striker might be able to turn the ball and face the goal he or she is attacking without pressure. Because the striker can play the ball forward, teammates should attempt to run forward and get behind defenders. Figure 13.12 shows 10 v 8. Striker 2 has checked back and is able to turn. Striker 1 and left-flank player 3 make vertical runs behind defenders to get on the end of defender 2's pass. Left-back defender 7 also runs forward to exploit the space created by defender 3's run. Defender 6 also runs vertically.

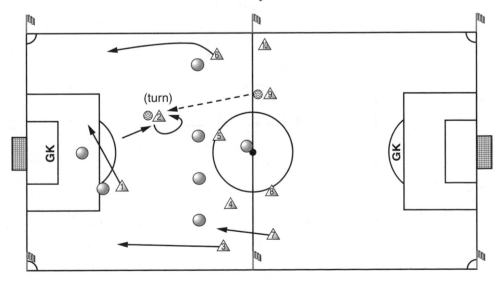

Figure 13.12 10 v 8 action.

As strikers arrive in the scoring areas, defenders draw closer together to reduce space in the central area in front of the goal. The goal line reduces space vertically and necessitates flatter passing angles by attackers.

Basic options are to try to outflank the collective defending action, go wide and cross the ball into shooting spaces, or penetrate the massed defense through combination play or improvisational dribbling.

To score from crosses, strikers must arrive at the spot the instant the ball arrives. The spot is where the striker and the crossed ball arrive simultaneously in the same space to be struck at goal. UCLA's winning goal in the 2002 NCAA men's championship game is an example of an attacker arriving in the spot the instant the ball arrived and striking the ball first time into the goal.

Figure 13.13 shows an attack being developed on the right flank by attackers 3, 4, and 5, as strikers 1 and 2 begin drifting to the left side of the field. The strikers will bend to the weak side of the field to empty attacking spaces in the box, take away the defenders' vision (they can't see the player and the ball at the same time), and to receive the ball running at the goal.

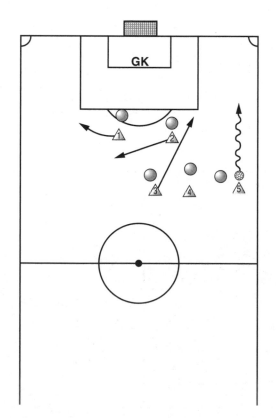

Figure 13.13   Attack on the right flank.

Attackers try to arrive in the attacking spaces in the box the instant the crossed ball arrives (figure 13.14). The first space is the near post (NP), second is the far post (FP), third is the second six-yard box (#2), and last is the top of the box (TB). Assuming a correct service, the goalkeeper won't be able to cut out any of these crosses.

The secret to arriving on time at the spot is to hold the run until the last possible instant so that the attacker arrives at the spot in a full sprint a step ahead of the defender the instant the ball arrives at the spot.

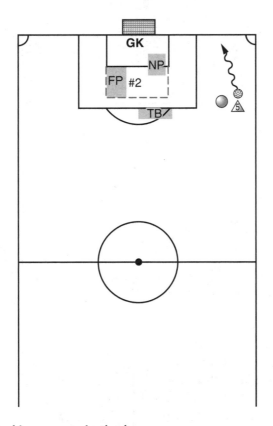

Figure 13.14   Attacking spaces in the box.

Combination Play

Achieving penetration to a scoring chance through combination play requires good technical players and repetition of training. An example of a module for teaching the takeover appears in figure 13.15.

Mark a field appropriate to the level of the players. For a college team, begin with an 18 × 25 yard area with goalkeepers at each end. Begin each attacking repetition with a takeover. The key to the exercise is for the ball to be played to the marked player. The defender 3 marks one of the strikers. Attacker 3 must play the ball to the marked player; then a takeover must

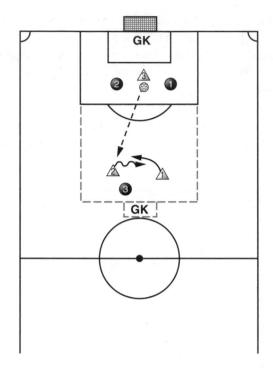

Figure 13.15　The takeover.

be executed before going to goal. The same procedure then goes the other way.

In figure 13.16, we increase the numbers to 3 v 2 in each half, but each repetition must begin with a pass to a marked player who then executes a takeover before going to the goal. This specific module teaches a specific type of combination play.

Figure 13.17 shows a general exercise for strikers to execute combination plays and improvisational dribbling. Begin with two strikers and a marker for each positioned at the top of the box. Use three supporting midfield players marked by two defenders. The 3 v 2 setup allows midfielders to keep possession and have windows to

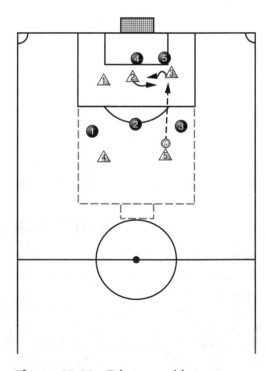

Figure 13.16　Takeover with 3 v 2.

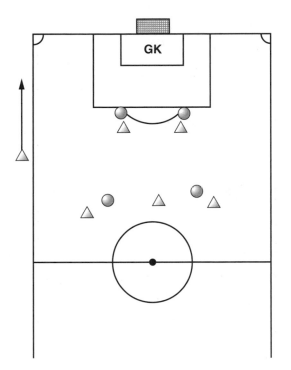

Figure 13.17   Combo plays and improvisational dribbling.

make passes to the strikers. They dribble, combine, or pass for each other to achieve penetration. Gradually build up the numbers to make the activity at the top of the box more gamelike.

Finishing

Soccer literature is replete with exercises for finishing. Finishing includes shooting from distance, slotting (playing the ball past or around the goal-keeper) dribbling, heading, and toe poking.

One of my favorite finishing exercises is shown in figure 13.18. Play 4 v 4 in the box. Have four servers, each with a supply of balls. The servers play a ball to the attacking four. The attackers play until there is a shot or a clearance. Another ball is immediately played in, and the exercise continues. Rotate the 12 players so each four has a chance to finish.

Figure 13.19 shows a field 40 yards long with full-sized goals and goal-keepers at either end. Have plenty of balls available at each goal. Make a halfway line 20 yards out. Play 1 v 3 in each half. All players must stay in their own half. The ball is rolled to any of the three, and he or she can shoot or pass to another teammate to shoot or play to the one attacker in the box. When you increase the number to 2 v 3, one player may go into the other half but he or she must play into a teammate in the other half before

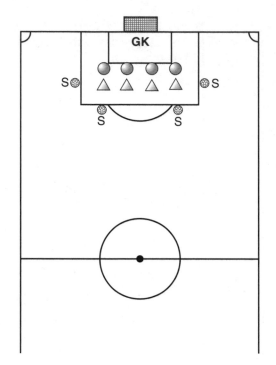

Figure 13.18 4 v 4 in the box.

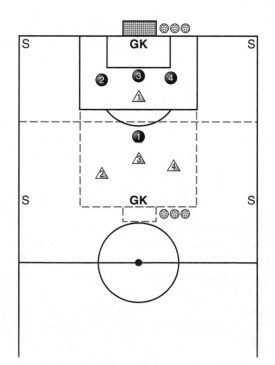

Figure 13.19 1 v 3, short field.

proceeding. Add servers in the corners and the players can play a ball wide to be served into the box. This is a two-way exercise with an emphasis on finishing.

Figure 13.20 shows an 8 v 8 exercise on a 40 × 75 yard field. Today's players must be able to play technically in tight spaces, so their training should replicate the game. Play 8 v 8, 9 v 9, or 11 v 11. Arrange teams in their normal positions in the system in which they're accustomed to playing. Or, you might have the reserve team play in the system and style of your team's next opponent.

Goal scoring and the play of exceptional strikers might be instinctive, but you can positively affect the quest for goals by including finishing exercises in your training sessions. As much as possible, design all exercises to conclude with a strike at goal.

Once strikers are consistently making correct tactical decisions, coaches need to examine the strikers' technical abilities. Whether the skill is correct striking of the ball on the ground, striking the ball out of the air with the feet, or heading the ball to the goal, functional training (training players, under the pressure of an opponent, in and around the goal area where they typically play) should be instituted to refine striking techniques. This repetitive training will develop your players into more refined scorers.

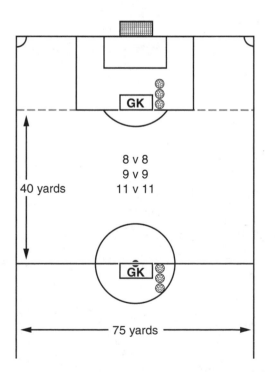

Figure 13.20   8 v 8 on a 40 × 75 yard field.

CHAPTER 14

Goalkeeping Excellence

Peter Mellor and Tony Waiters

An old soccer saying goes, "If you can't pass, you can't play!" You could say about goalkeepers, "If you can't catch and dive, don't bother playing in goal!" A goalkeeper who lacks these basic techniques—catching and diving—will always be at a disadvantage. Catching and punching the ball, diving to hold the ball, diving to deflect a shot, kicking, and throwing are all fundamental skills a goalkeeper needs.

This chapter covers more than just these basic techniques. We'll emphasize the importance of goalkeeping smarts—game savvy—to make correct decisions that set apart a technically efficient goalkeeper from the accomplished, effective goalkeeper. The former keeper will make decisions that result in losses; the latter player relishes making the "big save" and will keep the team in the game.

Developing Goalkeeping Techniques

Solid goalkeeping techniques are required to enable good decisions and reach a successful conclusion. Whenever possible, goalkeeping practice should be done within a team environment. The revised back-pass rule has really brought the goalkeeper back into the team. This rule is welcome as a major step forward in goalkeeping. We both wish we had played under this rule because the goalkeeping position is much more exciting and rewarding now.

The back-pass rule has extended the role of the goalkeeper within the team system. The sweeper-keeper position is now a requirement of every keeper.

Big Shot

In the big shot practice (figure 14.1), goalkeepers are always in the action—organizing the defense and dealing with realistic shots on goal—often during situations in which the keeper is unsighted or a shot takes a deflection.

Mark an area 24 × 24 yards with a halfway line. Set up two full-sized goals. You can use portable or improvised goals made with cones, poles, or corner flags. If you use cones or corner flags for the second goal, change ends frequently so that each keeper gets equal time in a regulation-size goal.

The drill is run as a 3 v 1 (plus the goalkeeper). Play is restricted to half the field. The sole attacker, the sniffer, looks for scoring opportunities from rebounds off the goalkeeper, defenders, or goal posts. Most shots come from 12 to 15 yards out from the other half of the field. Shots can be taken only from within the sniffer's own half. Goalkeepers can't shoot.

The goalkeeper must take charge and play good balls by hand or feet to his or her teammates. After playing the ball, the keeper supports the team and is prepared to receive a back pass to relieve pressure and restart the attack.

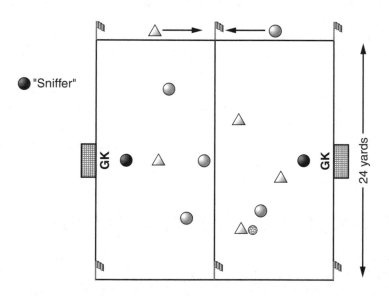

Figure 14.1   Big shot setup.

Two Goals

If a phase of team practice is not goalkeeper specific, set up the two-goal practice, as shown in figure 14.2. In the absence of regulation-size portable goals, use cones or flags.

Set goals up 15 to 20 yards apart. The two goalkeepers work together. Play begins with a throw or kick (including volleys and half-volleys). Although this drill can be done without supervision, it's best for a coach to supervise

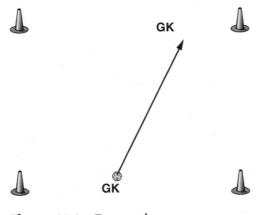

Figure 14.2   Two goals.

and direct the practice, if possible. In the absence of a coach, keep an eye on the keepers as the field players work to make sure they're challenging one another enough.

Back Pass

Because of the back pass, many team passing and possession practices are beneficial for goalkeepers, but you must also replicate game situations to produce the realism and distances involved in 11-v-11 play.

Use half a field for a 6-v-6 game (figure 14.3). The goalkeeper acts as the odd man for the defending team. The two attackers start from outside the

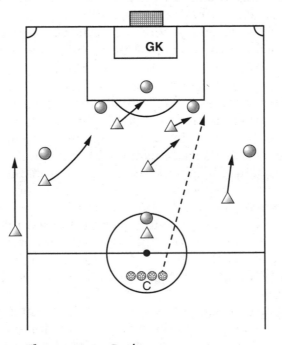

Figure 14.3   Back pass.

penalty area. Begin the exercise by delivering the ball to a central defender or wide back.

Once the ball is rolling, the two attackers combine with their teammates to pressure the ball, win possession, and score. They do whatever they feel will disturb the goalkeeper, working together to reduce the keeper's options of playing out of the penalty area. The keeper must be careful not to be closed down and must select the best way to deal with the situation. Keepers might have to play for safety, but when allowed will attempt to keep their team in possession by delivering a penetrating pass to the coach at midfield. The keeper should look for the possibility of switching play by playing to the open side after receiving the ball from one flank.

Principles of Goalkeeping

As a team coach, you will likely get the goalkeeper you deserve. Spend time planning practice to incorporate goalkeepers into team practice in realistic circumstances. Spend another 10 minutes with keepers at the end of practice. They'll appreciate your efforts, and there's a good chance you'll be rewarded.

In 1998, the NSCAA Goalkeeping Institute was established to provide information and practice for the benefit of the team coach working with goalkeepers in a team environment. In the six-hour course, much time is spent identifying and putting into practice the key principles of goalkeeping. We recommend this course to any coach who hasn't taken it. It's offered through both the NSCAA and state associations.

The first principle covered in the course is maximizing the use of the hands. This is such a great advantage for the goalkeeper in the defending penalty area. In the easy save (the welcome position), the goalkeeper uses the hands and body to ensure no mistakes (figure 14.4). In the bad save, the lazy goalkeeper gambles and effectively loses the use of one hand—the right one—and the insurance of the body behind the ball (figure 14.5). Had the goalkeeper not been lazy, he would have made a collapsing side dive save to optimize the advantage of using the hands (figure 14.6).

A second key principle taught in the course is the shape of the goalkeeper. *Shape* refers to side-diving technique as well as the importance of maintaining an open body position in relation to the ball.

A third key in the course, staying alert and alive, might sound like a BGO (blinding glimpse of the obvious), but keepers often lose concentration when play is in the other half of the field and can be caught out when situations quickly change. The keeper must try to be a split second smarter than the opposition.

Another key course principle—"stay on your feet"—might seem contradictory to a previous principle, but there's a proviso: "for as long as possible." Many inexperienced goalkeepers try to anticipate plays and consequently

Figure 14.4   Easy-save (welcome) position.   **Figure 14.5**   Bad hands.

Figure 14.6   Collapsing side-dive save.

make early, incorrect dives, giving the shooter an easy score. Keepers need to practice waiting until the last possible moment before committing themselves.

The goalkeeping course also teaches "DCO"—decision making, communication, and organization. Obviously, these key factors can make or break a goalkeeper. There used to be a saying, "If you're strong right down the middle, you've got a good team." What that meant is that if you had a goal-scoring center forward, a ball-winning and incisive passing central midfielder, a strong stopper center back, and a dependable goalkeeper, you were in the business of winning games. Not much has changed. For best success, put your keeper in gamelike situations that test and train the DCO principle.

Mixed Bag

The objective of the mixed-bag exercise (figure 14.7) is to place goalkeepers (and field players) in decision-making situations with attacks developed from the width of the field. In this exercise, goalkeepers work on making good decisions in crossed-ball situations; staying alert, alive, and open; staying on their feet; and optimizing the use of their hands.

Do the exercise on half a full-size field. Mark an eight-yard channel on each side of the field and a halfway line. Play 3 v 2 with a goalkeeper in each half. The wingers in the channels have no allegiance—they play for both teams. When the goalkeeper has the ball and is restarting play, he or she always throws to flank players of the keeper's choice. Wing players can pass to one another, overlap, and cross the ball, or they can play the ball in or out to the three attackers. Have field players rotate periodically to give them experience in the different roles.

Goalkeepers work on accurate throws to wide players. Encourage them to switch play, to communicate their requirements, and to organize the defense. Goalkeepers must observe the changing circumstances, adjust accordingly,

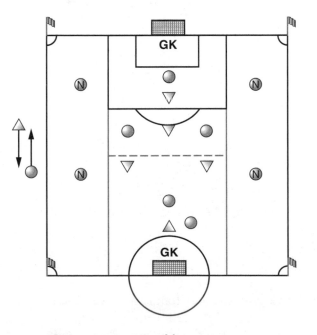

Figure 14.7 Mixed-bag setup.

and take the required action. For field players, encourage good attacking runs (near and far post), and make sure field players are skillful and cooperative when defending against greater numbers.

Practice can begin with simpler numbers, such as 2 v 1 in each half with a single flank player. You can increase player numbers as they master their roles. As coaches and players become familiar with this exercise, it can be further developed. For example, defenders can play the ball directly to attacking players without the ball having to go wide. A defender can be released to go forward over the halfway line to support an attack. One defender and one attacker can go into the other half to assist play (player's own choice) but must get back quickly when the ball goes to the goalkeeper. One of the flank players can follow the pass or cross to assist the attacking team. These modifications produce a mixed bag in terms of developing the judgment and decision-making abilities of goalkeepers.

Super 8s

Most teams have a roster of 14 to 18 players. While 11-v-11 play can be advantageous in developing team understanding, most teams can't organize in-house 11-v-11 play during practice. This being the case, drills of 7 v 7 or 8 v 8 are fine. The super-8 drill produces most of the situations found in 11-v-11 play, particularly those that arise when the game plan is not working and players must think for themselves. Super 8s put it all together, covering most facets of goalkeeping.

Set up a line and regulation-size goal 18 yards beyond the center-line (figure 14.8). If a portable goal is not available, use corner flags. Mark two

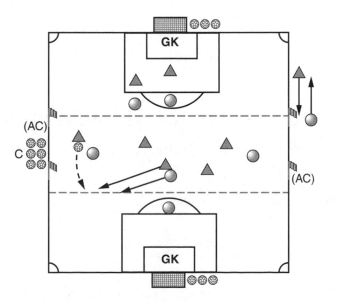

Figure 14.8   Setup for the super 8.

25-yard lines with coaching disks; use corner flags to emphasize the 25-yard lines, if possible. Two linemen (assistant coaches or parents) are stationed on opposite sides of the field to coach at the 25-yard lines.

Play under the normal rules of soccer, except that each team can be offside only beyond the attacking 25-yard lines. Consider narrowing the field by 5 to 10 yards on each side.

Encourage goalkeepers to organize rear players to use the offsides, keeping opponents away from the goal. Encourage total soccer with players moving up and downfield, playing both offense and defense, with no set positions. Keepers must communicate well. Encourage them to stay on their toes as situations rapidly change and develop. Encourage awareness, attacking support, width, and defensive cover. Encourage keepers to organize the team.

If you have too many or too few players for super 8s, play super 7s or super 9s instead. The demanding nature of these drills help develop the two-way player so desirable in modern-day soccer.

Because of the fast-changing end-to-end nature of the game and the offsides rule, most of the tough situations goalkeepers face in the 11-v-11 game will occur here in this drill, including through balls, crossed balls, long shots, and short-range shots. The difference is that 10 times more action occurs in super 8s than in a normal full-sided game. Also because of the smaller field, goalkeepers have a tougher challenge in distributing the ball. A long kick often ends up in the other goalkeeper's hands. A thrown ball to create an attack might be the better option. Bad decisions and irresponsible throws are punished with poor results.

Both the mixed-bag and the super 8 drill produce end-to-end action and multiple and complex goalkeeping situations. With numerous attacks from crossed balls—always a challenge for goalkeepers at any level of play—the keeper is put into a cauldron of goalkeeping. Younger goalkeepers won't be ready for these drills; take care not to overchallenge them to the point they're discouraged.

The Importance of Technique

Goalkeeping techniques are the building blocks on which goalkeepers base their game. These techniques should be a planned part of every goalkeeper's practice sessions. Break them down into parts, including footwork, diving, catching, kicking, and throwing. Pay close attention to detail; don't allow faulty technique.

Footwork

In most cases, the feet get the hands to the ball. Good footwork gives the goalkeeper good mobility and positioning around the penalty area. During the game, goalkeepers must remain constantly active, continually making little positional adjustments. By keeping their feet alive, goalkeepers stay in touch with the game.

Three types of footwork movements should be developed: sideways shuffling movements, forward movements, and backward movements. For sideways (lateral) shuffling movements, each shuffle step should be roughly shoulder-width apart (figure 14.9). Forward movement from the goalkeeper's set position is used to attack a through ball. Be sure the first step is forward and not backward. Backward movements are used to get to a ball that has been chipped over the keeper's head toward the goal. The keeper needs to learn to step out, make a crossover step, and then shuffle backward, maintaining good shape and balance. The initial step out and crossover step give the goalkeeper a big advantage in getting back to the ball.

Figure 14.9   Side shuffle step.

Dives to the Side

The most important coaching point in diving is to attack the ball. Go to the ball! Many young goalkeepers tend to dive to the side or even backward. Good shape in diving is *to* the side and *on* the side of the body, with the hands leading, using the body to block the goal as much as possible (figure 14.10). If the keeper is going to hold the ball, he or she should use the ground as a third hand by getting one hand behind the ball and the second hand on top of the ball, pinning the ball against the ground.

Figure 14.10   Diving to the side.

Shots and Crosses

Top goalkeepers have what we call *soft hands*. They seem to be able to absorb the ball, holding most shots and catching most crosses. When the goalkeeper is in training or practice sessions, pay attention to detail in this area. The keeper should give up as few rebounds as possible.

One-on-One Breakaways

Goalkeepers need to know how to protect themselves when going down to get the ball at an opponent's feet. The technique is not much different than diving to save a shot. The keeper needs to stay on the feet as long as possible. To go to the ground to get the ball, the keeper leads with the palms, looking through the space between the arms (figure 14.11). The hands and arms protect the face. The keeper needs to make as big a barrier to the goal with the body as possible.

Figure 14.11   Saving the ball at the attacker's feet.

Foot Skills

Since the introduction of the back-pass rule, the role of the goalkeeper has changed. The keeper is now the 11th field player. Incorporate goalkeepers into possession games to help them develop and become more comfortable with their foot skills.

Back Pass

In the back-pass exercise, the keeper is challenged to put all the tactical demands of keeping into practice. The keeper must be ready, alert, and alive at all times. A possession box 44 yards wide by 15 yards deep is marked with discs or cones. The keeper stays in line with play in the possession box and makes all necessary footwork and positional adjustments. Target gates are set up 5 yards apart and marked by corner flags. The keeper must make good decisions about which target to play to. The keeper should focus on kicking technique and be able to use both feet to play the ball, based on the attacker's pressure. As the exercise progresses, the goalkeeper should exude confidence and remain consistent in execution.

Create two teams of six field players (figure 14.12), each team with its own goalkeeper. A third team of six plays behind the target gates. The other two teams play for possession in the possession box. A team that possesses the ball for five consecutive passes, plays the sixth pass out of the possession box. The goalkeeper must decide how to play the back pass using his or her feet and which gate to send the ball to.

At first the unpressured goalkeeper uses his or her feet to find one of the six target gates and deliver the ball to a player standing behind the target gate. The goalkeeper has to decide which gate to use. At this time, no pressure is being put on the goalkeeper. Pressure on the keeper is added when the team that played the ball to the goalkeeper follows the pass, trying to win the ball and score. The goalkeeper finds an open gate and plays the ball to that area. Bring in the third team after a few repetitions of the exercise. The third team replaces one of the teams in the possession game. The players on the third team try to receive the ball from the goalkeeper once it passes through the gate.

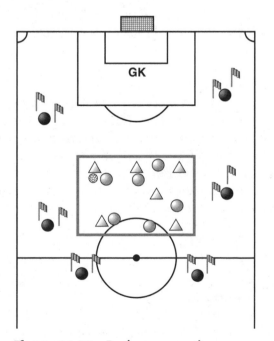

Figure 14.12   Back-pass practice.

Kicks and Passes

Goalkeepers must be able to pass the ball with their feet and make both short passes and long ones. Encourage young keepers to work on kicking with both the right and left foot, particularly in relation to the back pass. This helps them distribute the ball without concern about which side an attacker is pressuring.

There are four other types of kicking: the punt, the drop-kick, the sidewinder, and the goal kick.

The punt is the most common kick used by goalkeepers. Punts get distance down the field. However, a punt usually goes high in the air and is often easily intercepted by the opponent's defense. To punt the ball, the goalkeeper throws the ball up in the air about 18 inches in front. As the ball drops, the goalkeeper locks his or her kicking-foot ankle and follows straight through the center of the ball with the laces of the shoe. The goalkeeper's body and shoulders should follow through toward the target once the ball has been kicked.

The drop-kick has a much lower flight than the punt. Because of the ball's lower trajectory, forwards have a better chance of controlling and keeping the ball from the opponent. The ball gets to the target player or area much quicker and more directly than does the punt. This kick is more difficult to execute consistently. To drop kick the ball, the goalkeeper drops the ball in front. As it hits the ground and pops up, the goalkeeper follows through with the kicking foot, ankle locked. The keeper keeps shoulders and hips square to the target area.

In reality, the sidewinder is a side volley. It was developed and used in Mexico and Central America and is becoming much more common in the world game. This kick is used mainly as a counterattacking kick when a quick and direct route to an attacking teammate up field is needed. This type of distribution is probably the most difficult to master and should be encouraged from the ages of 14 and up. The goalkeeper releases the ball from the hands and chops down through the side of the ball.

The goal kick is probably the most neglected kick of all. Back in youth soccer, some coaches would have the strongest player on the team take the goal kick instead of the goalkeeper, who often lacked power. It's of prime importance that coaches develop this technique in goalkeepers. When the keeper takes the goal kick, it gives the team an extra player up the field and helps avoid offside penalties.

Throws

There are three types of throws: the underarm bowl, the sidearm or baseball throw, and the overarm throw or bowl.

The purpose of the underarm bowl is to move the ball along the ground to a teammate who is close to the goalkeeper in an area where there are no opponents between the goalkeeper and the target. This makes the ball very easy to receive and control by the target. This serve is very similar to the "10 pin" bowling action. The goalkeeper releases the ball low and on the ground.

The sidearm or baseball throw allows the goalkeeper to send the ball a good distance in the air to a teammate. This type of throw is used when there are no opponents between the goalkeeper and the target. The throw stays low and is easily received and controlled. This serve falls between the underarm bowling action and the overarm bowling throw. The ball is delivered shoulder height, similar to a baseball pitcher throw.

A keeper uses the overarm throw or bowl to get height and distance and put opposing players out of the game. When executed correctly, this throw can be a safe and accurate counterattack option. The ball is grasped in the hand and brought from the side of the body in. An overarm bowling action is used. The ball is released when the arm and hand are extended at the 11-o'clock position.

Game Savvy

Goalkeepers with game savvy always know where they are in the game, tactically. Goalkeeper reaction is based on this information. The keeper is asked many times during the game to make decisions. Usually, game savvy comes from many years of playing the position and is better known as experience or the ability to read the game.

With the recent rule changes, the sweeper-keeper role has become a required tactical role for the goalkeeper. A goalkeeper is required to play off the goal line and be responsible for the space between him or her and the last defender or unit. Keepers also should to be able to balance this responsibility in relation to the space behind them and the goal. They must recognize when there's sufficient pressure on the ball. Degree of pressure on and off the ball determines whether the keeper advances forward from the goal line to support the defenders or drops off to cover the goal. Without pressure on the ball, the goalkeeper risks being chipped or having to deal with a long-range, dipping shot. This is particularly critical when the ball is 30 to 35 yards out from goal.

Game Savvy Drill

All types of shot-stopping are required in this keeper savvy drill. The key to the activity is constant high-pressure defense.

In this drill, the defending team is not to allow a shot on their goal. If they do, the resting team (the third team) replaces them. The third team is spread out along the touchlines outside the field of play. These players can be used by the attacking team in the game but are restricted to one touch play on the outsides. The shot must be on target or force the goalkeeper to make a save. If the shot is wide of the target, both teams continue to play.

Create three teams of five or six players. Set up a field 36 yards long by 44 yards wide marked by discs. At each end, set up a 6-yard box marked with discs as a goal. Also mark a center-line with discs. Two teams play freely in the field (figure 14.13). The third team waits on the outside of the field. Players on the third team are restricted to one touch only to send the ball back to the team that passed it to them.

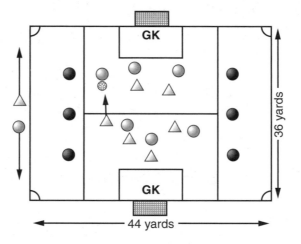

Figure 14.13 Game savvy drill.

The goalkeeper's team tries not to allow a goal or a shot on goal. The goalkeeper's role is to organize the team's marking, communicate, and get players to pressure the ball. If they don't, a shot will be taken on them. That team would rotate with the team that was on the outside.

The keeper must make many positional adjustments to support the team, including assuming the sweeper-keeper role. The keeper also communicates with defenders to keep pressure on the ball so that no shots are allowed. Keeping pressure on the ball ideally means man-to-man defending. If there's pressure on the ball, the keeper must recognize it and adjust as necessary in the goal.

Summary

Decision making, communication, and organization are just as important as technique, if not more so. The most efficient technical and tactical goalkeepers in the world would still struggle if they could not make early and confident decisions. Early decisions and quality communication give defenders confidence in the goalkeeper's ability and encourages them to cover the goal when the goalkeeper is coming off the line to attack the ball.

An important role of the goalkeeper is to organize the defense tactically. Prevention is better than cure. With clear communication, good tactical information, and tactical organization, a goalkeeper might be able to prevent a wide attacking player from serving the cross. Perfecting this tactic, though it's not as spectacular as a diving save, is often the hallmark of good goalkeeping.

CHAPTER 15

Shutting Down Opponents

Jay Hoffman

The best teams in the world defend well. Strong defense is no longer the main focus of a certain few—it's a collective team effort. Every player on the field needs to play good defense.

This is what we asked of the 1999 U.S. Women's World Cup team. We wanted to confront the squads we faced, defined by their multitude of attacking personalities, with well-disciplined defenders who were both skillful and tactical. To succeed, we needed to be ready to win individual matchups, defend against any attacking scheme, and control the defensive rhythm of the game.

Our three-year preparation for the 1997 Youth World Championships also demanded a team focus on defense. Young players competing on professional clubs on a daily basis populate this under-20 age group (U-20s) throughout the world. These players are technically competent, tactically astute, and professionally motivated. We designed our defensive training of our players to meet two objectives: (1) to increase defensive abilities and thereby accelerate attacking skills and (2) to create a way to regain possession from opponents whose exposure to the demands of the game, as compared to ours, was greatly enhanced through their professional playing environments.

Although the 1999 U.S. Women's World Cup and 1997 Youth World Championship teams were different in many ways, both teams relied on defense for success. The women won the World Championship. The U-20s advanced to the second round in Malaysia. However, the true success of this team was in the development of players such as Olsen, Wolf, and Victorine, who are all playing in MLS today.

As we watched the 2002 Men's World Cup and the U-19 Women's World Championship, we were once again reminded that defending requires hard work and commitment. It also requires an intelligent application of the principles of play and the concepts that enhance them by the individual player within a system and a defensive scheme of play.

Principles of Defense

A team's ability to deny goals, limit opportunities, and recapture the ball depends on individual and collective application of basic defensive principles. All players, regardless of position, have a responsibility in this effort. Although there's room for some interpretation of the principles, players must stay focused on them to meet the defensive demands for the duration of a game.

The first principle is that of immediate chase. Immediate chase applies to both the player who loses the ball and to the team overall. Can the player who loses the ball immediately win it back by dispossessing the opposition? Can the team regain possession by making the opponent make a poor decision? In our collective defensive effort, chasing also requires remaining players to immediately recover into positions that establish a defensive shape. They must delay penetration while giving teammates opportunities to recapture the ball. It's best if these can occur while the ball is still in transition.

The second principle is to delay the attack and deny penetration. This allows players to recover and get organized behind the ball. Pressure needs to be applied quickly to the opponent with the ball. In today's game, this pressure can be exerted at various angles and degrees with one collective thought in mind: to recapture the ball based on either team's collective strengths or weakness. The pressuring player always wants to exhibit control and restraint backed by an aggressive "you can't beat me" attitude. The more effective the individual pressure, the more time allowed for teammates to collectively recover and organize.

The third principle is to cover the organization of the players behind the pressuring defender. Cover can involve any number of players. Several factors in the game dictate a covering player's position, including the pressuring defender's body position, angle, and speed of closing down; the distance of pressure; the body language of the player on the ball; and the desired play in a particular third of the field. Player movement off of the ball, by both the opposition and teammates, also affects positioning. Primarily, covering players want to position themselves to deny penetration. If the pressuring player is beaten, covering players want to deny the advancement of the player on the ball. Covering positions should also allow covering players to be able to intercept, tackle, and defend if the ball is played to a player in their area of responsibility while limiting passing lanes for the player on the ball.

Balance is the fourth principle. Players who aren't in the immediate vicinity of the ball provide balance in the team shape. The team's shape should restrict space centrally, denying penetrating runs. To restrict space, balancing players want to get into position early and be able to see both the ball and the players away from the ball. An open body position, no ball watching, and a constant surveying of the field helps ensure proper positioning. To deny the opposition space behind the defense, defenders attempt to use good starting positions, goal side and ball side. They also should use their bodies to step across an attacking player's run, maintain team shape, and, when appropriate, use offside tactics.

The fifth principle, compactness and concentration, refers to team shape in defending. This principle involves the distance from our goalkeeper to our forwards and from the left side to the right side of the team. This shape is designed to limit time and space, making it difficult for the opposition to penetrate. The ability of a team to maintain this shape depends on many factors, including stepping up to press, dropping back to restrict space behind the defense, and squeezing play to the flanks or central. Pressure on the ball, movement of the ball and players, speed of play, and the role of the goalkeeper all affect team shape. Players need to understand their roles and functions, the laws of the game, and offside tactics; they should be able to make good tactical decisions to keep a compact team shape.

These principles are the basis of our defending. Regardless of the system of play, the defensive scheme, or the line of confrontation, the principles must be cooperatively imposed for successful defending.

Teaching Defensive Principles

Players must know the principles and understand how they relate to each other. They must be aware of and trained in the concepts that bring these principles to life. As soccer has increased in technical, tactical, physical, and psychological speed, this training has become even more important. Player's decision-making skills are significantly enhanced once they can combine soccer principles of play and concepts.

Defensive Concepts

The first concept is communication. During a game, communication is divided into verbal and visual. The visual aspect is the most important because of the increase in playing speed at the highest levels of the game. When time allows, verbal communication is also very effective, but the information needs to be specific and simple to allow for clear understanding. Visual communication requires an understanding between players; it can change with each touch of the ball or movement of a player. Visual communication demands every player's concentration and the ability to adapt quickly to defensive demands. Figure 15.1 illustrates the visual communication provided by a pressuring defender. The pressuring defender uses body

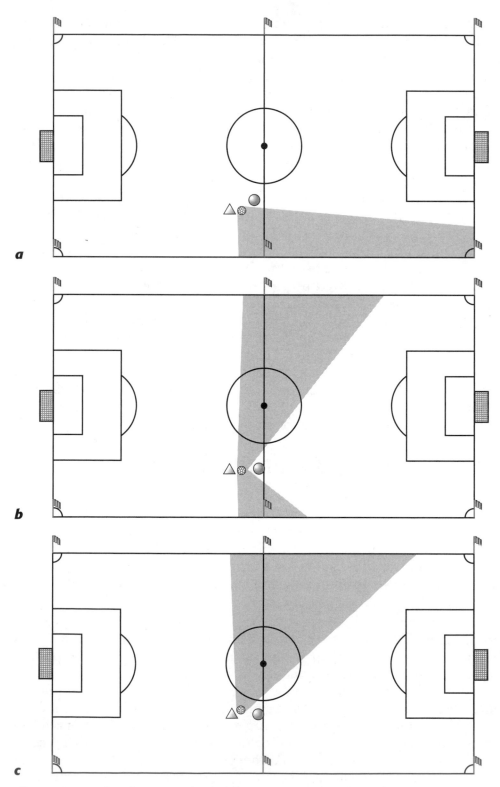

Figure 15.1 Visual communication from a pressuring defender.

position to inform his or her teammates where the opponent with the ball will be pressured to go. Figure 15.2a shows an attacker with greater playing options due to the defender's positioning, whereas figure 15.2b shows the visual communication provided by the pressuring defender who has been more effective closing down the attacker.

If we relate this to the principles of play, we can see that recovery runs, cover positions, balance, and team shape are all affected differently in each example, as indicated by the shaded areas of possible penetration.

The second concept is transition, the speed at which a player changes roles in the game. This includes moving from attack to defense, from defense to attack, and from one role to another in the attacking and defending processes. In the speed of today's game, players must be able to alter their defensive roles as the ball is played from one player to another. If this change in roles is slow or late its effectiveness to limit the opposition is greatly reduced.

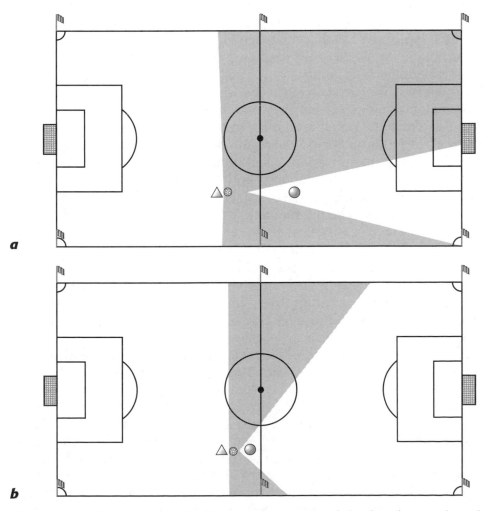

Figure 15.2   Visual communication from a pressuring defender who can close down the attacker.

The third concept, defensive vision, involves a player's ability to read the thought and movement of the opposition as well as those of teammates. Players must be trained in advance to think defensively. Even when in possession and on attack, players must know what's taking place around them and how to deal with the loss of the ball.

Defensive vision also includes reading the body language of attacking players: head up or head down; shaping up to pass or shoot; preparing the ball close to the body or on the final touch away from the body. The physical and psychological dimensions of players influence these cues. Improving defensive vision requires players to establish good defensive positions early to see the ball and players, not just watch the ball, as well as develop a high level of technical competence and fitness.

The fourth concept is the tactical application of technique, in which skill and decision-making work together to enhance defending. We don't defend just to destroy play but to attack. The application of tactics to technique improves the ability not only to regain but to maintain possession. It provides the opportunity to take advantage of the opposition when their team shape is not conducive to defending. This application requires a high level of skill to be done consistently.

Examples include a defensive player stepping across a player dribbling the ball or a defender stepping across an attacking player's path as the attacker tries to penetrate in combination play. In both cases, the defender's movement puts him or her in position to regain possession rather than just break up the play. Tactical application of technique might also include a player's ability to clear a ball to the opposite end of the field, easing the pressure and providing time to reorganize or establish a good starting position that might allow the pass to be intercepted and possession maintained.

The final concept is speed of play, which is a combination of all the concepts in relation to the principles of play. Coaches have devoted a lot of training time to increasing players' speed of play. In attacking, speed of play is characterized by one- and two-touch plays, increased technical, physical, psychological abilities, and decision-making. As might be expected, increased speed in attacking elicits an increase in the speed of defense play as well.

To increase defensive speed of play, players need to know the difference between action and reaction. In defending, speed of play is defined as how quickly, efficiently, and cohesively players can apply the principles of defense through tactics. Instead of reacting in an attempt to defend an attack, individual players and the team act defensively to pressure the opposition. This is action. The development of action might include a well-trained tactical plan tailored to either team's strengths, weaknesses, and playing personalities. It could involve a team's ability to constantly change from low pressure to high pressure. It also involves variations in the setting of the defensive line of confrontation with a defensive scheme to force play wide, central, or square within any such plan.

Action might not always be immediately possible during loss of possession. Reaction is sometimes necessary. Defense might be based on reaction until individual players and the team can organize and dictate play.

Throughout a game, moments of action and reaction are the norm. For example, it might not be beneficial to push play central, especially if the attacker is wide. (Here the touchline can be used as an extra defender.) There will be times when defensive shape won't support the action of a player applying pressure. Players need to make these decisions. A goal in coaching is to have our players read the tactical situation and quickly apply an effective defensive action.

Training Exercises

The following are exercises I have used to train defensive principles and concepts. These activities have been useful training for U-14 boys and girls, as well as WUSA, MISL, NASL, and MLS professional players, Youth National Teams, and the 1999 Women's World Cup champions. As with any training activity, replicate the game as closely as possible to provide opportunities for players to make decisions under gamelike demands.

1 v 1

Set up a rectangular grid 15 × 20 yards (figure 15.3). The server has several balls. The players play one-on-one soccer. Goals are scored by dribbling over the endline. Play restarts when a goal is scored or when the ball is sent out of bounds. The defensive player needs to read the pass from the server and close down the attacking player while the ball is in flight. Focus on individual defense, stealing possession of the ball, and counterattacking. For variety, change the starting positions of the defensive player or the server or change the type of service.

Defenders work on reading the body language of the server. When the defender is closing down on the attacker, watch for speed and angle of approach, body position, and controlled aggression. Watch for individual defense skills such as body position, the ability to win the ball, and the ability to dispossess the attacker. Watch for application of the principles of defense.

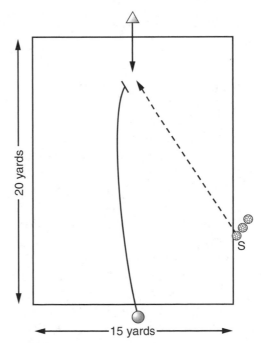

Figure 15.3   1 v 1.

1 v 1 (II)

This exercise reinforces individual defending, dispossessing, and counterattacking. Set up a rectangular grid 15 × 20 yards. Set balls around the outside of the grid (figure 15.4). The players play one- to two-minute games of one-on-one soccer. Goals are scored by dribbling over the endline. If a ball goes out of bounds, a new ball is brought into play. For variety, set up one, two, or three small goals. Goals are scored by dribbling or passing through a goal.

Defenders work on closing down skills: speed and angle of approach, body position, and controlled aggression. For individual defense, watch for correct body position, the ability to win the ball, and the ability to dispossess the attacker. Watch for application of the principles of defense.

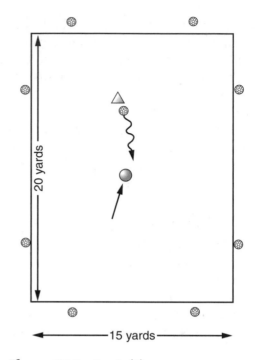

Figure 15.4   1 v 1 (II).

1 v 1 With End Players

This exercise focuses on individual defending against a player with or without possession of the ball, tracking down and defending off-the-ball running in combination play, and dispossessing and counterattacking. Set up a rectangular grid 15 × 20 yards (figure 15.5). Set extra balls around the grid. Players score by getting the ball across an endline using combination plays with either end player. The end players move to create passing angles for support. Play one- to two-minute games, then have players change positions. For variety, play two on two, three on three, and so on, adjusting the field size accordingly. Players can score

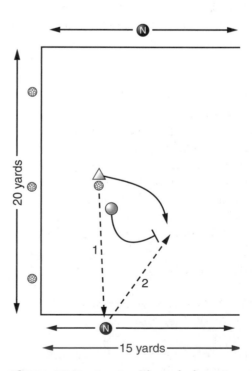

Figure 15.5   1 v 1 with end players.

by combination plays or on their own. Any player can score through a combination play (two on two, etc.).

Defenders work on closing down skills: speed and angle of approach, body position, and controlled aggression. For individual defense, watch for correct body position, the ability to win the ball, and the ability to dispossess the attacker. When defending combination plays, defenders need to know when and how to step across the attacker and when and how to drop between the player and the goal. Emphasize transition, immediate chase, and recovery runs. Watch for application of the principles of defense and the maintenance of team shape.

3 v 3 v 3

This exercise can also be played with three teams of two or four players. Create three teams, assigning each a different colored vest. Set up a grid the appropriate size for the number of players. For teams of three, set up a field 20 × 30 yards (figure 15.6). Set balls around the outside of the grid. Two teams try to maintain possession against the third team. The team that loses the ball immediately defends against the other two teams.

Figure 15.6 3 v 3 v 3.

Defensive players should not allow the attack to play through them. By applying the principles of play, the defensive team works to reduce the number of playing options, allowing the defense to win the ball, find an attacking option, and maintain possession. For variety, limit the number of touches for the attacking teams to one or two.

Watch for correct team shape during transition. Observe how players read the game. Make sure they apply the principles and concepts of defense, such as communication, closing down, and individual and group defending.

4 v 4 v 4

This activity develops individual defensive skills and the team's ability to organize and defend as a unit. It can also be done with teams of five, six, or seven with or without goalkeepers. Demands on players will vary depending on their positions when the ball is served.

Create three teams, each with a different colored vest. Set up a grid the appropriate size for the number of players, complete with markings. For teams of four, set up a field 44 × 60 yards (figure 15.7). Use regulation-size goals. The server stands outside the grid with the balls. Put a team at each end of the field and another in the center.

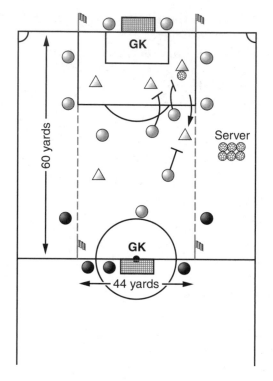

Figure 15.7 4 v 4 v 4.

All play starts with the server. Restarts play appropriately. Teams play for five to seven minutes. The ball is served to one of the end teams to begin an attack. The team at the middle of the field defends and can counter attack. After a goal or goal attempt or after a set period of time, the server serves a new ball to the other end team to begin a new attack. The initial attacking team goes to their end of the field.

For variety, play with more attackers than defenders or more defenders than attackers. Limit the number of touches for the attacking team. Play without goalkeepers to one, two, or three small goals.

Watch for individual defensive skills, team skill during transition, and correct application of the principles of defense. Players need to communicate well. If you use a goalkeeper, watch for correct execution of the keeper's role and function. Watch for correct team shape and the ability of players to read the game. Assess safety and risk factors. Watch for appropriate defense throughout the field.

5 v 5 Plus 1

You can also do this exercise with teams of four, six, or seven. Use goal-keepers.

Set up a field 60 × 44 with normal field markings and regulation-size goals (figure 15.8). Be sure extra balls are available. Create teams of five. One extra

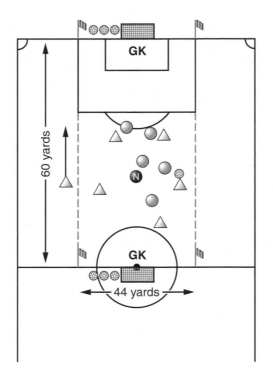

Figure 15.8   5 v 5 plus 1.

neutral player always plays with the team in possession of the ball, while the defensive team defends as a group in a numbers-down situation.

For variety, limit the number of touches for the attacking team. If the game is played without goalkeepers, play to one, two, or three small goals. Organize players by position. Add more neutral players.

Watch how defenders execute in a numbers-down situation. Defenders need to execute individual defensive and transition skills. Watch for application of the principles of defense, including good communication. If using a goalkeeper, watch for the correct execution of the keeper's role and function. Observe team shape and how players read the game. Assess any safety or risk factors. Watch for defensive play throughout the field.

At any level, to affect a positive change in playing behavior, constantly raise the demands of the game to challenge your players. Make sure your players are aware of the basic principles during training time. They are the foundation on which you can build and develop a collective effort to defend.

Team Defense

At the highest levels of the game, the demands on your players are increased; each player must contribute to the defensive process. We select players based on their playing personalities and position them where they can be most effective on both sides of the ball. Each position and group of players on the team has a unique role and tactical function.

Regardless of the system of play or player demands, the laws of the game influence defense. Teams knowledgeable and experienced in professional fouls, time tactics, and offside tactics have an advantage when trying to recapture the ball. Make sure your players understand that applying these tactics involves risk. As necessary, remind them that the referee and assistants interpret and judge their behavior, leaving them open to discipline, including being sent off.

The use of offside tactics and the space behind the defense does not necessarily mean we win the ball by catching opponents in an offside position. The correct use of this space and tactic is to allow the team to remain compact at all times, enhancing opportunities to win the ball in more advantageous positions. To effectively keep compact, the team needs a goalkeeper who can cover the space behind the team and play with his or her feet. It also demands understanding, cohesion, and application by every player. Teams should realize that while the correct use of this tactic can be beneficial, any mistake or misjudgment by the referee or players can result in a goal-scoring opportunity for the other team.

Tactical Roles

All players have the common defensive responsibilities of heading to clear the ball or to gain possession, passing off the interception, clearing the ball, tackling, dispossessing the attacker with the ball by stepping across the dribbling player, dispossessing the attacker with the ball by stepping across the runner after the ball has been played, closing down the player in possession of the ball, establishing correct starting positions, and transitioning to attack.

Goalkeepers are further responsible for stopping shots; catching, boxing, or redirecting crosses; closing down the shooter; clearing balls; heading to clear and to gain possession; and passing off the interception to transition to attack. The keeper also needs to organize the defense; provide cover and balance; play as a sweeper; move in relation to the movement of players and the ball, with a line between the ball and the goal; be ready to come off the line to close down players; cut shooting angles; handle crosses; and be able to transition to attack.

The sweeper is responsible for executing positional play behind the defense, even with and in advance of the defensive line. The sweeper also helps to organize the defense; provides cover and balance; tracks down players, executing zonal and marking responsibilities; helps establish and control the line of retreat; uses offside space as appropriate; executes recovery runs; knows when and how to dispossess the opponent; and is able to transition to attack.

The marking backs have marking responsibilities; depending on the defensive scheme, their responsibilities vary as to player assignments and movement on the field. Their starting positions are established in relation to player, ball movement, and pressure. They use offside space, are able to execute individual defensive techniques, and know when and how to dispossess the opponent. Marking backs also provide cover and balance, track players, and execute recovery runs. They might have roles in man-to-man, zone, or combination defensive schemes. They must be able to transition to attack.

Outside defenders have marking and zone responsibilities, both laterally and forward. They provide cover and balance and must be able to execute individual defensive skills in establishing starting positions, tracking down players, making recovery runs, and dispossessing opponents. They must also be able to transition to attack, providing width.

As a group, organization is the key for midfielders, who need to be able to transition quickly and make recovery runs to provide the first block of defensive pressure. They need to execute individual defensive skills and provide cover and balance. Midfielders can change the defensive rhythm of a game by establishing defensive pressure and dictating the progress and direction of the attack. They have zone or man-to-man responsibilities. They must be able to transition to attack.

For the defensive midfielder, who organizes the midfielders and forwards, individual defensive skills are particularly important. He or she has zone and man-to-man responsibilities, provides cover and balance, and tracks players. The defensive midfielder's position is established in relation to the attacking and defensive scheme of the team. This player must be able to transition to attack.

The flank midfielders execute individual defensive skills, provide cover and balance, and must be ready to transition to a pressing defense. They have marking and zone responsibilities, both laterally and forward. They track down players and make recovery runs. These players are prepared to transition to attack and provide both width and support in advance of the ball.

The attacking and game-making midfielders execute individual defensive skills and transition to pressing defenses. They provide cover and balance, track down players, and make recovery runs. They have marking and zone responsibilities, both laterally and forward. They must be able to transition to attack.

As a group, forwards must be able to transition quickly, begin the pressing defense, delay the attack, make the game predictable, execute individual defensive skills, and transition to attack.

The wingers execute individual defensive skills and transition to pressing defenses. They have marking and zone responsibilities, both laterally and behind. They provide cover and balance, track down players, and execute recovery runs. They must be able to transition to attack.

183

The central strikers execute individual defensive skills, transition to pressing, make the game predictable, delay the attack, and have marking and zone responsibilities laterally. They must be able to transition to attack.

Within any system of play these roles and functions might be expanded, limited, or finely tuned for specific individuals or groups. You must carefully observe, analyze, and decide how each player's playing personality will best serve your defensive scheme.

Systems of Play

Which system of play is the best? The one that provides the greatest number of opportunities for scoring goals while eliminating chances and goals for the opposition. When selecting a system of play, use your players in a way that gives them the greatest opportunity to positively influence the game.

No system guarantees success. For example, having five defenders instead of four does not mean a team will give up fewer opportunities. All systems have both positive and negative defensive aspects. While the following systems might be the most common, each will vary depending on the interpretation of the defensive scheme, including organizing players within each group, forcing play wide to specific areas, varying the line of defensive confrontation, using pressing or low pressure, and using zone or man marking or a combination of the two.

In the 4-4-2, the deployment of players makes the field more manageable in terms of lateral and forward positions of responsibility. Players are evenly distributed. In this system, nine plus players can be defensively oriented. There's an equal balance of players at midfield and at the back.

In the 3-5-2, nine players can be defensively oriented. The distribution of players in the back and midfield are unbalanced, creating greater demands on the wide midfielders. Three defenders might have the responsibility to cover the width of the field. Concentration and organization of players in the midfield can provide pressure earlier and limit space for the opposition.

In the 4-3-3, the lateral and forward positions of responsibility can make the field more manageable. Depending on the organization of the midfield and forwards, players might be more evenly distributed. The distribution of players to the midfield and forward positions allows pressure to be applied earlier and limits space away from the goal.

Team Tactics

The final step of developing team defense is applying team tactics. Defending, as a team, the run of play and all restarts requires every player to be well organized and knowledgeable in applying the principles to deny the opposition goal-scoring chances. At the highest levels, teams also need to be trained to vary their tactical approach throughout the game. Defensively, that might mean playing low pressure then, on cue, pressing the opposition. These variations in defensive rhythm are designed to disrupt the opposition's play and increase opportunities to regain possession.

Pressing can be exhibited in various aspects and times of the game. A team that loses possession in their own attacking third might be immediately confronted, closed down, and pressured by a well-organized defensive unit. Pressing can also occur if the defending team reads cues that make the opponent susceptible to losing possession in a critical area of the field. This tactic requires great physical and psychological effort. The ability to press for a long time is limited. The team must be well organized and work together in applying this tactic.

Whether a team should press or not depends on several factors, including the overall ability of each team, the climate, field size, field conditions, and numerical advantages. Take into consideration the game situation, including time remaining, score, and your opponent's psychological state of mind. Know the particular style and strategy of the team you're playing.

Cues to press include when a player who loses the ball immediately applies pressure; when the player in possession of the ball is playing toward his or her own goal with limited support; and when the ball is played behind the defense, and defenders chase it toward their own goal or toward a goalkeeper who lacks technical competency under pressure and might have limited playing options. You also might want to press when defending or attacking on a restart and the opposition has committed numbers and shape to solve a demand of the game.

Apply pressure to the opponent immediately to make the play predictable. The team must defend with the objective of creating an interception of the next pass, stealing the ball from the player in possession of the ball or the receiver of a pass, or getting into defensive positions to continue the process away from the goal. Demands are placed on players to double-team the ball, play even or numbers-down away from the ball, read zone and player responsibilities, use offside tactics, and force play where it's most beneficial. Although application of pressure is based primarily on the game situation, some systems (3-4-3, 4-3-3, and 3-5-2) might provide greater opportunities to press.

If not pressing, the defense is reorganizing and developing a line of defensive confrontation. This line might appear anywhere on the field and requires the team to be patient, organized, and disciplined. After losing the ball, players recover and organize behind the ball quickly.

There are several factors to consider in low-pressure defending, including the overall defensive ability of each team, the climate, field size, field conditions, and numerical disadvantage or advantage. Consider game situations such as time remaining, the score, and the opponent's psychological state of mind. Are you playing against a team with a particular style or strategy? Is it a home game or an away game? Is a particular result desired?

Depending on the position of the ball, repossession might not be the imme-diate focus. The line of confrontation, team organization, and tactical scheme are designed to limit space in front of the goal while creating space behind the attacking team. The team must be compact, balanced, and ready to defend intensely. Offside tactics, defensive schemes to win the ball in certain areas, double-teaming on the ball, or a change in systems with more players behind the ball (5-4-1 or 4-5-1) can lead to success when applying low pressure.

Exercises

The following training exercises combine everything we have discussed in defending. These exercises have been used with more advanced players. Organize players by position to improve their decision-making and execu-tion of their roles within the team tactic.

Midfield Defending

This exercise reinforces midfield defensive organization and player roles. In the midfield third of the field, mark an area approximately 40 × 75 yards (figure 15.9). Play to three goals. The extra players on the ends of the field play for both teams. Players on the endlines have only one touch and may move to support play by attacking or defending the three goals.

As a modification, have players who are supporting the attack from behind enter the game to develop midfield defending with numbers down. Players supporting the defending team from behind can enter the game to develop numbers-up defending (for example, the outside back stepping into the midfield or central defender). Add an attacking or defensive third of the field and the respective players for each team, who now defend two thirds of the field.

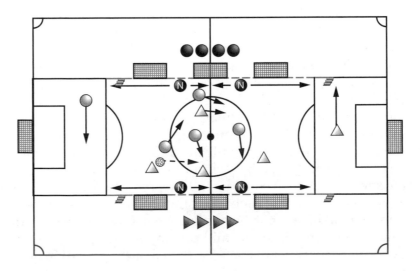

Figure 15.9 Midfield defending.

Focus on developing individual defensive skills and team shape. Players work on tracking down and defending with numbers up or down. Both pressing and low-pressure defending can be executed, as well as offside tactics. Observe how well players understand their roles and transition to counterattack.

Pressing

This exercise varies defensive tactics—pressing and low pressure defending to pressing. Set up a field appropriate for the number of players (use from 6 to 11 players per team). For 7 v 7, the area is 55 × 75 yards (figure 15.10). Divide the field into four zones. Each zone is assigned a point value. The zone closest to one's attacking goal is worth four points, then three, then two, and then one. Players are organized by positions. When a defending team gains possession of the ball in a respective zone, maintains possession, and scores, the goal is worth the point value of the zone where the ball was won.

Players should work on transition skills and individual defensive skills. Look for proper team shape. The goalkeeper works on properly executing his or her role within the defensive scheme. Players should try to change

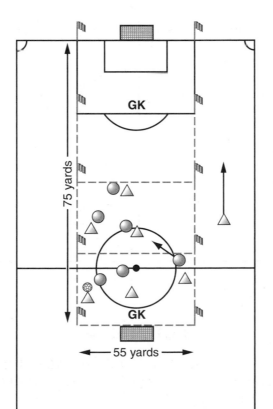

Figure 15.10   Pressing 7 v 7.

the defensive rhythm of the game and counterattack. Players should read cues to determine the appropriate defensive action, based upon their roles and functions within the team.

Team Defense

The aim of this exercise is for the team to defend as a whole, keep the team shape compact in length and width, and defend restarts. Set up a field big enough for the number of players (use 8 to 11 players per team). Divide the field into zones, as shown in figure 15.11. Players are organized by positions.

If goalkeepers are not available, you can play to two or three goals. Assign the team to set a defensive line of confrontation. Let players experience game situations, such as being goal down or goal up with a set amount of time remaining.

Players work on individual defensive skills and executing their roles. Observe the team shape and how the team defends through the thirds of the field. Practice offside tactics, low pressure, pressing, changing the defensive rhythm of the game, counterattacking, and the role of the goalkeeper.

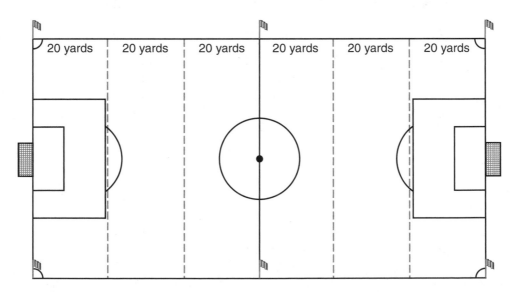

Figure 15.11 Team defense.

Summary

As head coach of the Men's U-20 National Team in 1994, I established at every training camp that our first focus was to improve defense. Over the next three years, this priority was discussed, coached, and demanded of every player in all aspects of training. The evolution of this team over the years required us to change from playing a modified 3-4-3 to a 4-4-2 alignment. This system allowed us to present the opponent with varied defensive schemes through-out the game. The organization and the player's defensive responsibilities allowed us to defend in a 3-5-2, 3-4-3, 4-3-3, 2-5-3 or 2-4-4 system of play regardless of our line of defensive confrontation. Players were required to defend in their respective groups and in the group in front and back of them. Figure 15.12 shows our defensive rotation versus a 4-4-2 system.

The figures show the team's defensive rotation when the outside back is in possession of the ball. Defensively, the outside midfielder pushes forward to defend the outside back as the outside back pushes forward into midfield. Note the ballside positioning of the deeper defensive midfielders and backs. Figure 15.12b shows that the initial 4-4-2 has been reformed into a 3-4-3 defensive formation.

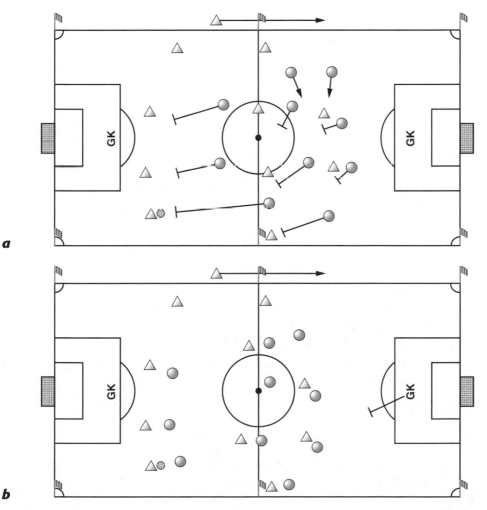

(continued)

Figure 15.12 *(a)* 4-4-2 v 4-4-2; *(b)* transition from 4-4-2 to 3-4-3; *(c)* transition from 3-4-3 to 2-4-4.

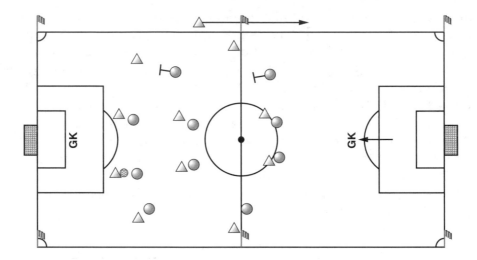

c

Figure 15.12 *(continued).*

In figure 15.12c, the central defender is in possession with the possibility of pressing. Both wide midfielders and backs look to push forward, leaving back players in a one-on-one situation, presenting a 2-4-4 defensive framework. This allows our central strikers to remain central while decreasing the area they have to cover defensively. The pressing tactic puts more players on the attack quickly once the ball is won. Pressing positions players where they are the most effective. Note the advanced position of the goalkeeper who here serves a sweeper role.

While coaching in the WUSA for the past two seasons, we again worked with varying defensive tactics throughout the game. Although each opponent had a unique playing personality, system, and style, our team had the ability to change the game defensively. Our system of play in Boston was 4-3-3 with variations in the positioning of one or two defensive or attacking midfielders. Playing against a 4-4-2 system of play required an outside back to push into the midfield, showing a 3-4-3 defensive system (figure 15.13a). When playing against Philadelphia's 4-1-4-1, both outside backs moved into the midfield, presenting a 2-5-3 defensive framework (figure 15.13b). This allowed us to defend any area of the field as a unit, remain compact, and take advantage of our players' personalities in their respective positions when the ball was won.

Collectively, we need to dedicate our coaching efforts to make soccer an attractive, exciting game. To do so, we must continue to expand player knowledge, individual ability, physical capabilities, and the mentality to defend. Defending is no longer just hard work and effort for a chosen few; it's now a collective process applied intelligently and focused on leading to what fans (and players) really enjoy—attacking. If we instill in our players the mentality that "we defend in order to attack," they are more inclined to give their all on defense.

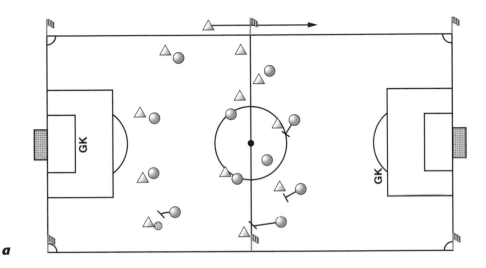

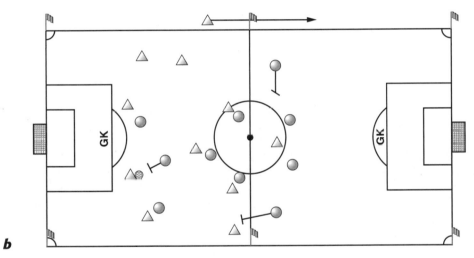

Figure 15.13 *(a)* 4-3-3 vs. 4-4-2; *(b)* 4-3-3 vs. 4-1-4-1.

CHAPTER 16

Competing in Tournaments and Playoffs

Schellas Hyndman

Postseason, second season, NCAA playoffs, "the big dance"—these phrases evoke a sense of excitement for every sports fan, and even more so for every team involved. Receiving an invitation to the national championship tournament is every college soccer team's goal for the season. If such invitations occur with regularity, they establish a program among the nation's elite.

Teams don't make tournaments by chance or survive them through luck. Preparation for the playoffs begins well before a team receives a bid. Your challenge is to have your team prepared for the "winner take all" environment of tournaments at whatever level of competition.

In this chapter I'll describe how the coaching staff at SMU perceives and deals with the pressures of postseason tournament play. While the shared experiences are those of a collegiate coach, most of the coaching problems at the college level are common to high school and club levels as well. This chapter covers how we attack those problems. Even if your own systems are vastly different from ours, I think some of what we do can be transferred to your program and be modified to suit your team's style and needs.

Seasonal Planning

Preparation for tournament play begins before the season starts. Returning players and new recruits set the stage for a great season and provide a positive mentality. Above all, the most essential factor for a successful season is to formulate a thorough plan from preseason training, progressing to the regular season game schedule, to, finally (we hope!), preparation for tournament play.

Your plan must be realistic and take into account your team's level of commitment and the way training will develop both individual players and the team as a unit. Your plan should include effective scheduling of competitive games in different settings, combined with a solid conference schedule. It must be a step-by-step outline that culminates in the playoffs. You sometimes hear of teams backing into the playoffs even to their own surprise, but in general, if you don't have a plan of action, the playoffs will elude you. Most important of all, once you have your plan in place, don't deviate from it unless you have to. Implement your plan. A plan without action is a hallucination.

At the first meeting of the season, as coach, you must sell the season plan to your players and establish individual and team goals. The players must believe in and commit to your plan and to each other for the plan to be successful. I rely on my 27 years of experience to chart a course of action to prepare my teams for the rigors of the coming season. At the first meeting, I dissect the season by examining each opponent and each game, home and away. Working together, we establish our team's goals. This prepares us for the task at hand and confirms that each segment of the season is an important step on the successful trip to a berth at the College Cup. It's imperative that your team make a commitment to themselves and each other because it's their team and their journey.

To help the group dynamics in this quest for collective commitment, I have my team sit in a big circle. Within this setting, the team arrives at their objectives for the season. The circular setting requires players to look teammates in the eye as they commit to the season. This helps establish mutual trust, unity, and loyalty to the team's common goal.

Every good team will agree that the ultimate goal is to win a national championship. For some teams, this goal is unrealistic. At SMU, we try to be both realistic and challenged. We try to accomplish goals on a sequential basis, starting with a productive preseason followed by winning the conference championship. Finally, we want to be on the ascent and playing our best soccer as we enter the NCAA tournament. I firmly believe that a team needs to be focused on the process rather than on the end product. Fundamentally, the season's foundation is based on continued learning in an enjoyable environment. At the end of the day, games will be forgotten. It's the journey that matters the most.

Early Season Play

As the journey progresses from the preseason to the season, individual and collective playing styles are established, and player roles are developed. Our overall focus week in and week out is to play good, attractive, effective soccer. At SMU, we try to play at 80 percent of our capacity during the first week of competition. It's the coach's responsibility to establish each player's individual and team roles. Once these roles are defined, the only obstacle remaining is to establish the playing rhythm, which is built through familiarity and a collective understanding among the team. While this is occurring, the team settles into the season and prepares for the NCAA playoffs.

For playoff preparation, try to create a challenging regular season schedule. Play teams with different styles and in different environments. Engaging in two-day tournaments in various parts of the country is an excellent way to achieve this goal and simulate postseason play.

Since conferences reward champions with automatic NCAA berths, conference games occupy the middle and late part of our schedule. Early in the season, we play weekend tournaments hosted by competitive schools, including or own school. These early season tournaments help develop the team. Success in these tournaments can pay huge dividends in postseason play.

First, tournaments give your team a chance to play teams at a neutral or away sight. This forces your team to adapt to different environments and fields, which helps when it comes time to play in the NCAA tournament. Second, these tournaments expose your team to squads from different areas of the country and allow you and your assistants to assess how your players cope with different playing styles. Third, it gives you a chance to test your team in an environment where they are out of the running for the championship if they lose or play poorly.

In our last couple of seasons at SMU, we played teams from every area of the country except the northeast. Perhaps by coincidence, and perhaps not, in championship play, a team from the northeast ultimately eliminated the Mustangs from further play. We now make every effort to schedule a game with a team from that area of the country. We hope this gives our team an opportunity to learn the style of soccer teams from that region. Unfortunately, we had to learn the hard way the importance of learning to adjust to varying styles of soccer.

Conference Play

Once the early season tournaments and the nonconference schedule are complete, the team settles into the season's routine. By now, players are used to daily training, and the team structure is pretty well established. As a team enters conference play, players need to understand their roles, team tactics, and, most important, the mentality needed to succeed in both the short and long term. This should be embedded in every player.

Conference play is the way most teams advance to the NCAA playoffs. Every game is important. One slip can cost a team its automatic bid. Within every conference, rivalries develop. Games test both the soccer ability and will power of each player. These games are proving grounds that can establish the mental toughness needed to advance to the later rounds of the national championship.

In 2000, two teams from the Missouri Valley Conference, SMU and Creighton, advanced to the semifinals of the College Cup. That year, the conference was as competitive as any in the country, and the battle for the top spot was very difficult. Every game was a tough test, and teams had to play consistently well to win. Our spirited conference schedule no doubt aided in the progression of two of its teams reaching the Final Four. Every week, players performed in big games—games that had to be won. By the time the playoffs arrived, playing under pressure was second nature.

Tournament Play

The NCAA playoffs are single-elimination matches. One poor performance immediately ends the season. Pressure is magnified, and player preparation from the season is put to the ultimate test.

At SMU, preparation throughout the season puts players in situations in which winning is rewarded and losing punished. This teaches players to get accustomed to the pressure to perform and thrive on that pressure. Training for us has always incorporated small-sided five-on-five games to two full-size goals in a "world cup" format (see figure 16.1, five on five plus four). When the games are over, winners go inside and take a shower. Losers pick up the gear, carry the goals off the field, and maybe do a few extra sprints. This kind of play immediately establishes the mentality of what it takes to be a winner and how one mistake can cost a season. With this in mind, the team continues to play elimination games with the emphasis on performing skills correctly and playing tactically error-free soccer. We also emphasize playing in a free, creative fashion but not carelessly.

The NCAA tournament forces every coach and player on the team to perform at his or her best. We all know that 89 minutes of good soccer and great concentration can be ruined by one second of carelessness.

A major difference between regular season and tournament play is that tournament games don't end in a tie. It can be difficult to score when two good teams are playing their best. If there isn't a winner after regular time and four overtimes, penalty kicks ensure a result. The pressure on a player to convert a penalty kick in the environment of an elimination game is almost impossible to replicate. But, as coaches, we must find five players who are strong and confident enough to step up and take the responsibility.

Although the pressure of the situation can't be duplicated, I still work with my kickers on how they take penalty shots. We work hard to make shots routine and try to create pressure situations in which the kicker must make the kick. Players must practice kicks so often that technique and execution become natural and the player can stand up under pressure. You also need to put your goalkeeper in the mindset of believing that he or she can save penalty kicks. Keepers must have confidence to be effective. Just one save of a penalty can be the difference between advancing and going home.

5 v 5 Plus 4

This exercise creates a demanding environment that requires players to attack and defend under the pressure of elimination.

Play 5 v 5 in a field 36 × 44 yards (figure 16.1). Each team has two flank players and two goal-line players. The flank players are responsible for getting down the line and serving dangerous balls. Occasionally, they should send some early services into the goal mouth area. The goal-line players are restricted to only one touch and are used as targets for wall passing. The five players on the field have no restrictions. They try to get forward and create scoring opportunities.

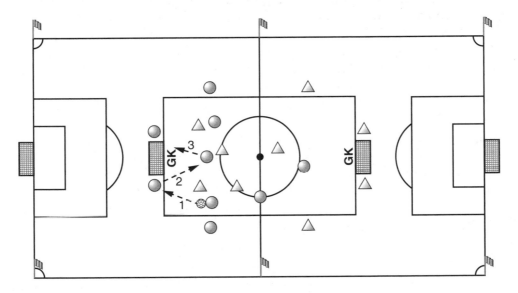

Figure 16.1   5 v 5 plus 4.

The game is designed to challenge every player to perform at maximum intensity and ability. Matches are five minutes long and require full concentration. One mistake can lead to a goal. Players have to fight for every loose ball and must always be prepared for the unexpected.

Players can play direct to a target, build wide through the flanks, or play down the middle. Every aspect of the game is magnified. Players are constantly playing one-on-one attacking or defending and numbers up or numbers down, as in a real match. Players not only develop soccer skills but are mentally put to the test.

Once a team receives the official bid for the NCAA playoffs, and opponents and game sites are established, the coach immediately puts all of the team's energy and concentration into preparation for the first opponent. Use all your resources to acquire intimate knowledge of your opponent. This phase of the preparation should include four or five scouting reports, video analysis, and examination of personal files related to the opponent. Training sessions should be planned for the needs of the team and any tactical adjustments required to deal with the opponent.

Training Intensity

With my years of experience, I feel I have a pretty good idea of the playoff picture. In my early days of coaching, I rigorously trained my team before postseason matches. My idea at that time was to make training more difficult so that players would understand how much they had given to the team, which would make it harder to give up in an important playoff game. Today, I have moved almost 180 degrees away from that. Our practices are now geared toward learning more about the opponent and fine-tuning and perfecting our normal patterns of play. Our training is no different than it was during the season. Generally, the length of training sessions reduces as the season progresses. We start the season with two-hour training sessions and gradually decrease the time to one hour and 45 minutes, then to one hour and 30 minutes. By the time we reach the NCAA tournament, training sessions are no more than one hour and 15 minutes. Players leave the training session hungry for the next session or the next game. The last thing a coach needs is exhausted, burnt-out, or injured players.

By game time, players should be tactically prepared, physically rested, and excited to play. Each time we win, the entire process starts over. As a coach, you must have your team prepared for the opponent, but more important, ready to play its own game.

The Playing Site

Playing at home or playing on the road, whether in the championships or the regular season, requires different preparation. The obvious benefit of playing at home is environmental. Players stay in their comfort zones in terms of eating and sleeping in a familiar setting. There's also the benefit of an extra day of training and preparation because there's no travel day. Playing on the road takes a lot of preparation time for nongame factors such as arranging an itinerary for the team's travel. Arranging mode of transportation (bus or plane) and planning meals, lodging, and workouts tends to eat up time. One advantage to being on the road is that the team can completely focus on the game without any outside distractions. Most likely you'll have some players who prefer to be in the less hectic away environment.

Whether at home or on the road, try not to let any stone go unturned. Game preparation should include obtaining three to four scouting reports combined with video analysis on team strengths and weaknesses and tendencies. We usually put together 15- to 20-minute films that profile the opponent. This lets our players see how the opponent plays. We focus on playing against opponents by training reserve players to mirror the opponent. We try to identify a team's passing tendencies, its special players, its set pieces, and so on while enforcing the idea that we need primarily to play *our* game. As a coach, you don't want to adjust so much for the other team that you lose your own team's identity.

As the playoffs continue and your team advances, repeat the weekly process for each new opponent. If your team plays well enough to reach the finals, focus on preparing your players to avoid the distractions surrounding the final round. With the media attention and excitement that accompanies the College Cup environment, you need to keep everything in place and focus on the importance of the next game. This is when players need to be focused but relaxed and able to play their best. Remind them that no matter how important the next game is, it's still only a game. If you've done your work over the season, your team is prepared to play, so all they have to do is go out there, relax, have fun, and play the way they always do.

Planning, commitment, practice, and experience make for a successful season. It's your job to outline the season and facilitate your players' growth. The road to the NCAA tournament is not an easy one, but the rewards are great and make for memories that last a lifetime. For a team, the opportunity to win a championship is a dream come true. In the grand scheme of things, individual games fall away, while the journey is always remembered.

V

Player and Team Development and Motivation

CHAPTER 17

Managing Players Effectively

Al Miller

After 40 years of coaching and managing at the top levels in college and professional soccer, I have an indelible impression that everything a coach does—every word spoken, every pat on the back, every criticism or punitive action—affects the team. In my mind, this notion makes the difference in winning or losing, in calm or chaos reigning, in strong or weak players emerging, and in acceptance or nonacceptance of team rules. Player management is far more complex than any other aspect of coaching, and, unfortunately, many are ill-prepared to deal with its many nuances prior to becoming coaches.

Leaders have a persona, a strong, trusting character, a confidence in their beliefs, and are the best salesmen on the planet. Every day you sell yourself, your program, your team, your ideas, your tactics, and your preparation. Most of all, you sell players on going further than they ever thought possible. Player management is all about convincing players to take the high road you have chosen.

Optimal working conditions, good leadership, delegation and division of responsibilities, fairness, honesty, and open communication are characteristics of a successful organization. Short-term and long-term planning dictate short-term and long-term success. Success is not accidental. As someone once said, "The challenge for every organization is to build a feeling of oneness, of dependence on one another . . . because the question is usually not how well each person works, but how well they all work together." It requires tremendous leadership and a group of people working diligently to reach a common vision. Believing, preparing, and sacrificing are necessary on everyone's part. Creating a family atmosphere helps provide strength in numbers. Getting all the necessary elements to work correctly is a major exercise but well worth it.

Success Starts at the Top

Everything starts at the top. My first pro job was in Philadelphia. The team's owner was Tom McCloskey. Tom was a giant in the building industry and a giant of a man who had many strong qualities. I soon learned that he would support me every way he could. By the end of the year, the players loved and respected him, affectionately referring to him as the "Big Booter." He never meddled with me or the players but was always there. He came to parties, organized some himself, and took a genuine interest in the players as people. They got to know his family and saw how important they were to him. His employees loved him, which soon became obvious to us. We always knew we could trust him. He provided a perfect work atmosphere, and we responded. Our 1973 championship team was the first pro franchise in any sport to win the league championship in its expansion year, a fact I'm very proud of. Tom McCloskey never played a minute but had a lot to do with that accomplishment.

When the college president thinks winning is important for the student body and community, the coach has an important thrust from the top. It doesn't guarantee success, but it's a great start. When I was hired at Hartwick College in the 1960s, Dr. Fred Binder, a former naval officer (and a fierce competitor), made it very clear that he chose me because he believed I could produce a winner. Hartwick never beat their neighbor West Point. When I arrived, I was introduced at the annual faculty meeting as the new soccer coach who could finally defeat Army. In my six years, we never lost to them. The president set the mood right from the start.

The athletic department and athletic director have to help you succeed. The AD facilitates a winning program by showing genuine interest, listening to your needs, and helping you get what it takes to be successful. That relationship is vital to every college coach. One of my ADs was Jim Konstanty, the former Philadelphia Phillies and New York Yankees pitcher and MVP of the National League in 1950. He was a winner, thought like a winner, and gave me a lot of insight into a champion's thinking. He and I talked daily for four years about many subjects. It was easy for me to see why he had made it to the top. I was blessed to work with him and learn from a professional. He was a big influence on the formation of my personal methods of coaching and leadership.

We had a president at our local university who would start every annual board meeting by saying that there should be only two items on the agenda. The first was a question the board should answer: Do you want to fire the president? If the answer was no, the second agenda item should be: How can we help the president achieve his goals? That speaks volumes to me. If a leader has the support of those around him, he has a good environment to create success. Unfortunately, for many coaches the environment is not supportive—garnering support becomes another sales job.

Developing a relationship with the front office and owner is critical. After that, select players who fit your style of management and coaching. Next, build an environment that makes players and staff feel comfortable. The team setting must generate enthusiasm and respect of the players for the organization and the people in charge of their destiny.

The organization's structure, expectations, rules and regulations, working conditions, and mutual respect are all part of the winning mix. Every individual should have a defined role and should agree to fulfill that role. I wanted my assistant coaches to be ambitious. I wanted guys who dreamed of being head coaches. I told them my expectations very clearly, and they were with me sink or swim. Behind the scenes second-guessing was unacceptable. They were part of the decision-making process.

Include the administrative team in most of your coaching plans and decisions. Weekly meetings to answer questions and confront concerns are tedious but healthy. Information shared at these meetings is privileged and should be treated accordingly. The worst thing that can happen to an owner or administrator is to be surprised or left out of the loop. A good coach keeps the front office team informed. This way, you're all in it together and support each other.

When I was a general manager, the coach decided to bench one of our star players. At halftime, the owner was furious and blamed me for not informing him. I didn't know the reason behind the benching either and was just as upset. After calmer heads prevailed, we agreed that it would not happen again, and after my private talk with the coach, it didn't. Coaches must understand that although they have been chosen to lead the players, they are a part of another team. For some coaches, that's difficult. Power to make decisions is one thing; taking over the organization is another. The coach had the power and the right to bench the star player. He did not have the power or right to keep it from the owner and the general manager. It was our team, too.

During my years in competitive sports, I have observed that winning programs are always a reflection of a passionate leader dedicated to winning. That is the main objective, and everyone knows it as soon as they enter the organization. Goals are clearly defined, and players are carefully screened to make certain they have the right attributes. The organization's strengths and weaknesses are identified, and everyone in the organization makes decisions based on one goal—will it help us win?

Player–Management Tools

Players need structure and work most effectively with a clearly defined organizational plan. They need a fair set of rules and regulations and a good work environment. All successful organizations have good leadership and an environment that makes all employees feel that they have a stake in the organization's success. Industries spend millions of dollars for consultants to get an organizational operational plan that maximizes employee productivity and builds company loyalty. A team has the same needs, and a good coach employs all his experience and savvy to create a similar environment for his or her team. Orchestrating players and staff to work harmoniously and feel that it's their team is a big step to successfully managing players.

Good practice conditions, up-to-date equipment, a well-managed dressing room, a private training and medical room that has all the necessary treatment and rehab equipment and supplies, a weight-training facility, and a home stadium that players take pride in are all parts the coach has to organize. Getting a one-up on opponents starts with paying attention to these details.

I always insisted that the equipment manager take pride in the position and provide better things for our players than other clubs did. It came back a thousandfold. When I coached in Dallas, I hired a senior citizen who had retired from the corporate world. The players respected him, and he took delight in adding perks to the dressing room. Elly was a big part of our player-management success. He was kind and considerate and made players feel special, but he had the ability to control the equipment and dressing room.

A big part of player management is catering to players but also demanding responsible behavior from them. "To whom much is given, much is expected," was always my guideline. I tried to give players the best organization they could ever play for. I wanted them to brag to other teams about how they were treated. My personal goal was to make our club the best organization players would ever experience. High expectations require that kind of thinking.

The other part of this player-management philosophy was to include families and friends. Every Christmas, we had a party that included dinner and gifts. I liked to host it at the owner's home. This reaffirmed the owner's team standing, got his wife and family involved in the team, and was an important building block in creating a family atmosphere in the organization. It also helped to build front office staff morale because it was one of the few times players and staff got together socially.

Little touches go a long way in building a successful organization. Early in my first year in Philadelphia, I had a small get-together for the players' wives at the stadium. I bought them all a beautiful silver locket with the team logo inscribed (Atoms). I thanked them and told them I fully understood what a big role they played in helping me make this a championship team. I made them feel important that day, but more crucial, I included them in the organization. I am quite sure this was a first for most of them. I also made certain that they had a comfortable place to retire to after games as they waited for their husbands. Sometimes that wait could be an hour or longer. To mingle with other wives and have staff with you certainly was the right thing to do and one more reason for them to feel good about our organization. I learned a long time ago not to ostracize wives if you want their husbands to fully buy into your organization.

What am I saying here? Player management is about considerate individual treatment and great working conditions. Once you have established the right atmosphere, you can raise the bar on player expectations, and they'll respond in a positive fashion.

The owner in Cleveland, George Hoffman, was great in helping me create this type of atmosphere. He had a way of slipping guys $100 bills when they contributed in a game. He was subtle, but every player got his dollar blessing sooner or later. Our players weren't rich, and those gestures went a long way. If I suggested anything that I thought would help us win, he cooperated. He has three championship rings to show for his willingness to listen to someone who understood the chemistry of managing players to win.

I realize you can't give college players $100 bills, but I'm sure you can come up with some type of "atta boy" that will make them feel special. Football coaches use decals on helmets. Doesn't sound like much, but players stretch themselves to get the recognition.

On the negative side, I created the yellow jersey award. It was an ugly yellow soccer shirt. Every day at the end of practice, we awarded it to the player who had a bad day, a bad practice, or just couldn't get things right. The players hated the award ceremony and having to wear the ugly shirt the next day in practice. I know of few people who like being criticized openly in front of their peers. When we had a great practice, we didn't present the award. This little gimmick did more to get players to bust their backsides in practice than anything we coaches could say or do. It also gave the guys a laugh at the end of some difficult practice sessions.

Rules, Regulations, and Punishment

Looking back at my coaching career, I conclude that high expectations are much better than a player manual of rules and punishments. Creating an image of what you want from players, what you want them to look like, how you want them to behave, should be constantly communicated. Ultimately, whatever they accept will be the rules.

For many seasons, I had my senior players make the team's rules. Most of the time, they were tougher than I would have been. When it comes to making rules for players, I try to ask one question: Does this action hinder our ability to win or harm our image? If the answer is yes, then it can't be allowed.

Take, for example, the issue of proper rest before a game. I once had a star player, Hector Marinaro, stay up all night with his wife while she was bearing his first son. There were serious complications because the baby was born prematurely. I told Hector that we were okay with him not playing that night, although the game was extremely important. He showed up after the team's pregame warm-ups, dressed without saying a word to anyone, and went out and played the game of his life. If rest is that important, how do you explain this story? To me, public perception is just as important. If your team loses and the public finds out that players were out late, they'll immediately blame the loss on that reason and consequently blame the coach for lack of team discipline. If the public sees a player having a drink the night before a game and you lose, the player was drunk. Rules are invoked for image control as well as for giving your team the best chance to win.

It's a challenge to college coaches to construct minimum rules with strong reasons for why the rules are essential—for example, going to classes, achieving academic success, and learning to be different than the rest of the student body. The athlete's peers don't have these restrictions, but neither do they receive the recognition. Selling the word *sacrifice* is a big job, particularly when the next big social event is scheduled. It's so tough for an athlete to abstain from alcohol and drugs when their friends are doing it. How does an athlete stay macho, build his profile, and abstain? The great ones deal with it; weak, average athletes have a harder time.

You can't ignore all the temptations or assume athletes are above them. That's dangerous. You need to sell, sell, sell and also monitor their actions. Being a championship-caliber athlete requires a lot of going the extra mile, not just for athletes but for coaches as well. Assistant coaches have to understand their roles regarding discipline and not try to be pals with the players. They have to buy into your goals and ideals 100 percent.

Any act that could destroy a life, career, or team's ambitious objectives must be discouraged and prevented, no matter what level you're coaching. Alcohol results in many athletes using poor judgment and ruining their careers. More than ever we hear of famous athletes getting arrested for DUI, fighting, and behaving disorderly because of alcohol abuse. If you're truly committed to winning, you have to find ways to prevent this irresponsible behavior. It's part of your coaching responsibility and can't be ignored.

Enforcement

The biggest challenge is when a player violates one of the important rules and forces you to make a tough decision. This is when you earn your salary. Dismissal or suspension can be damaging to the team. My decisions were always based on how I could reprimand the player and make sure it didn't happen again. Often I brought in senior players to discuss the ramifications before making the decision. I thought if they agreed with my thinking, they would help me sell it to everybody else. I always encouraged the guilty player to apologize and make things right with his teammates. If I ever thought that I could lose my authority, I would go to the fullest extreme because I didn't want a player on my team whom I couldn't trust and respect. It was far better to get rid of the player.

At the first meeting, I used to tell my players that I, as head coach, had the responsibility to chart the course. I was the boat's captain, the general in battle, the father, and that meant that I was chosen to lead this team as best I could. I always liked to have their input and help in making tough decisions. My ultimate goal was for them to take as much responsibility as I did for the team's success. I knew I had succeeded when they started to monitor problem players for the good of the team.

I can't put into words the excitement I felt when I participated in my first week of practice as a freshman in college. I wanted to be accepted by the upperclassmen, and I wanted to start. It became bigger than life to me, and I was going to run every wind sprint and go through every practice session as if it were my only opportunity to make the team. Fortunately, the coach noticed my intensity and soccer ability and gave me the chance to start as a freshman.

The first three-fourths of the season were like a dream unfolding. We won every game. I scored some big goals, and life was good. Then came the game on our schedule that everyone was talking about. It was our big rival, and the entire campus came alive. Signs were up on all the dorms, and this game took on a different kind of importance.

Two days before the game, our coach, John Eiler, said that the game on Saturday would probably determine our chance to go undefeated and possibly be considered for national recognition. Our football team was playing our rival on Friday night in a town about two hours away, and we had all made plans to go to the game. Coach Eiler said he was not letting us go because he felt we wouldn't get proper rest. He said, "In life you have to be able to make difficult choices to succeed" and this was one of them. He set our normal before-game 10:30 curfew, and we all accepted it.

That Friday night, I was awakened from a pregame restless sleep by Coach Eiler. He asked me if I had seen Karl, our top player. I sleepily responded, "No. Why are you asking me?" He replied, "He's not in his room, and it's well past curfew." Karl had decided to go to the game and drive his girlfriend, who was a cheerleader.

The next morning as we boarded the bus to leave for our trip, I saw Karl and Coach Eiler talking. Coach Eiler boarded the bus and said that Karl would no longer be a member of the team. He had broken the rules. The bus was dead silent all the way. When we arrived, Karl was waiting to talk to the coach. He was devastated. He did not play, but we played one of the best games of our lives. We won 1 to 0 and learned an indelible lesson about risk versus reward. Karl paid a big price (probably too big), but the coach made an indelible impression on a group of young athletes for life. The lesson was that if you make a rule, you have to have the guts to enforce it no matter how high the stakes.

This event had a profound effect on my disciplinary attitudes when I became a coach. As I look back, I truly believe that every player somehow knew I was unwavering with the few demands I made on them. Rules are necessary, but enforcement is what makes them work.

Rules Versus Expectations

Everyone understands there has to be structure, guidelines, or rules and regulations for any organization, whether it be a volunteer organization or one with paid employees. The coach must provide this structure. Guidelines must be well thought out and presented as simply as possible.

Ultimately, though, it comes down to leadership skills and the passion you have to drive yourself, your staff, and your players. You have to accept the responsibility for every detail of the program. Some might interpret this as micromanagement. I consider it being well informed about everyone and everything. Another essential to success!

At the professional level, the players' union required us to have player manuals that spelled out in vivid detail the rules and the punishments. I agonized over those rules every off-season because I felt if I listed an offense and attached a fine, I allowed the player to buy his way out of breaking the rules. Consequently, my list was short and to the point. The rest of my rules were inferred, with the understanding that players understood their intent. Somehow, I was lucky. I believe I can count on one hand how many times I had to deal with a serious problem over all those years. Players knew I couldn't tolerate bad behavior, respected that stance, and met my expectations.

Winning was my focus, and I sold it every chance I got. I didn't want problems that would become obstacles to that achievement. I always blamed the player who violated the rules for using bad judgment and putting himself ahead of the team. I really didn't care if he drank a few beers or lost some sleep. I cared that he couldn't conform to the rules we created for winning. His violation made it more difficult for us to win as a team. Team violations were big with me, and I had little patience for those who couldn't get in line.

Team Leadership

Internal team leadership is the best type of leadership. Team leaders are not easy to find or develop. They come in many different packages.

When I was general manager in Cleveland, I had two profound leaders with diametrically opposite styles. Hector Marinaro was the most prolific scorer in the history of the league. His father was a former professional player and coach and a solid family guy, and you could easily see his influence on Hector. Hector said all the right things to the media, he was a darling to the fans, and his teammates gave him the highest level of respect. Hector was laid-back, always smiling, and spent most practices taking it easy and enjoying himself. Whatever side he took on an issue, players followed him and trusted his judgment. During games, he was brilliant and consistently scored big goals, making it look easy. However, he was never our real leader or captain. He didn't appear to have the fire in his belly that others did. It was too easy for him, or so it appeared. I knew better. He was one of those rare athletes who had the passion to excel. He didn't need to do his thing in practice; he saved it for when it really mattered. He was league MVP and leading scorer a bunch of years, an incredible feat.

The other player was Zoran Karic, a highly skilled player who led the league in assists for about eight years and was always in the top five in scoring. Karic was a perfectionist. He hated to lose and had no patience with a player's carelessness. He knew the game and was always challenging players to play to his standard. He couldn't stand bad passes and would get in a teammate's face if he didn't give the pass the right way at the right time. In intersquad practice scrimmages, Karic would be wild if he wasn't winning. Every careless mistake increased his anger. His teammates hated him on more than one occasion, but he drove them far beyond what any coach could do. That demand for perfection made us a better team as individuals became much better players. Also, Karic couldn't stand selfish play—if someone was open, he should get the ball. Karic almost singlehandedly eradicated selfish play by his Crunch teammates. He also had a problem with referees. He often had defenders taking cheap shots at him. The referees hated him because he always challenged their calls. He had this insane look to him because every game was so important. He couldn't control his passion to excel, and even the fans would get upset with him. Then he would score an impossible goal to get us back into the game, and they would love him again.

Together Karic and Marinaro were unbelievable. They took apart defenses and set scoring records that will take a long time to duplicate. Karic was a brilliant passer with great vision. Marinaro found the openings, Karic delivered the perfectly weighted pass, and Marinaro finished. They did it for nine years for our Cleveland team.

Strange as it may seem, they led our team to great heights, and neither was thought of as a team captain. Both Marinaro and Karic were leaders and had a profound and positive effect on our team's success. They didn't have to wear the captain's armband to be leaders in my eyes.

I had some great leaders over the years who did wear the captain's armband. First, I'd like to tell you about Derek Trevis. Derek was a unique individual. Everyone loved him. His smile, sense of humor, and ability to give a player a pat on the back during play were infectious. Off the field, he was a comedian; on the field, he was a serious professional. He was handpicked from England as a leader for the Philadelphia franchise and will always be at the top of my list of captains. He was a born leader. When he came to our team, his extensive playing experience was a real asset to help him guide young players. They looked up to him and could still have a laugh off the field with him. But, most important, he knew when to draw the line.

My second great leader was Gert Trinklein. He came from Germany and had played for the great Eintracht Frankfurt team. His personality was like Derek's. He had the ability to be totally professional in the game and crazy off the pitch. Gert controlled our back four and made everybody around him stay focused. He perfectly understood how to make players view him as their leader. He, too, had a lot of experience to draw on and was no shrinking violet when it came to expressing his views.

Excellent captains like these are essential, particularly if you have a lot of players with limited experience who are overachievers. Experienced leaders give good advice and motivate players to keep improving. They become an extension of the coach on the field.

Leadership is vital and must receive careful consideration. Picking your leaders is an important part of team management. Over the years, I observed some great leaders in soccer. Franz Beckenbauer would get my vote as the best ever. He had every quality you would want in a leader. He was a great player and a great personality; every player on his team respected him, as did his opponents. Later, he became a great national team coach. He combined innate leadership talent with other elements in his soccer culture working in his favor.

Winning and Losing

Winning is an instant cure for most team ills. When you win, players have a satisfied feeling of accomplishment, they receive plenty of compliments, and they avoid the negatives of defeat.

The same emotions apply to the coach, staff, and entire organization. If you walk into a club's office after a game, it takes you about 30 seconds to know if the team won or lost. Winning and losing even permeates the community's attitude and mood. Studies have shown that a city's work production goes up and down with victory and defeat.

Winning also forestalls most team problems. It's amazing how many problems there are when a team is on a losing streak. And the problems just keep coming! When the team is winning, everything is beautiful. Even injuries are affected by winning and losing. In the dressing room of a losing team, the training room is full. In the dressing room of a winning team, the players with injuries are few, and they are in and out in a flash. If coaches could find the answers to this psychological phenomenon, they could become wealthy overnight.

Player management is one of the most important challenges a coach faces. How a coach handles players has a profound impact on winning. Success is not accidental and can never be taken for granted. It requires a lot of preparation and preplanning and an intelligent, honest approach to handling players. Players deal with personal problems, injuries, fear of failure, bad patches of play, and a garden variety of other distractions. The coach must find a way for players to feel comfortable and secure, though with the knowledge that you might disrupt their careers for the good of the team. Players are not indispensable but must feel loved and wanted. How's that for a challenge?

CHAPTER 18

Inspiring Today's Players

Tracey Leone

I remember sitting in a meeting room as a student at the NSCAA national coaching school, listening to a lecture on team management from one of my lifelong coaching mentors, Anson Dorrance. He shared a statement that has stayed with me for many years: "Coaching is about effect, about influence." Another coaching mentor, April Heinrichs, echoes that thought by stating, "Coaching is about inspiring players." The longer I have the honor of being in this wonderful field of coaching, the more I see the absolute truth of these philosophies.

I know of no secrets, mysteries, or special formulas regarding inspiring players at any level, but coaches all over the world are constantly challenged to get the most out of their players while providing the most positive experience they can. There's no one right way to do this; in fact, I think several approaches can yield success.

Today's Coaching Environment

Coaches today face different challenges regarding inspiring players than coaches of generations past. Just a decade ago, opportunities for players to play in soccer events and tournaments or on different teams in a variety of sports were not as available as they are today. Today, players run from one soccer team to another, from one sport to another, or from one tournament to another on a weekly, sometimes daily, basis. The calendar used to be fairly empty of organized activities; now there isn't enough room for everything.

Because of these changes, the environment has become more "coach-run" or "coach-dependent" than "player-run." Each environment has plusses and minuses. Benefits of the coach-run environment include the invaluable experiences, both personal and athletic, provided by a multitude of competitive opportunities. Decades ago, players were begging for this. The downfall, though, is that the balance has been tipped to the far extreme. Today we have almost too much programming.

This scenario has created a situation in which the number of games outweighs the number of practices. There's too much of a gap in the training-to-games ratio. Although games are critical for player development, players are playing so many games that the games become less special or important. Games should always be the highlight of the week. Through games, players see the benefits of practice. The overemphasis on games reduces opportunities for players to practice together to improve techniques and team play.

Players today depend more on the coach to create an organized, structured environment. Rather than young boys and girls training by themselves or playing pickup soccer with friends, most athletes wait for the coach to organize training sessions. The tremendous opportunity for experience is being counterbalanced by the huge loss of creativity that can be gained by players setting up their own training regimens, spending time with the ball, and playing on their own. The ideal is a compromise. This is a challenge today's coaches face. In addition, busy schedules mean scheduling conflicts will arise, putting more pressure on young players to make difficult choices. Little League game or soccer practice? We want them at the practice, but they'll usually choose the game. They're being pulled in several different directions, and they feel the detriments of the tug-of-war. Sometimes players end up quitting because of the stress.

Another difference between today and generations ago is that the level of coaching has improved. As a result, both U.S. players and teams have improved tremendously. However, this success is a double-edged sword. Increased expertise in coaching is a must, but with progress has come increased pressure on coaches to win and succeed because many are now paid professionals and coaching is their livelihood. These pressures can have damaging effects on players and on the sport if coaches, in their drive to win, resort to methods that aren't in the best interest of player development.

3 "E's": Energy, Emotion, Enthusiasm

As coaches, how can we cope with today's challenges and inspire our players to reach new heights? I think of inspiring players in a holistic way, beginning with the coach's personality and demeanor. Players feed off and follow the coach's lead in several respects, one being the coach's emotion.

April Heinrichs coached at the University of Virginia when my husband, Ray, and I co-coached at Clemson University. She once asked us, "What do you feed your team before you play us?" She saw that when her team played Clemson, we came out with great energy and emotion. Of course, we had games in which we did not, which concerned Ray and me more than anything. When we investigated the reason for the players' decreased energy level, the answer was usually multifaceted. Fatigue might be caused by school schedules, tests, team travel, or personal dilemmas. Combining a competitive college season with an academic load is challenging, and players become extremely tired, which of course affects their motivation.

Over the years, we learned a great deal about keeping players fresh, rested, and excited so that they would consistently play with tremendous enthusiasm and inspiration. We wanted to come into every practice and game with those qualities because we felt they often made the difference between winning and losing, between enjoyment and drudgery, and between being inspired or being bored.

Energy and enthusiasm are qualities Ray and I possess, and our team mirrored those qualities most of the time. Amidst the ambition, goals, and areas of improvement, players must enjoy themselves. Simple acts of smiling and laughing are critical. A team needs to know, without doubt, that the coach has an undying passion, love, and excitement for the team and for coaching.

Coaching the Person

Regardless whether your team is male or female, a club team, high school team, or national team, your players want to know that you care about them as people, students, and athletes. Showing them you care might mean phoning an injured or discouraged player; sending flowers and calling when a player has surgery or a family member or friend is ill; using e-mail to stay in touch with players, share news about teammates, motivate them for the next game, or brighten their day; being available and offering individual help before or after practices; and maintaining regular communication with players about both their soccer lives and their lives outside of soccer.

At Clemson, I had a player who was struggling to learn Spanish. I offered to tutor her so that when she went to study hall she could get help in other subjects. I thoroughly enjoyed this time but, more important, through our off-field relationship, I knew she knew that I cared about her. She played so hard for us at Clemson; she put her entire heart into our program.

During the U.S. U-19 national team's run toward the 2002 Youth World Championship, players were required to e-mail me their fitness results and training regimen every Monday of the two-year preparation cycle. Partly I wanted to monitor their training, but I also wanted to stay in touch with them and thus continue to build our relationships. This type of behavior is contagious. Players tend to follow the coach's lead. Each of the Women's National Team players, who won the first-ever U-19 World Championship in 2002, stayed in virtually daily contact. This bonding affected both training and games and inspired our players to work hard for themselves, each other, and the coach.

Communication

Regular communication is important to every relationship, including the player-coach dynamic. Along with corresponding through e-mail, there are many other ways to improve or maintain a dialogue between coach and player.

When I played on the national team, Anson Dorrance had five-minute individual meetings on game day, which I still try to organize with the U-19 national team. In addition, at the end of each event, I meet with each player for about 20 minutes. Included in our agenda is an evaluation of the player's performance in the event, a discussion of training at home, and feedback on areas in her game that need attention. The players' reactions indicate that they find these postevent meetings very helpful. Sometimes my assistant coaches and I divide the team, seek out the players we're responsible for, and have unplanned, spontaneous, informal individual meetings throughout events.

At Clemson, we usually had two long individual meetings with every player each semester. These meetings allowed players to set individual academic and athletic goals, evaluate and receive feedback on their performances, and discuss ways to improve their play. The meetings also allowed us to get to know players as people.

Of course, we have team meetings at which we set team goals. Sometimes with the U-19 national team, we also set game goals derived from our training themes. For example, when we were in Europe, we set a goal of getting 10 successful combinations in each half of each game. (Combination play was a major theme in our training.) Attempting to reach these goals proved to be a great motivation for players. Another tradition was to hold a team meeting in which we divided into small groups. Players devised and eventually voted on a team motto. The U-19 motto leading up to the 2002 World Championship was "USA: Unity, Strength, Attitude. In it to win it." The team constantly referred back to this theme. Ray and I did this with our team at Clemson, and I still do it with the U-19 national team.

Over time, I have significantly improved in the area of communication, and it has made me a better coach. The art of being honest but sensitive is a critical balance, and experience is the best way to improve communication skills.

Small group meetings, by position for example, are also beneficial, as are captain's meetings. With the U-19 national team, we have lecture meetings focused on tactics, but we also hold many interactive, problem-solving meetings. Coaches should investigate as many areas to expand and improve player communication and interaction as possible.

Challenging Players: COMPETE

One of the greatest ways to inspire players is to challenge them. As a coach, you should organize diverse practice sessions that move and flow for 90 minutes or so (less for very young players). Practice should be both fun and valuable. No standing around. Players run to water and back, and then the next exercise or drill begins. Make sure the session is intense and competitive—this inspires players to play on their edge.

You can have a physically light session that's still competitive and intense. To make sure it's competitive, keep score. One of my golden rules with the U-19 national team is that coaches don't keep score—players do. They must know the score at all times. Many coaches plan *training* days, when players get several repetitions of a skill, along with *teaching* days, on which the coach teaches a tactic or technique. Either way, it should end with a competition. Teach, then compete. Even if you're working on flighting a ball, end with players competing on flighted balls in some way. After competing, have the losing team endure some kind of harmless and fun consequence, such as getting (not buying) lunch for the winners.

There's always the question of whether the coach should record and post training results. Do posted results motivate players? Sometimes. In any case, I think recorded results can be useful for the coach. For some teams, it's beneficial to post results Some players are motivated to work or compete harder because their peers can see their rankings. It's been a tradition at the University of North Carolina for years to record and post every result in training.

But for some teams or players, posting results might not work or might not work all the time. Look at your team and decide what's best for them. For decades, UNC has been the standard that all college teams measure themselves against, but every team has its own dynamic. My team at Clemson was different from UNC's team, and we motivated them differently. We frequently recorded results, but we rarely posted them.

Tournaments

Tournaments within training sessions can be wonderful coaching instruments. With the U-19 national team, we organized what we called Competition Days. Coaches picked two or four teams, however many they liked. The entire session was devoted to competing in predetermined games—some technical, some tactical, some problem-solving, some small-sided—that concluded in identifying a winner for the entire day. Players were in charge of their own teams and had to find ways to win. These proved to be the U-19 national team players' favorite days of training.

We took this one step further later in the two-year cycle and held 11 v 11 self-coached games. We felt one of our most important jobs was to teach players to become problem-solvers. They had to become coaches on the field, so to speak. At the international level, players can't even hear the coach sometimes because of crowd noise. So we instituted more problem-solving situations for them. The 11 v 11 self-coached games were very simple, and the rewards were countless. We chose two teams and told them they had to compete to win three 30-minute games. They were in charge of their own team for the day. They decided on systems, styles, lineups and changes, restarts, tactical changes to hold a lead or go for the win, and everything else. If the period ended in a tie, we went to penalty kicks to simulate the pressure of a game. Our role as coaches was limited to evaluating and helping individual players. This exercise fostered group problem-solving, developing leadership, competitiveness, tactical organization, and gamesmanship. Plus the players loved it! It inspired them to lead their teams to success.

Setting Standards

One of the highest rewards of competition is establishing standards. One of the most impressive qualities of the 2002 U-19 World Championship team is that they set standards, met them, and then raised them constantly. In the beginning, coaches have to set the standard, which is how it started with the U-19s, but then the players have to run with it. With the U-19s, the players ended up raising fitness, training, and competitive standards. When this happens, you know you have an inspired group of players who strive to excel.

Setting, meeting, and raising standards is critical for the development of a team and individuals. Without standards, you have nothing to shoot for and no measure of where you are or want to be. Standards also challenge and motivate players. Find the balance of being positive and demanding. When you do, you'll inspire players to reach the next performance level.

Accountability and Responsibility

Fostering accountability among your players can work as a motivational tool. It also provides players with ownership and a greater appreciation that it's their team. With all our national teams, daily player duties are posted. Yes, even Mia Hamm carries the balls or the water for practice. If I were a youth coach, I would require every player to bring a ball and a water jug to every practice. This is a beginning.

Another way to teach responsibility is to give players homework and test them. Several coaches have fitness tests, but you can run technical and tactical tests as well. One year at Clemson, the first preseason meeting was on restarts because about 75 percent of the goals scored on us the season before were off restarts. Players took notes, which helped the visual learners, and we trained on the field, which helped the hands-on learners. We had a written test on restarts in preseason, and at midseason we had a pop quiz. The players and staff got a kick out of the tests, and we saw improved results.

Try to give your players some time of their own at the end of training. We did this after almost every training session leading up to the World Championships. Players had 10 to 15 minutes to work on whatever they liked. Many worked on restarts or a weak area of their game, but it was always the players who chose what they wanted to improve. Coaches were allowed to guide, but mainly we wanted players to be self-coaches and be responsible for their own development.

More Ideas

There are many other positive methods you can use to inspire and motivate your players. Use videotapes for teaching and motivating. We watched video frequently at Clemson and with the U-19 team. Year-end awards, or even awards after games or tournaments, can be used as extrinsic motivators for players. Team-building activities, such as team dinners, community service projects, or cooperative exercises, always help inspire players and teams to accomplish greatness together.

Finally, one of the most critical elements to keeping players inspired is to work hard and rest hard. Keep your players fresh and excited about playing soccer. During the demanding rigors of the college season at Clemson, we shortened practices and gave players more days off toward the end of the season. Once games began at the U-19 World Championships, our main goal was to keep the players fresh. We might have tweaked something small in training, but the work had to be done before we arrived. Have days for playing flag football or another fun activity that's not soccer; or on some days, just practice for 45 minutes and go home. Shorter training sessions allow players to rejuvenate mentally and physically and thus compete as hard as they can every day.

At the end of the day, I hope we all remember why we're in this profession in the first place. Amidst the seriousness of competition and achieving goals, our job is to provide an enjoyable and inspiring soccer experience for players while developing the total person. Soccer is the vehicle for countless life lessons; it's our job to use this great game to develop character, impart principles, and, in the end, watch our players grow and thrive in the environment provided by the sport they love.

CHAPTER 19

Establishing Pride and Tradition

Jay Martin

Establishing a program or team with pride and tradition is difficult but pays dividends. Operating with pride and tradition means doing everything with class and being consistently competitive. The team with pride and tradition will be very good and play at a high level every year. Losses will occur, and there might even be an off year, but the team will rebound and be competitive again soon.

Under the leadership of Red Auerbach, the Boston Celtics first used the term *pride and tradition* to describe their phenomenal success in the 1950s and 1960s. For the Celtics, pride and tradition was an attitude. That same mindset can be seen in soccer clubs such as Real Madrid, Bayern Munich, and Manchester United. These teams have established a standard of pride and tradition for players, coaches, staff, and fans. Everyone involved with these programs expects success—not just now and then, but every year. Such expectations raise the team's level of play and also affects how others play against the team. Games against these teams are pressure filled as up-and-coming programs try to knock the kings off their hill—or at least stay up there with them until halftime.

As a coach, to establish pride and tradition, you must create an atmosphere that helps your players reach their maximum potential. Such an atmosphere must encompass every facet of the team, on the field and off. Some new coaches seem to think that coaching focuses only on the two hours of training each day. Nothing is further from the truth. Establishing pride and tradition takes 24 hours a day. In fact, the two hours of training are the *easiest* two hours. The coach must immerse his or her players in a soccer subculture that allows for total development. The burden of fulfilling potential lies with the player. The burden of creating the proper environment is up to the coach.

Preseason:
Setting Expectations and Goals

To create an environment in which players can reach their full potential is the philosophy of the Ohio Wesleyan University program. The philosophy might sound vague, but it's actually very specific and all-inclusive. The philosophy demands that all aspects of the program be created in such a way that the player can achieve his best on the field and off. Preparation for this level of achievement is a year-long activity, but the real preparation begins in the preseason.

Developing a proper expectation for your team is the first step. Your expectation should be challenging but realistic. If your team has 10 new players, a national championship might not be a realistic expectation. The conference championship might suffice, but never settle for the middle of the pack in the conference. Even a team with new players must be challenged and learn to be successful. The expectation along with the philosophy is the foundation for all that happens with the team and program for the coming year.

Developing expectations is not simply goal setting. Expectations are general, not as specific as goals. You must answer the question, "What is my outlook for the team? What type of player behavior on and off the field is necessary to reach our expectations?" On the surface, the answer might seem easy, but expectations are not situational. They are enduring and long-range in nature. Because of their impact, it's important to choose them carefully.

A team that wants to establish pride and a winning tradition must create an atmosphere with positive expectations. Positive expectations create success, and success creates positive expectations. This is the cycle that builds a winning team or program. Achieving it is not often easy. As coach, you must attack and eliminate any and all negative thoughts and actions. Everything that happens with the team must be viewed as positive. Even traditionally winning teams lose games occasionally, but that's not a negative. The loss is treated as an aberration and an opportunity to get better. Once a positive cycle of success is established, it's almost self-perpetuating. Teams begin to believe they can't beat your team, and your team believes that they can't lose. Keep everything positive, and success will come.

Have a vision that deals with all aspects of the program, and make it clear to all your players. One of the most difficult aspects of coaching soccer is getting all the players on the same page or getting them all to understand what they should do in all situations. Write down your expectations so you can refer to them when necessary. If you don't have a clear understanding of the desired action or behavior in all situations, how can you expect your players to understand? As coach, you should clarify player expectations in these areas:

- The type of soccer you want to play. What's your definition of good soccer and bad soccer?

- The type of players you want. What's your definition of a quality player?

- The principles of the system you want to play.

- The role of each player in each position on the field.

- The different ways you can and should play the game in different situations. For example, what do you do when you are down a player?

Once the philosophy and expectations are established, it's time to set goals for you and your team. Goal setting is difficult at first and must be learned. To be effective, a goal must be specific, realistic, measurable, comprehensive, understandable to all involved, and time constrained. A goal to become a better soccer player is not a good goal because it's not specific enough. A goal to win the conference championship might not be realistic every year. If you set a goal that's not realistic, the goal-setting process loses credibility with the players. It might take some time to perfect goal setting with targets that are both realistic and challenging.

The first step is to develop season-long objectives. After these realistic goals are in place, you can create weekly and daily goals. It's often a good practice to split the season into thirds or fourths and list goals that must be completed by the end of that time. For example, Ohio Wesleyan doesn't practice attacking restarts in preseason—that's not a preseason goal—but we do work on defensive restarts. Understanding the defensive responsibilities for all restarts is a goal we aim to accomplish by the end of the preseason. This goal is specific, comprehensive, measurable, realistic, understandable, and time constrained. Attacking restarts wait until October.

With goals in place, you have developed a road map for your team for the upcoming season. You know where your program is going and how to get there. This plan is the basis for everything that happens in the program, from behavior on and off the field, to elements of each training session during the season, to the substitutions made during a game. Philosophy, expectations, and goals must be written down and accessible for review during and after the season. It's always a good idea to review these aims as the year progresses to reaffirm expectations, especially when things aren't going well.

The Season: Steps to Success

Although the psychological aspects of soccer are discussed in great detail in other chapters, I do want to mention the mental preparation we do at Ohio Wesleyan, which might be the most important part of the program.

When a player arrives for preseason, he receives a notebook divided into chapters that move him toward what we call *competitive toughness*, the ability to play at the same level all the time. Only great players can do this, but all players can improve in this area and become more consistent. To get our point across, we use the coaching cliché, "You always know what you're going to get from Joe." Joe has reached a level of consistency.

Many good books are available with materials specific to the needs of your team. Three I would recommend are *Mental Toughness Training for Sports* by James Loehr (Tim Stephen Geneve Press, 1982), *Focused for Soccer* by Bill Beswick (Human Kinetics, 2001), and *In Pursuit of Excellence* by Terry Orlick (Human Kinetics, 2000).

Here's what we do at Ohio Wesleyan. Our goal is for our athletes to focus on the process of the game of soccer, not the outcome. An Ohio Wesleyan player should never think, "We have to win this game or we won't make it to the tournament." Rather, the player should focus on the course of action needed in the game to be successful. The two major parts of this process deal with mental toughness and emotional toughness. Mental toughness is preparing to play the game; emotional toughness is reacting to unexpected situations presented during a game or season.

Mental Preparation

The following is a summary of each of the chapters in the players' notebook. Many of these chapters have homework. Players keep their notebooks in their lockers and must keep them up to date. If a notebook is not up to date, the player doesn't train. If the player doesn't train, he doesn't play.

Player self-assessment. Before a player can create goals, he must have a point of departure, a baseline. Self-assessment covers game situations, attitude, motivation, confidence, attention control, and a commitment (to the game or team) rating scale. These instruments serve to describe the player in all these areas at the beginning of the season. Once this is established, the coach and player work together toward fulfilling the player's potential.

Lifestyle. The Dutch were the first to understand the relationship between a player's lifestyle and performance. In the college environment, it's very important to discuss lifestyle options and decision-making. This chapter of the notebook deals primarily with decision-making on and off the field as it relates to team standards. The decision-making discussion deals with how to make correct choices in all aspects of life.

The team standards section is an important part of the total process. Captains lead a discussion with the team (without the coaching staff) that defines goals in each of the three important areas of student life—academics, social life, and soccer—and the behaviors that are acceptable and necessary to reach those goals. The result of these discussions is used as the guideline for the season. The captains and the council deal with any deviation from the stated behaviors. The council is composed of the captains and a member of each class. The council meets weekly with the coaching staff and discusses anything and everything. The council also deals with discipline. The creation of the standards and the council gives the players a sense of team ownership.

One year a behavioral standard stated, "There will be no alcohol consumed 48 hours before a game." The night before a big game, the captain saw our senior sweeper drinking a beer. The captain told me the next day, "Mark won't be playing today." Mark didn't, and he was very upset, but the standards were the team's standards, not the coaching staff's. If Mark thought the standards were unfair, he should have said something earlier, before the standards were final. By the way, the captain was Mark's roommate. The team always comes first!

Goal setting. This is the focal point of the steps program. Although there's not enough room to discuss this in its entirety, an overview is important. Players set goals three times each year: at preseason, during the winter, and before the spring season. They are asked to assess their strengths and weaknesses, list their personal goals, list potential obstacles for those goals, and develop an action plan. The action plan is the most important part of goal setting. The plan must be specific and must lead the player to his goal.

Game goals are created the day before each match. Players are asked to list three or four goals for the game, potential obstacles, and their action plan for the game. Both individual goals and game goals are used to internalize motivation and emphasize the process, not the outcome. We want players thinking about their roles in each situation.

A few years ago, a player came to me before his junior year with his goals. He wanted to be an All-American, score one goal a game, and break all the Ohio Wesleyan University scoring records. We assessed his strengths and weaknesses. Although he was a great athlete, had a great left foot, and was great in the air, he could hardly stand on his right foot. We planned for the player to work with the goalkeepers and me every day, using only his right foot. During practice scrimmages, I'd blow the whistle for a turnover any time he used his left foot. The keeper practice allowed many repetitions under low pressure. The game condition forced him to use his right foot under pressure. He ended up a two-time All-American, still holds all the Ohio Wesleyan scoring records, and averaged 1.25 goals a game for two years. In fact, in his senior season, he scored one more goal with his right foot than with his left foot. The key is that he was self-motivated and focused on the process. He wanted to be an All-American.

Preparing for victory. There are two parts to this section. First is a discussion about habits and training expectations. Players in every sport develop habits during their formative years, some good, some bad. We examine what habits are, what good and bad habits are, and develop a plan to change negative behaviors. We ask each player to change five routines each season, either on the field or off. This process is something players can use their whole lives. We also examine the role of the training session and the expectations of everyone during the training session, including the coaching staff and players. Every aspect of the training session is discussed and analyzed, and expectations are developed for everyone. We stress that the sessions last two hours or less, so it's important to use the time effectively.

Winning through unity. As the season progresses, the roles on the team develop. This is a very important aspect of team unity. All players want to start and play 90 minutes, but as the season unfolds, players develop roles. Whether they start or not, players need to understand their roles and how they are important to the team. All members of the team (players and coaches) describe their roles in writing, develop goals within these roles, and analyze the responsibilities of the roles. This process is a key aspect of team chemistry. This is an important time to assure each player of his worth on the team. Although a player might not be good enough to start, we might think he's very valuable coming off the bench. To be really effective, the player must understand and accept his role on the team.

The right attitude. Here we deal with the benefits of having a positive attitude at all times. We spend time eliminating negative thoughts and changing them into positive thoughts. In a sense, soccer is a negative game. More bad things happen than good things. So it's tough to completely erase negative thoughts. But a team that thinks positively will be successful. The process takes work and practice.

The right energy. We want our players to concentrate while on the field. What is concentration? How can we improve it? Every coach tells players to "get it" or that they "must have it," but few say how. Soccer is a game in which concentration for 90 minutes is almost impossible, but most players can improve in this area. We present ideas and strategies to promote flow or mental calmness that leads to improved concentration.

Pressure. The player learns what pressure is and how to deal with it. We know pressure can't be eliminated (and we probably wouldn't want to), but by understanding the nature of pressure, players can avoid flat performances and prepare for big games by making pressure more of a challenge than a threat.

Emotional toughness. The preceding topics deal with mental toughness. As noted, mental toughness is preparing to play. Emotional toughness involves how players react to something that happens in a game. For example, an unexpected goal against the run of play can devastate a team that isn't emotionally tough. Developing emotional toughness takes work and practice.

Not long ago, Ohio Wesleyan played a game on the road in the NCAA regional championship. A strong wind was blowing, and we decided to defend the wind and win in the second half. With seven seconds left in the first half and the score tied 0 to 0, one of our backs made a bad foul 30 yards from the goal. The opposing player simply hit the ball at the goal. It was not a shot, simply a player playing the ball on the goal. With his face in the wind, our keeper caught the ball and took a step back to maintain balance. The official called a goal. It was clearly not a goal, but we went from being tied at zero to being down 1 to 0 to the host team in the NCAA regional championship game. A tough situation. How our team reacted to the bad call and being down at the half would determine the outcome of the game. As our players walked in for halftime, they were talking only about what they had to do in the second half to win the game. Ohio Wesleyan won 4 to 1. That's emotional toughness.

Academic Preparation

In addition to mental and emotional preparation, creating a successful environment includes academic considerations. All players have a strict regimen to follow off the field in terms of academic preparation. Any player who doesn't follow these guidelines doesn't train. Once more, players who don't train don't play.

We have an established mentoring program at Ohio Wesleyan. Every incoming freshman soccer player who attends the university is assigned a junior or senior who serves as a mentor. In order to counsel newcomers, all mentors must have achieved a minimum academic standard. The mentor meets with the freshman player four times in each of the first two semesters. The coach develops the agenda for each meeting. The mentor acts as a resource for all academic questions or concerns, and often this relationship becomes personal, and close bonds develop. This program is great for team building.

The mentor system is also used to develop time-management skills. Each player receives a day planner that lists all games, training sessions, and departure times for road trips. It's the mentor's job to review the freshman's class syllabi and place all pertinent information into the day planner. The freshman keeps a record of all tests, papers, and assignments in his planner. A member of the coaching staff can ask to see the planner at any time. If it's not up to date, the player doesn't train or play in games.

Each senior must present to the freshmen a seminar on some area of academic skill. These presentations can include note taking, test taking, writing a paper, and other academic skills. Handouts that supplement the presentations are placed in binders that remain in the freshmen's team lockers.

Creating the Environment

Certainly the work on the field and in academics is important. They are tangible outcomes of a program with pride and tradition. But manipulating the total soccer environment is equally important.

The right atmosphere sends a message that soccer is important and that this program is unique, that there's an element of class associated with this program that others don't exhibit. Creating an environment means manipulating everything that the players see or do. This is a never-ending process. As coach, you can easily facilitate some of these things. Some demand longer planning as well as money. Here are some considerations for creating an environment.

Facilities. Soccer facilities in this country are often abysmal, and sometimes that can't be helped. But with good facilities, soccer games turn into events. Players should want to play at the facility, and fans should want to attend each game. The field comes first. Make sure the field is perfect: it must be maximal in length and width with a good grassy surface. Irrigation and drainage make a huge difference. The installation of bleachers and lights should be next on the list of facility priorities. A building with locker rooms, rest rooms, and concession areas is a great addition. The facility at Ohio Wesleyan is modeled after a European soccer club. There's a clubhouse, and the bleachers are close to the field to give spectators a real sense of being at a soccer game. Building such a facility takes time and money, but the effort is well worth it.

Equipment. As with facilities, having the best equipment shows players (and opponents) that this is a first-class program. Ohio Wesleyan has always had a relationship with Adidas, which has been involved with soccer for a long time. Staying with one manufacturer over many years keeps our program consistently stocked with fine equipment. The right equipment also includes practice gear. It's important that players look and feel the same when training as when on the field. When players come to train, they should know that this is business. They change into training gear and get ready to go.

Memorabilia. Teams with great tradition display their memorabilia as part of their history. Don't put it away—display it! All trophies, signed soccer balls, pennants from international games, and any other soccer memorabilia should be prominently displayed. New players in the program should know the program's history. In fact, in an orientation period, veteran players share the team's history with new players. This is a formal and specific process that guarantees all your players know the history and traditions of the program. The coaches' offices and the team meeting room should house memorabilia. The locker room, for example, should have pictures of championship teams, past All-Americans, and any great action photos that paint the picture of history and tradition. You might also display your program's library of books and videotapes. At Ohio Wesleyan, we have more than 400 videotapes, including teaching videos and game tapes going back to 1970. Our soccer library has more than 200 volumes. All of our resources are accessible to players. In the players' lounge in the locker room are copies of *World Soccer, Four Four Two, Soccer Journal*, and other soccer periodicals for players to read while waiting for training to start.

Soccer ambassadors. From the first day on campus, Ohio Wesleyan soccer players are introduced to the concept of being soccer ambassadors. They represent the program and the university. In addition to their work as team members, players have duties to perpetuate the pride and tradition of the program. Players send out a newsletter, via regular mail and e-mail, to all alumni. This biweekly publication keeps former players in tune with the program. For a fee, alums can join TEAM OWU. The price includes a piece of Adidas gear, the newsletter, tickets to games, and more. Our TEAM OWU organization keeps all players, present and past, connected.

Team members also work in the community. Each player must be an assistant coach for a youth team in the area. Young players in the community learn about our soccer team and come to our games. These youth teams play one game in the main stadium, usually before a varsity match. This aids community relations and gets people in the stands.

Developing pride and tradition is time consuming. A coach willing to put in the time to develop a program such as the one at Ohio Wesleyan will find that the 2 easiest hours in the day are spent training. The other 22 hours, if used correctly, develop a program. Once the groundwork is developed, however, the program is self-perpetuating. The key to the entire program is a focus on the process and not the outcome. If you develop a program with pride and tradition, your team will be consistently competitive as they strive to live up to great times past.

CHAPTER 20

Making Teamwork a Priority

Miller Bugliari and Tim Schum

Much has changed since we began coaching, but one coaching aspiration remains as much in place today as it was at the onset of our coaching careers—the coach's desire to consistently place a competitive, cohesive, well-trained, and highly motivated team on the field. To what degree a coach achieves this objective relates to how well he or she motivates individual players and the team.

The process of motivating is quite different today from how it was four decades ago. Certainly, player expectations are a major difference. Most players today are not satisfied to simply be a part of a team. Most players who spend long hours practicing with a team are no longer willing to warm the bench for the regulars. They expect to play at least part of the game. One of the more difficult challenges for coaches is to keep the lower skilled players interested and invested when playing time is not part of the equation (at least a "reasonable" amount of playing time, as far as the player is concerned).

Coaches have several methods for dealing with players who typically see little playing time (especially at the start of the season).

The Selection Process

One method is to hold tryouts to trim the squad. Tryouts bring some semblance of reality to marginal players. For instance, by paring off the team's best players versus those competing for their positions in small-sided practice games (1 on 1 up to 3 on 3), players can begin to realize their potential to unseat someone for either a starting spot or for a greater share of playing time.

Orchestrated small-sided games also allow coaches to evaluate players' abilities in terms of strengths and weaknesses. The coach can compare players vying for starting positions to those who have already been selected to assume major playing time on the team. The coach's powers of observation must be keen during the tryout process. Even if players are not quite ready to start games, they might show enough promise during tryouts to indicate they'll at least be able to compete for playing time. Along with evaluating the ability to understand and execute the technical, tactical, and physical components of the game, when determining the value of players to the team, coaches also need to consider their players' psychological makeup.

Once a coach has made as objective an analysis as possible about a player's ability to contribute to the team, he or she needs to share it with the player before the playing season. At this point, the psychological component is extremely important to the coach and the team. If a player is able to understand and accept the evaluation of the coaching staff and realize that playing time is earned based on coaching objectivity, then perhaps the player will be inspired to work hard at individual improvement to make headway within the team structure.

Unfortunately, when players can't accept the limited roles that lie ahead of them, it might be in everyone's best interests for them to leave the team. I've generally found that if I can't predict a role for a player within the team, then I have two choices: (1) try to work for better understanding of the player over time (particularly for less mature athletes) or (2) cut our losses.

Another objective for the coach during tryouts is to determine what roles nonstarters might play on the team. The overall complexion of a team is multifaceted.

Team Makeup

First there are the starters. This is probably the easiest of a coach's decisions. Some players bring experience to a team and have earned their places. Some newcomers are so talented that it's obvious they must play. If the key players are at the upper age (club team) or upper class level (school team), then the coach must use more long-range vision in selecting the team. Which players should be brought along in terms of an investment in playing time? Can they be substituted at times for veteran players or play complementary roles relative to those players? If a player is injured, how can the coach shift players (including substitutes) so that the team maintains its stability? Obviously, nonstarters will have playing characteristics different from those of the starters, so the coach must try to forecast how the team will play with substitutes.

Generally, as the playing level of a team increases in complexity, the role of the bench becomes even more crucial to a team's success. If starters and nonstarters don't understand their roles, team chemistry can rapidly dissipate.

Examining the complexions of great teams reveals that there are other roles within a team that must be assumed for the group to be a well-functioning unit. For instance, when the talented Los Angeles Lakers team that featured Jerry West and Elgin Baylor added the great Wilt Chamberlain to the roster, the anticipated juggernaut never quite came to fruition. Off-court chemistry wasn't ideal. Wilt tried to be the team humorist, a role that was Baylor's prior to Chamberlain's arrival. It was a small thing but affected the team in a big way.

Some roles must be assumed on every team, such as humorist and cheerleader. Every team needs a player who can pick up other players when the going gets tough. Teams need players who are mature enough to understand and make certain that the team's goals are kept in the forefront throughout a season. Even certain players' social skills can add to a team in the absence of first-line playing ability.

Coaches should take inventory of the various roles that need to be assumed if a team is to emerge as both a force on and off the field and try to identify players who can assume these roles.

Three Stories

Sometimes it can help to relate stories that epitomize success in being a good team member. Over the years, these tales have helped soothe the psyches of discouraged players on my teams and encouraged them to carry on.

Some of the shared experiences involved self-sacrifice; others had more to do with persistence. But all were shared with players either individually or collectively to lend some understanding of what it took to assemble a true team of players dedicated to a common goal.

The Runner

A player we'll call Jim was not the ideal team selection. He was, to be kind, a bit disheveled (as were the great majority of the enrolled student body in the 1960s). He was a likeable, kind lad if left-footed and a bit slow off the mark, but he seemed to fit in. In the coach's estimate, he held some promise. In particular, he was the team's best juggler. In fact, he was an exquisite juggler, able to do all the tricks. Other than that, though, he might have been better suited for the cross country team because his endurance was something to behold.

Jim was kept on the roster, and as the season progressed, he maximized his team contributions. He worked with less-skilled teammates to improve their juggling skills. In fact when the coach inserted juggling as part of a team warm-up, the coach raised the players' confidence and self-esteem by having Jim demonstrate the skill. Further, when the team worked on various forms of endurance training, Jim was always in the lead, even when the distances were increased.

Jim also began to improve as a player, showing a versatility that allowed the coach to use him either at the back or the midfield. Most important, over time Jim earned the respect of his teammates, even from some he passed in terms of playing time. At season's end, there was no question when it came to voting for the annual team player of the year. Jim "The Runner" was an almost unanimous choice.

The Missing Shoes

The coach always required players to take their shoes home to clean and shine them before the next day's match. The idea was to have players focus on the next match outside of the normal team setting. But boys will be boys, and one starter in a hurry to pack his bag in the team room before departure for an away match somehow forgot to pack his most important equipment—his shoes.

Word spread quickly on the bus about the missing shoes. Not wanting to let the coach know the situation right away, the team quickly took an inventory of its shoe sizes and discovered that a player who didn't see much playing time had the same shoe size as the starter who forgot his shoes.

Once it was worked out, the captain told the coach what was going on. The player who didn't see much playing time would give up his shoes to the starter. Was the solution justified in terms of the coach teaching the starter a lesson? Maybe not. Was it an example of what teamwork is all about? Absolutely.

The coach knew the player who didn't see much playing time would not resent being asked to volunteer his shoes, particularly when he was involved in the team's decision-making process. Perhaps another player would have caused a problem.

Years later at a team reunion, the shoe episode was fondly recalled by the starter, who saluted his teammate, now a physician, for his unselfish behavior. The recollection was a highlight of the team's reunion, indicating the long-term significance of the unifying gesture.

The Quiet Man

Knowing a player's background and interests can help a coach determine whether the individual can withstand the rigors of being a nonstarter. The quiet man was such an individual. He was very centered, possibly because of his religious beliefs. In terms of playing ability, he was average. His strengths were good technique, a strong body, and a willingness to play several positions. He was also an accurate striker of a dead ball.

After a year's JV experience, he moved onto the varsity team. He generally worked diligently in practice as a midfielder, and in scrimmages the coach would use him to play in that part of the field with other starters to allow for continuity if he were inserted in a game situation.

During the nontraditional season, the team worked hard to improve team play and to raise funds. By keeping the team together throughout the year, the coach strengthened the team's solidarity. The quiet man could always be counted on to work on his game and lend a hand during these months.

One of the coach's jobs was to prepare the team to meet its season schedule. Typically, this team participated in two or three back-to-back tournament games at season's end. During the week's preparations for those games, the coach indicated that, if possible, he would like to spread out the workload. He asked every player to be willing to come off or go on in order to meet the physical demands of the tournaments.

During the second day of one of the tournaments, the quiet man, now a senior, came on in the second half of a tie match and delivered a long-range goal, laid a brilliant cross on the head of the center forward, and crashed home a free kick to account for three goals as the team clinched the tournament title.

For his play on that occasion, the quiet man was named to the all-tournament team. While his performance that weekend was outstanding, it also cemented in the minds of his teammates how well he had played his role on the team over his career. The quiet man was that year's recipient for best team player.

What lessons do these stories hold for the coach trying to develop the concept of teamwork? First, try to be objective in the construction of the total team. Recognize that playing roles and team roles are sometimes distinct. Second, inventory the various roles on a team and, as much as possible, assemble a team in which individuals serve the team in selected capacities. Third, if an athlete can't immediately play a role on a team, you must make a decision. If the athlete has redeeming characteristics, then nurture those qualities. If that isn't the case, don't muddy the team environment by keeping such a player.

Next, always be on the lookout for incidents in which a nonstarter contributes to making a team better. In some cases, try to acknowledge both to the team and to the media the play of the unsung player. Involve all players in the team's decision-making. Assign bench personnel to observe play in their playing areas of the field and ask them to share their information with the coaching staff. This input can be valuable in evaluating halftime tactics, preparing for subsequent postgame practices, and examining the team's tactics. Why have some of baseball's marginal players become some of the best managers? They had plenty of time to observe what worked both on and off the field.

Prepare players to assume roles by letting them mix with the regulars in team training exercises. Sometimes you might find a nonstarter's playing style merges better with the starters than those that you have been starting.

Detail the characteristics that an ideal team player exhibits. Honor those with an appropriate award within the team structure. Soon it will be an honor that all team members will aspire to.

In the end, you can use many approaches to achieve harmony on a team. The key to this management aspect of coaching is to let players realize that you care for them totally and will do your best to help them realize their potential.

But players must understand that some of life's lessons are best learned within the team environment, and such lessons are not always easily mastered. How a coach orchestrates this aspect of the learning process is part of the art of coaching.

12 Steps to Building Teamwork

First, speak to the whole team and explain the importance of every player ("our team is only as strong as its weakest link"), reminding everyone that varsity players hone their skills while practicing against the second string. In turn, scrimmages also give the bench personnel a chance to compete and impress the coach relative to future playing time. Emphasize the concept of *team*.

Second, don't focus on standout players. It isn't healthy. One or two great players cannot replace an entire team.

Third, appreciate the importance of the role of the captain. Try to use the captain as a sounding board. Make sure the captain understands that his or her role is not just as a leader on the field but also as a conduit between players and coaches. Often, newer or younger players are more comfortable talking to another player than to the coach. However, the captain should keep the coach in the loop so that the coach can oversee relationships that develop over the course of the season.

Fourth, during practice, invest positive attention to the substitutes, making them feel they are an integral part of the team. Keep statistics on goals, assists, and playmaking. Publicly and privately note these accomplishments, either after practice or before the next day's workout. This positive reinforcement in front of the entire team builds confidence and helps reinforce nonstarter roles with the rest of the team.

Fifth, allow all players to share in the team's success. At Pingry, we have had a long tradition of soccer success. We always try to share the glory among all team members.

Sixth, devote extra time after regular practice to work with players who are anxious to improve their individual skills. If you're there working with small groups, no one will feel overlooked. After practice is also an ideal time to reinforce your expectations of a player, build player confidence, and maintain communication on an individual basis.

Seventh, during practices, have nonstarters occasionally serve as interim captains and choose sides for small games such as 4 on 4 or 5 on 5.

Eight, subtly remind the big egos on the team that the rest of the team is not on the field solely to deliver them the ball.

Ninth, use regular positive reinforcement to note team improvement and individual success. Keep the team moving forward by focusing on the positives. You can't motivate effectively by just pointing out individual and collective mistakes.

Tenth, know the importance of how you handle playing time. This affects the entire season. Before the game, set the stage for different eventualities. Discuss with the group what the team should expect if the team is winning and what changes might occur if they're losing. What happens if a player isn't playing up to the team's expectations? Before putting in a sub, remind the player what is expected of him or her. A few constructive comments to the departing player are equally valuable.

Eleventh, maintain player interest and involvement in the game. Nonstarters can run the sidelines, keep statistics, or videotape games. We've also encouraged input from nonstarters about their game observations and acknowledged their contributions to improving the team's play during a match.

Finally try to have a well-constructed plan for substitutions. Forgetting someone in the sub rotation can be devastating to your players. A roster on a clipboard can help you chart player substitutions. Or ask assistants or captains to help you remember to use everyone. Handle substitutions with sensitivity, especially when young egos are involved.

Open Communication

Good communication is basic to the construction of any team. Get to know all of your players on a personal level. Learn about their family and their academic and personal goals. Try to make eye contact with each player during team discussions. During a game, address particular players directly during halftime, asking them how they felt about a particular play. Engaging your players this way makes them feel that they have a say in the team's tactical planning. Be open to suggestions. Players should feel that they're being heard. The players involved on the field experience the game differently than you do, so ask for their input.

The postgame ritual is an integral part of coaching. It provides an opportunity to get ready for the next game, inspire the team, and adjust the team's mental attitude. The coach's job is to ready the team both mentally and physically for the next match.

Occasionally, postgame is not the right time to review failures. Assess your team's mental and emotional status before launching into your lecture.

If you choose to analyze the game, be organized and to the point. Dwelling on a loss and the negative aspects of a game can quickly lose a team's interest. Likewise, allowing gloating over a victory is neither constructive nor healthy.

A short practice immediately after a game, win or lose, can focus players on the things they need to improve and keep them focused on the learning process. Postgame practices should be fun and organized and should move quickly. Don't try a postgame practice after a particularly grueling game.

Your team should always be growing and changing. The inspirational component of team growth comes from constant reminders of team goals and the value system that the coach has put in place. Humor is a valuable tool in this process but should never be used to embarrass a player.

Being flexible, adjusting to the personality of your team, is of utmost importance. Finding the inherent magic in each new group of players is the challenge. Chemistry changes from one year to the next. Your response to that chemistry and the ability to read the personality of each new team is as important as assessing technical skills.

Playing as a team and achieving success toward meeting a common goal can be among the most meaningful experiences of a youngster's life. At a time when many players experience burnout at a young age, our responsibility is to make the experience positive for every player. Coaching is not about the coach's ego or the win-loss record. It should be about the life lessons of teamwork and responsibility. It should be about the ability to win or lose with honor, knowing that you and your team did your best on that day, on that field, against that opponent.

CHAPTER 21

Developing Responsible Decision-Makers

Chris Petrucelli

The results of making the right decisions can be found everywhere in life, so it's no surprise that making proper decisions is an important part of soccer. Decision-making takes place at almost every moment in our lives. Every morning we decide whether we're going to get out of bed, if we're going to brush our teeth, and what we're going to wear. These decisions don't take much thought for most people. We get out of bed, and we brush our teeth. It's almost automatic. This is the mindset we want for our players as they play the game.

Players make decisions during every second of the game. When players have the ball, they decide whether to dribble or pass. If they choose to pass, they then decide to pass either on the ground or in the air. Should they drive the pass or bend it? If they bend it, do they bend it toward a teammate or away from the teammate? Players not in possession of the ball but who see that a teammate has the ball must make other decisions. Do they run away or come to support? If they support, at what angle should they support from? How close should they support?

Defensive players make other choices, such as whether to run with the player with the ball or stay in space. If they stay in the space, do they press the ball or drop off?

These are just a few of the many decisions players make over the course of a game. As coach, your job is to help your players make the right decisions given the circumstances at hand. Here are some ideas.

Repetition

We talk about repetition constantly during technical training, but repetition in tactical training is just as important. Place players in decision-making environments. Offer certain sets of circumstances so that they must make choices. The key for the player will be to identify certain visual cues that point toward the right decision. For example, if a player receives a ball on the right side of the field and sees that the defense is totally shifted to that side, then the visual cue tells him or her not to try to penetrate there but to find another area on the field to penetrate the defense with a better chance of success.

How do players know not to penetrate the crowded space? Players recognize this because they have seen it in training, have tried penetrating there and failed, and have had success in training by changing the point of attack and penetrating elsewhere. With repetition, making the right decision on where to play the ball becomes like brushing your teeth.

Decision-making can affect technique. The decision to use a certain technique should come from replication in training. Often, players try things in a match they have never accomplished in training. How many times have you seen a player shoot from 40 yards out during a game only to see the ball roll harmlessly into the goalkeeper's arms? Players make the decision to shoot when it's not the best decision. The shot is beyond their shooting range. These players know their shooting range from training. Training shows how accurate and dangerous a player's shot is from certain areas of the field. If a player can't succeed in training from 40 yards out, then it's a poor choice to shoot from that distance in a game. I've always believed three times in a row is a habit. If a player can pull something off technically three times in a row, then he or she has it down. At that point, the decision to shoot is the right decision.

Tactical Quizzes

Sometimes having players take tactical quizzes that actually match situations can be helpful in fine-tuning their decision-making skills. *Soccer Journal* ran a series of these quizzes over the course of several issues in the 1980s, and they have proved helpful in offering players mental practice in various soccer situations.

Each quiz can be converted into an overhead transparency and flashed on the screen of a classroom. Allow a few seconds for players to view the situation and make one of four possible tactical decisions relative to the situation presented. Here are four typical tactical situations. Take a look and make your decisions.

Defender's Choice

Figure 21.1 relates to a defender's decision in the final defensive third of the field. The situation depicted relates to collective fundamental defensive tactics, specifically that the closer the attacking team is to your goal, the tighter the defensive pressure on the ball and the players in possession of the ball must be. Another tactical adjustment for the defense is for the angle of cover to be very shallow. At this point, the actual covering defender is the goalkeeper. To make the keeper's job easier, the defender's approach to the ball must allow for some predictability on the possible direction of the shot. Finally, the defensive team must seek to compact itself, giving the least attention to the player or players farthest from the ball.

Option 1 is the correct choice. Immediate pressure must be put on the ball at all times in and around the penalty area. The player's approach should be at an angle to cut down the shooter's opening to the goal and give the goalkeeper some idea where the shot might be aimed. Option 2 would allow a shot. Option 4 finds a teammate already marking the attacker, and there's no need to cover a defender whose attacker doesn't have the ball. Option 3 is obviously the worst decision because the player farthest from the ball is in the least dangerous attacking space.

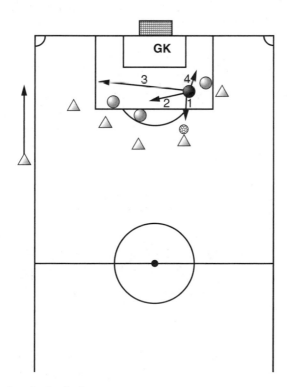

Figure 21.1   Defender's choice.

Midfield Passing

Figure 21.2 reflects a midfield passing situation. In constructive attacking midfield play, the object is to maintain possession of the ball and work to penetrate toward the goal. Part of the attacking team's objective is to create a numbers-up advantage. As soccer is a game of opposites, the defense seeks to prevent penetration toward its goal by pressuring the ball and not allowing the ball handler to make deep penetrating passes to teammates in good attacking positions.

All options shown have positive tactical merit. The player with the ball is under severe pressure in the midfield. Option 4, the pass back to the supporting defender who has both the time and vision to make a good decision with the ball, is the best option. In general, the midfield is the buildup phase for the attack. Next to penetration, possession is the best tactic in this area of the field. Option 3, a backward dribble to gain time to observe and select the next pass, is good but amounts to a slower version of option 4, and the passer is facing away from the goal. In option 2, the ball goes wide to a player who has space in which to play the ball forward. However, this moves the ball to the flank and out of the center of the field, which is the best distribution point for the team. A dribble forward, option 1, seems a bit risky. If the ball is dispossessed, it would create a numbers-up situation in midfield for the ball-winning team.

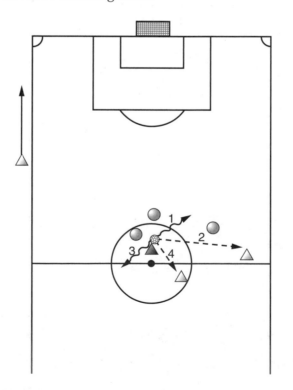

Figure 21.2 Midfield passing.

Attacking Third

Figure 21.3 calls for the player in question to make the correct decision in the attacking third of the field. In many cases, the attacking player's creativity is limited by the intense pressure applied by the defensive team in and around the goal. By delaying play, the attacking team allows the defense to compact even more, playing right into their hands. In this case, the defense has a clear numerical advantage near the ball. The attacking player must look to another area of the field with penetrating potential.

Option 4 is the correct choice. In this situation of four on seven, choosing the best pass is crucial. The four defenders closest to the ball are in relatively good compact positions. Choice 1 is a safe enough play and would maintain possession but delays penetration, which should be the objective in the final third. Option 2, dribble penetration down the wing, finds the defense ready to combat it and no strikers in good position to deal with a subsequent cross. Option 3, a pass to a supporting midfielder, maintains possession with the possibility that the midfielder can subsequently switch play. Option 4 clearly changes the field of play and takes advantage of a poor defensive position by the far-side defender. It offers the best potential for penetration by the wide-side attacker.

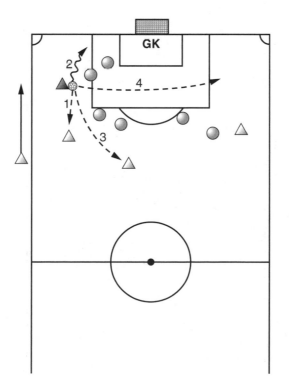

Figure 21.3   Attacking third.

Tactical Attacking

Figure 21.4 reflects a tactical attacking sequence in the final third of the field. In this area of the field, the team must not turn over the ball because doing so could present immediate counterattacking by the defense. It's particularly important not to lose the ball in the center of the field for this same reason. Dribbling in the final third of the field is not a good tactic for the attacking team. Playing to wide players changes the point of attack and can lead to further forward penetration, which is the basic objective for all attacking play.

Option 3 is correct. For the moment, no attack is obvious, so the question is how to maintain possession in a six-on-seven situation in the midfield. Lateral dribbling (shielding) does not offer much in the way of odds of possession, support of the other three attackers is not evident, and the dribbler would have to turn away from both the goal being attacked and his or her teammates. Option 4, keeping the ball in the center while awaiting team support, is the best of the two dribbling choices. Option 3, the long pass to the outside, is an improvement for penetration play. It would then create a two-on-one on the outside of the field. Option 2 plays the ball to space, where a two-on-two situation exists and does not offer good attacking odds.

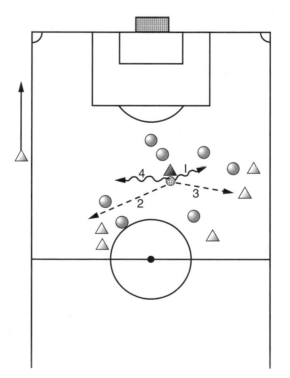

Figure 21.4 Tactical attacking.

Coaching Players, Coaching Positions

Coaching position is a key to helping players make proper decisions on the field. The coach needs to be able to see the same visual cues that face the player. Pat Summitt, the women's basketball coach at the University of Tennessee, makes her point guards sit in a chair at midcourt and watch the patterns of the offense in action. This gives players who make the most important decisions the ability to see all the choices as the other players move through the court.

This is easy to relate to our sport. Coaches must place themselves where their view is similar to that of the players. If the decision being made in training relates to runs of the forwards, the coach has to have a proper view of the angles of these runs. The coach must be on the field and behind the forwards to see this. To see which option a midfielder should choose as he or she tries to play a dangerous ball, the coach needs to view the action from behind the midfield. In like manner, as defenders play out of the back, the coach must be behind the defenders.

This is where the use of videotape comes in handy. Football and basketball coaches are masters at breaking down videotape. Its use has become more common in soccer in recent years. We have started to videotape training sessions to show players the decisions they might face in games. Again, the position of the camera is important. One of the most helpful things our players can see is the view behind the goal. After watching a game taped from behind the goal at the University of Colorado, the light went on for me. Bill Hempen, the Colorado coach, tapes all of his games from that vantage point. This gives us the ability to see what the players are seeing. We can now better replicate in training what players see in games.

We play our midfielders and forwards against our backs and another set of midfield players. We play 6 v 7 with the six attacking the big goal with a keeper and the seven trying to come out of the back and be in possession past two-thirds of the field (figure 21.5). A view from both ends provides just about all of the decisions that will be made in a game.

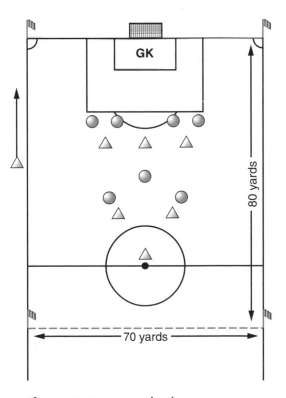

Figure 21.5   6 v 7 plus keeper.

Midfielders play forward, forwards make runs in attack mode, midfield players defend, and forwards defend. We can see the organization of the back four, the coordination of defending between groups of players, defenders starting the attack, the finishing options for forwards, and the goalkeeper's choices and more. This video is an invaluable teaching tool to review with players.

Watching video with players is always interesting. Often we learn what they were thinking at a particular moment in the game. The film doesn't lie. It shows exactly what choices were there, what decision was made, and the outcome of that decision. We can see a player missing the final pass or making the final pass that leads to a great goal.

Field Vision

It makes sense that decision-making and vision go hand in hand. To make the right choice, players must see all the choices open to them. This is why it's so important to train players to play with their heads up, looking before and after receiving the ball. A player must be able to see the defense, the field, and his or her teammates at almost every instant in the game.

Without all of the information, it's extremely difficult to make the right decision. The only way to get the information on the field is by picking up your head to look. This is a factor in defense as well as attack. If a player does not constantly assess the situation when defending, the situation will change for the worse. The attacking player will be in position to receive without defensive pressure, causing all kinds of problems for the defense.

Can vision be trained? I think so. Again, we must put players in an environment where the situation is constantly changing and the only way to succeed is to look and assess the situation. One of the best ways to do this for the defense is to have the back four train numbers-down. Play the back four and a forward against three forwards and three midfielders. Both teams play to full goals with keepers (figure 21.6). The back four must constantly deal with a changing environment as the free player runs forward. Defenders must decide whether to mark or pass. Free players

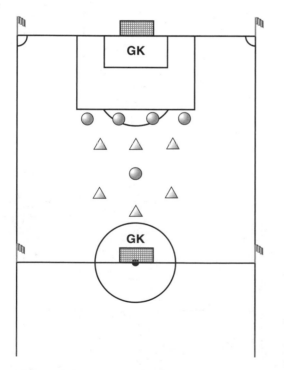

Figure 21.6 6 v 5 plus keeper.

are behind throughout the exercise. If the collective back four doesn't have the vision to see everything, they'll give up goals.

Off-Field Decision-Making

How best to develop responsible decision-makers off the field could be debated for hours. Questions such as, "Is this the role of the coach?" and "Can you actually affect a player's action off the field?" are all relevant.

I believe developing character is part of coaching. Coaches fill many roles. I remember watching Dr. Mick Franco, a sports psychologist at Notre Dame, list the roles of a coach on a chalkboard one day. The list filled the board and more. I remember thinking, "Do I do all of this?" The answer was "Yes." A few of these roles were motivator, tactition, psychologist, leader, mentor, and supervisor. Coaches do wear many hats. Of all these roles, I believe developing responsible decision-makers is the most important. We should try to influence the lives of our players. When players leave us, we want them to be able to make the right decisions both on and off the field.

I have always given my players a great deal of leeway when it comes to making decisions off the field. I believe the best in a person until he proves me wrong. I don't have curfews or bed checks. I have few rules on my teams. At the beginning of the season, I tell my team that only two things matter. The first is being on time. The second is doing the right thing.

If a person is on time, that tells you a lot about him or her. People who constantly show up late are of the opinion that their time is more important than the team's time. This is not a person you can count on. Over the years, my teams have come to appreciate the importance of being on time. They help each other to make sure everyone is punctual. This is something that will help them as they go through life. Mike Berticelli always told his team to be 15 minutes early. He called it Vince Lombardi time. Vince Lombardi used to punish his teams if they weren't 15 minutes early.

The best evidence of sticking to the rule of being on time comes from Pat Murphy, now the baseball coach at Arizona State. Coach Murphy was the baseball coach at Notre Dame while I was there. He had a player who was late to a meeting. Pat told the player that if he was ever late again, he would be kicked off the team. A few days later, the player was running late and knew he was in trouble. He intentionally ran his car into a tree so he'd have a good excuse for being late. When he told coach Murphy that he was late because he had an accident and ran his car into a tree, Pat's response was, "I'm glad you weren't hurt. I'm sorry for your car, and you're kicked off the team for being late." It seems no excuse is good enough for Coach Murphy, and I totally agree with him.

When I tell my team to do the right thing, this is an all-encompassing phrase. I'm talking about decisions that are made every day. Players are faced with many decisions that ultimately affect the performance of the team. I like to give players the freedom to make their own choices. If a poor choice is made, they must suffer the consequences. I'm not big on physical punishment, but I do believe if a player makes a bad choice off the field he or she must serve some sentence for it. This is part of the learning process. If I suspend a player for a game because of a bad choice, I hope he'll learn from it. It's the same as making a poor choice on the field. The consequence of making a poor choice on the field could be losing a game; a poor choice off the field might result in a suspension. Either way, the player is in an environment where he must make a choice and deal with the rewards or consequences of making that choice.

I don't believe a team has to lose a game to learn a lesson. But I do believe that losing makes those lessons stand out. Winning usually masks the mistakes made in a game. It's hard to make big changes in your team if you're winning. Those changes might need to be made but don't seem urgent until you start losing.

The 1995 NCAA Division I national championship team, I coached, needed some personnel changes in order to win a championship. Some of the players who needed to change had helped the team reach the national finals the year before. Because we lost several games early in the year, it became clear that this team was not going to win a championship unless major changes were made. This would not have been as clear if we had continued to win. Deep down, I knew changes needed to be made, but the losses brought it all to the surface. The choice to make these changes was the right choice and led to winning a national championship.

CHAPTER 22

Enhancing Performance Through Mental Skills Training

Colleen Hacker

Every sport, including soccer, is composed of four fundamental components: technical, tactical, physiological, and psychological. The technical components of soccer are the skills necessary to play, such as dribbling, shooting, heading, and passing. The tactical aspects are the strategies and concepts employed to showcase the technical components in competition, for example, what system to play, where to establish the restraining line for pressure, and whether to play a zone defense. Soccer's physiological components include the physical requirements to play the game, such as strength, flexibility, and cardiorespiratory and anaerobic capacities.

The fourth component is the psychological dimension. Soccer requires the psychological skills of mental toughness, motivation to compete, self-confidence, imagery, energy management, performance routines, team cohesion, and goal setting. This chapter focuses on these performance-enhancement principles, which help players enjoy playing soccer even more and to perform at higher levels. Once players have mastered soccer's mental game, they can focus on the physical dimensions of the sport and thereby fulfill their potential.

Importance of the Mental Game

Soccer is a fast-paced game based as much on strategies and split-second decisions as on quickness, strength, accuracy, and endurance. Often, deficits in the psychological game rather than errors in physical performance keep players from performing their best in practice or competition. Research and anecdotal evidence show that more physically skilled athletes are not always more successful than less physically skilled athletes. Why? Because of differences in their mental games. Sometimes it's more important to be strong mentally than to be strong physically. In fact, the mental game is often the primary explanation for sport outcomes and fluctuations in individual performance. When more than 600 U.S. Olympic athletes were interviewed after the Olympic Games and asked to list the top 10 factors essential for success at the higher levels of competition, mental skills constituted the top five spots. Not surprising, the single most important quality cited was mental toughness.

What can we learn from these elite performers to help us bolster our traditional training methods? Essentially they understand the importance of developing the psychological dimension of the game. No matter what your level of competition, recognizing and refining the mental game plan should be a top priority.

Goal Setting:
The Staircase to Success

Goal setting is one of the building blocks of a successful psychological skills training program. Coaches and players can use the goal-setting principles discussed in this chapter in each of the four pillars of soccer (technical, tactical, psychological, and physiological). To help you better understand goal setting and benefit most from its powerful effects, we'll start with a definition of goals.

For our purposes, goals are specific standards of proficiency achieved in specific areas of performance within a specified time. For example, a player could set a goal to improve corner-kicking ability by taking 30 extra attempts every day immediately after practice. All of the criteria listed in the definition must be met (along with several other important standards) in order for behavior to be considered a goal. The three key questions to ask to determine if a goal is set correctly are, "Can I measure it?" "Can I see it?" and "Have I specified a completion time?"

Goals are more than wishes, hopes, and dreams. Dreaming is important in sport and in life, but dreams lack the observable, measurable behaviors required for achieving the end result. This distinction is an essential ingredient in effective goal setting. For example, I might "wish" that I was an

Olympic performer, and I might "dream" about making an Olympic team, but when I set a goal, much more specificity and accountability are required of me if I am to achieve my goal standard.

Types of Goals

The three types of goals are performance goals, outcome goals, and what we'll call "do your best" goals.

Performance goals are those in which participants focus on process-oriented standards relative to the participants' own best performance capabilities. Performance goals emphasize the process by which a given outcome is achieved. Participants have much more control over the likelihood of a successful outcome with performance goals. Examples of performance goals are increasing the number of offensive headers taken in order to improve percentage, committing to a consistent pattern of three strength-training sessions per week in order to increase the amount of weight lifted for a one-rep max, or engaging in first-person imagery training four days per week for the next month of practice.

Outcome goals are goals in which participants focus on the end result. The outcome or a product-type measurement is the standard of comparison. Outcome goals are the most often used types of goals among coaches and players. Although participants sometimes think they have control over outcome goals, the fact is that athletes and coaches have only partial control over the ultimate successful accomplishment of outcome goals. Examples of outcome goals are to become a starting member of the team this season, to win the league championship, or to achieve the school scoring record before graduation.

"Do your best" goals are defined by the title. The focus is not on specific standards of proficiency, either process or outcome, other than asking participants to give it their best shot, try hard, and do their best. Someone making this type of goal might say, "I'll try my best to play well in today's game," "We'll try our best to play good defense," or "I'll try to be a better coach this season." What's clear in these examples is that "do your best goals" lack the specificity and detail of performance goals and outcome goals.

It might be easier and more convenient to set outcome goals rather than performance goals, but sport psychology literature clearly indicates that the most favorable results in performance occur when players and coaches set performance goals. In fact, if correctly and consistently used, performance goals make for greater success than either outcome or "do your best" goals. For more information on goal setting in sport, see *Applied Sport Psychology: Personal Growth to Peak Performance* edited by J. Williams (Mayfield Publishing, 2001).

Generally, the recommendation is that every outcome goal you set should be accompanied by at least four performance goals. For example, if the outcome goal is to become a starter on next year's team, the player should set four process goals that increase the likelihood of achieving that goal. These performance goals should be behaviors or activities over which the player has complete control, such as:

- I'll complete my strength-training program three days per week all year long.
- I'll stay after practice on Wednesdays and Fridays to take 50 extra shots with my right foot and 50 extra shots with my left foot.
- I'll watch game film at least two hours every week and write down three key tactical points from each video session.
- I'll complete five, five-minute imagery sessions per week throughout the entire season.

As these examples show, performance goals should be set so that players can completely control whether they engage in the activities; the activities lead to improvements in each of the specified areas of performance; the improvements increase the likelihood of achieving the outcome goal; and each goal includes a standard of proficiency and a specified time for achievement.

Determining Goals

Goals should be difficult but realistic. Unrealistic goals create anxiety and disbelief. Goals should be specific, observable, and measurable. Players should set goals in each of the four pillars of soccer: technical, tactical, psychological, and physiological.

When setting goals, have players set both short-term and long-term goals. Tell them to set performance or technique goals rather than outcome or "do your best" goals. Ask them to write their goals down—to ink what they think. They should discuss their goals with at least one other person. Most players will need to be taught and then guided through the goal-setting process. The level of difficulty, number, and sophistication of goals can, and should, be adjusted depending on the age and skill level of the player. Players should provide and receive goal support through interactions with important people in their life, such as their family, coaches, and teammates. Players should evaluate the effectiveness of their goals and adjust them as necessary to ensure the goals challenge their current abilities and future potential.

Once players and coaches set observable, measurable goals and specify the date for completion, motivation, excitement, and satisfaction increase as goals are successfully accomplished. Satisfaction leads to exuberance, which can quickly amount to trying to go too fast. Two common goal-setting problems are setting too many goals too quickly and setting unrealistic goals based on current level of performance.

Although there's no magic formula for how many goals to set in a particular time frame, in general encourage players to focus on no more than four goals a week. The challenge is to keep the goals meaningful, relevant, and motivating. Goals should not control a player's life or become burdensome to the training regimen. Rather, they should serve as guideposts and standards of excellence that are individually significant. They should be difficult but realistic, and only the player can determine what that might be. While coaches can facilitate the goal-setting process, it's important that players themselves create, adopt, implement, and adapt their goals.

For example, for an athlete currently bench pressing 125 pounds, it's an unrealistic goal to bench press 155 pounds within one week's time. That's a 30-pound increase from the previous best. However, let's say the athlete sets a long-term goal to be able to bench press 150 pounds. One effective use of goal setting is for the athlete to commit to completing three sets of 10 to 12 repetitions three days per week at 125 pounds for the next four weeks using perfect form. Bench pressing consistently each week after proper strength training is behavior completely under the athlete's control (barring injury or illness) and brings him or her closer to reaching the ultimate goal of bench pressing 150 pounds.

Let's look at a soccer example. Let's say a player's goal is to improve the accuracy of long-ball service over the last season. They establishe a realistic long-term goal of a 20-percent improvement in nine months. They then creates a goal-setting plan to achieve that outcome. Specifically, they commits to practicing an extra 100 long-ball serves each week for three months.

The key here is that it's better to design few, high-quality goals and commit to their successful accomplishment than to set too many goals and simply hope that several will be accomplished. Decide what aspects of performance are most important and which skills should be focused on for a particular week. Once that determination has been made, the player is ready to create weekly goals.

Players might want to use a small spiral notebook, index cards, or a goal-setting worksheet (figure 22.1) to track goals. When writing goals, be sure to clearly specify the observable behavior to be accomplished and list a method of accomplishment. Setting a goal to become a better offensive player is not specific enough. Instead, set the goal, "I'll stay after practice and take 50 volley shots on goal with my right foot and 50 volley shots with my left foot at least three times per week." A good tactical goal might be, "To become a better tactical player, I'll watch two hours of video each week and write down three offensive tips for success from each video session." These goals are specific, measurable, written, and time constrained.

With increased coaching, practice, and game play, players will undoubtedly become better at soccer. Thus, as coach, periodically review goals to ascertain whether they are still appropriate for the new level of performance.

Name_____ Date _____

Goal type	Goal (specific, measurable, dated, performance oriented, athlete controlled)	Completion date
Physiological		
Technical		
Tactical		
Psychological		
Team chemistry		

Individual concerns, feedback, suggestions:

Figure 22.1   Goal achievement worksheet.

A player asked to change positions needs to determine if there are new technical and tactical demands that should be addressed through goal setting. A player asked to play more minutes in each match will likely need an increased commitment to fitness. Alternatively, a player might experience a setback after an injury or illness. This player will need to adjust his or her competitive goals accordingly to facilitate rehabilitation and recovery. A rehabilitation goal might be, "I'll complete all rehabilitation exercises prescribed in each of my four appointments with the trainer this week" or "I'll spend five minutes every morning imaging my ligament healing and getting stronger."

This step-by-step approach to a few, well-constructed goals can result in tremendous athletic improvement. Don't forget to reward successfully accomplished goals. Positive reinforcement for success is both deserved and enjoyable. It's amazing how many people go through life simply hoping for good things to happen or dreaming of athletic fame and fortune but neglect the most basic tool—effective goal setting—necessary to help them get there. For the player who makes a commitment to work on goal setting, goals work.

Imagery Training

What the mind conceives, the body achieves. This is what imagery training is all about. Rehearsing performance in the mind, in the absence of overt, physical movement, is one of the most powerful training methods in our psychological artillery. During imagery, we vividly create or re-create performances or competitive experiences in our mind.

The underlying principles for the effectiveness of imagery are based on the complementary nature of psychological and physiological forces. Psychologically, imaging performances on the field exactly as the player would prefer to execute them highlights the powerful effects of the adage *seeing is believing*. Players can perform fundamental soccer techniques, team tactics, and even psychological skills—such as projecting confidence, dealing productively with setbacks, and maintaining effort in presence of fatigue—by vividly using images from the senses. Imagery can help establish a type of "mental blueprint" in the player's memory to facilitate effective, successful, and desirable performances.

Physiologically, imagery can stimulate submaximal electrical activity in the muscles associated with the imagery practice, thereby strengthening the learning and performance process. Players can "practice" away from the actual physical environment with no wear and tear on the body. Simply stated, imagery is a type of practice that helps performance become more automatic.

There are several plausible theories (psychoneuromuscular, bioinformational, and the symbolic learning theory, to name a few) to explain why and how imagery works. The most important conclusion gleaned from the literature and practical experience is that it facilitates performance over and above benefits derived from physical practice alone. For more information on imagery training and other aspects of psychological skills training, see *In Pursuit of Excellence* by T. Orlick (Human Kinetics, 2002).

As with other psychological skills, players need to follow established principles to improve the effectiveness of imagery practice. First, they should image using all of their senses—sight, touch, smell, sound, feel, and emotional content. They should image realistic performances done in the environment in which the skills and techniques are likely to be performed. They should image in real time, in color, and be able to control the images at will.

Some players imagine themselves from an internal perspective, seeing and experiencing events as though they're inside their own bodies looking out. Others prefer an external perspective and experience images as though they're seeing themselves as a camera would see them. The choice of imaging from an internal or an external perspective (or both) is less important than that the images are vivid, controllable, and composed of the corresponding emotional content present in the performance being imagined.

The applications of sport imagery to facilitate performance are limitless. Athletes use imagery to mentally rehearse performance; develop contingency plans; adjust mood, energy, and motivation; boost confidence; automate, refine, correct, or control technique; imprint tactical patterns of play; focus, refocus, or extend concentration; help prepare for competition and training; and recover and rehabilitate an injury.

The key to imagery's effectiveness is a commitment to consistent practice and application. Players are more likely to experience the positive effects of imagery training when their images are vivid and controllable and when they contain realistic emotional content.

Imagery is just like physical skill training in that players must practice intentionally and consistently to improve. It's not a technique that can be done with success just before the big game, important tryout, or qualification match unless it has been practiced thoroughly beforehand.

As with physical practice, progressions (simple to complex) are important in imagery training. Initially, players should attempt to learn and apply imagery techniques in a relaxed state. Then, gradually, they should increase the pressures and distractions. In a few short weeks, players will be able to practice imagery skills on the soccer field during dead-ball situations or before kickoff at the beginning of the game or second half. Actions should be practiced at game speed and with skills and tactics executed in their entirety.

Paradoxically, imagery training seems to follow a "less is more" principle, meaning that emphasizing quality and consistency of practice sessions supersedes the length or quantity of practice. Vividly imaging even three to five minutes a day is likely to facilitate performance more than less frequent but longer imaging sessions. Imagery is a foundational psychological skills-training technique that helps the body perform at a high level. Research shows that imagery boosts self-confidence, aids in optimal competitive focus and positive motivation, and enhances effective anxiety control.

Imagery, though valuable as a training tool, should not be used as a replacement for physical practice. Equally important, it should not be viewed as a frill or an extra but rather as an integral part of the competitive training environment. Coaches and athletes should strive to combine trigger words or phrases along with vivid images to facilitate effectiveness. For example, performance cue words such as "explode" or "drive" could be combined with images of powerful heading technique. Properly used, this form of mental practice should help automate skills, increase consistency, and help solve technique problems. Players can imagine their own technique errors and then correct them through imagery training to approximate a more desirable standard of proficiency.

When the mind is relaxed and receptive, greater insight can be gained. Imagery training also enhances other essential psychological skills, such as attention control, stress management, goal setting, self-confidence, refocusing, improving self-awareness, controlling interpersonal skills, and assisting injury recovery. Imagery practice should be done on a daily basis before, during, or after practice.

A postperformance review can help players recall what happened in competition and what should be reaffirmed or altered before the next match. Although it might seem more efficient and administratively tempting to conduct full-team imagery sessions, it appears most beneficial to provide individually tailored imagery sessions. Imagery cassettes or CDs with performance cues, personally selected music, and imagery descriptors to improve performance can be created. Some teams use highlight videos (either individual or team) to increase confidence and motivation. Finally, players can use written imagery journals to monitor their progress, performance benefits, and imagery experiences.

Controlling the Jitters and Negative Emotions

There are countless ways players manifest anxiety in response to situations that cause feelings of worry or insecurity. Some might feel wobbly in the knees, get an upset stomach, have their heart pound uncontrollably, sweat more than usual, or experience muscles that are tight, rigid, and quickly fatigued. These players manifest anxiety in physical ways. Other players might experience stress symptoms psychologically. They worry more about what might go wrong, think about ways they are likely to fail, or engage in self-deprecating language that lowers their confidence.

The most dangerous element of physical jitters or out-of-control emotions is not the feelings themselves or the thoughts that accompany them—it's the fact that players often don't perform to potential. A player who says, "I've done that a thousand times in practice; why couldn't I do it in today's game?" or "I don't know what happened; I just didn't know what to do" is demonstrating a kind of temporary paralysis by overanalysis or worry. A nervous soccer player might strike the ball straight into the air well over the goal. A player might be so preoccupied with worrisome thoughts that they don't feel the defender coming up for an easy tackle. Those who have played soccer for any length of time can relate to these examples. The focus of this section is strategies to overcome the debilitating effects of anxiety on performance.

Controlling the jitters and other negative emotions in sport is no easy task and can be a career-long process. So many variables can affect performance in constructive or destructive ways that learning to bring the psychological factors under personal, consistent control is one of the most important techniques a player can master. As players become adept at regularly using psychological-skills training in sport, they'll notice that implementation becomes automatic and are more likely to benefit from the synergistic effect of multiple techniques used simultaneously.

Players can, and will, be frustrated, disappointed, or even angry at times. Such emotions are normal, expected, and human. The problem arises when those feelings result in negative behaviors, attitudes, choices, and expectations.

Let's use an example of a soccer player who feels frustrated because he wasn't selected to start in a particular game. The player might perceive that the coach doesn't have confidence in him or that the coach believes that he lacks certain skills or expertise. Based on that interpretation, the player might respond by staying after practice every day to put in extra time on the field, participating in additional scrimmage opportunities, or seeking out an expert coach to assist in technical and tactical refinement. That player's choice to respond in a task-oriented, positive manner turns his frustration and disappointment into a competitive advantage. If, on the other hand, the player responds to that perceived injustice by quitting the team, badmouthing the coach, or losing confidence in himself, they have made choices that undermine the likelihood of future athletic success. Again, the choice is the player's. Both options are available. Players need to work at and practice making the right choice. To learn more about how these techniques can be applied in a soccer setting, refer to chapter 24 in this book and to *Catch Them Being Good* by T. DiCicco and C.M. Hacker (Viking Press, 2002).

How, then, can players learn to control the jitters, quiet the doubts and fears, and turn setbacks into opportunities? First, players need to realize they already possess the ability to relax and compete at a high level. They need to learn to trust their skills. Players should commit to the highest work rate possible and establish an appropriate expectation to compete in their ideal zone of optimal performance. Players allow doubts, anxiety, and worry to take residence in their minds—but these obstacles *can* be overcome, just as physical obstacles, such as the inability to kick effectively with the left foot, can be overcome. Through controlled breathing, the use of performance-enhancing imagery and productive self-talk, and a commitment to high-quality practice, players can clear many of the mental obstacles blocking their best performances.

Learning to Breathe

Although the jitters manifest in many different ways, let's begin the intervention process with something simple and effective. Athletes of any age, in any situation, can master breath control. In fact, this seemingly involuntary, automatic physiological occurrence is one of the great saboteurs of effective athletic performance.

At its most basic level, breathing can be divided into two fundamental types: belly breathing and chest breathing. Belly breathing is associated with calmness, confidence, and relaxation. Chest breathing is associated with stress, fear, and fatigue.

Try this simple experiment. Sit comfortably on a chair or lie quietly on your back on the floor. (If you have a sore back, prop your knees up on a chair in front of you so that they're elevated above your head.) Put one hand on your belly and one hand on your chest. Keep hands flat, with palms down. Practice taking a few chest breaths so that when you inhale, your chest expands, and when you exhale, your chest retracts. Keep your mouth open as you inhale and exhale. Notice how that feels. Now, take another deep breath, but this time breathe from the belly. You'll know you're breathing from the belly if your belly expands as though a string were pulling it out as you inhale, and your belly drops back down as you exhale. Note the difference between the belly breaths and the chest breaths. For the next few minutes, practice belly breathing.

Use the cues of feeling tired, stressed, or anxious as opportunities to practice belly breathing. Breathing from the belly provides greater control, relaxation, and energy. Belly breathing is a skill, however, and won't change automatically without attention and practice. For the next few weeks, create a goal to make belly breathing an automatic response to anxiety and stress.

Choosing a Response

Games, coaches, opponents, places, and situations don't make players tense—players do it to themselves. What's happening around the player isn't the culprit. Rather, the player's view, approach, and response to those circumstances or events is the problem. Many wise counselors have reminded us that success in life (and sport) doesn't depend so much on what happens to us but on how we react to and perceive those events. When players focus on problems, worry about failing, or fear the negative evaluations of others, their bodies typically respond with tension, stress, and anxiety. Alternately, players who view competition as a challenge and an opportunity to demonstrate excellence instead of as a source of pressure or adversity respond with greater freedom, confidence, and a heightened sense of control. The players have a choice in how to respond. It's wise to choose an option most likely to increase the chances for optimal performance.

For example, players cut from the team during tryouts might conclude that they're not good enough to play at that level, that the coaching staff knows little about selecting good talent, or that it's another instance of disappointing friends and family. Players who choose to respond to team elimination in one of these ways will likely quit practicing, experience lower self-esteem and confidence, and be disinclined to try out for the team in the future.

If, however, these players view being cut as an opportunity to practice more, sharpen their skills, and grow physically and psychologically until the next tryout, they'll likely respond with increased effort and determination. Such players persist in the face of adversity and challenge themselves to reach new heights. They are more inclined to dig in with greater resolve to prove their mettle and shine at the next opportunity. Remember that even the greatest players have been cut from high-level teams at some point in their careers. If they choose to view that setback as temporary and resolve to come back with heightened motivation to prove critics wrong, then the initial adversity serves as both a challenge and an opportunity. Which choice is in the players' best interest?

Developing Thinking Habits

Because players can control physiological responses and psychological interpretations of adversity, competition, and performance setbacks, they can choose to respond with confidence, hope, and positive expectations. Habits of thinking are just that—habits. We become what we think about. That's why it's vital for players to monitor their self-talk and keep track of their inner dialogue.

Often a player's greatest saboteurs are not opponents, scoreboards, or coaches but rather their own inner (and often negative) voice. It's critical for players to cultivate the inner winner that lives inside each of them. The inner winner must be fed before the outer winner appears. Attitude is like a paintbrush—it can color any situation.

Truly outstanding players are self-confident. Unfortunately, confidence is an illusive, transitory condition. Often it must be worked for rather than enjoyed as a permanent psychological attribute. Confidence results from honest, productive thinking and frequent reminders about previous successful experiences. Confident players are the ones who want the ball at the end of the game and seem to be at their best when the pressure is greatest. In essence, confident players think they can, and as a result they often do. Confident players imagine themselves being successful and focus on successfully mastering their own personal performance. They concentrate on variables over which they have control rather than worrying about the negative consequences of failure. Figure 22.2 is a sample worksheet for working on building self-confidence.

Putting It Together

Begin exerting effective control by combining breathing skills with thought-management strategies. While inhaling, players should focus on reasons why they're prepared, skilled, capable, and ready to perform. Repeat a short phrase that captures those factors on both the inhalation and exhalation. To calm the body as well as fears, the long, slow exhalation phase of the breathing cycle should be twice as long as the inhalation. For example, inhale on a two count (one-two) then exhale on a four count (one-two-three-four). Better yet, combine exhalation with an audible sigh or by putting your tongue in an "N" position on the roof of your mouth to help facilitate the relaxation of your jaw and neck muscles. Allow your shoulders to rise toward your ears as you inhale. As your belly expands outward with air, repeat the first part of an affirmation phrase, such as "I am ready, fit, and strong" (inhale) then repeat the second part as you exhale: "I can make this play."

Some people find it helpful to use technique reminders as part of their breathing cycle. Soccer players at the penalty kick line might say "relaxed and calm" as they inhale, then "smooth and steady" as they exhale to remind themselves to strike the ball cleanly and confidently. Additional examples of affirmation phrases to use with controlled breathing techniques are "I am powerful and fast," "I've done this a thousand times before," "I am prepared and confident," "This is my game," and "I love to play."

Consistently implement the performance phrases and combine them with well-practiced breathing techniques. Repeat this combination at practice until you master the skills, so that in competition, when the benefits are most needed, you use the techniques unconsciously.

As with most psychological-skills training, developing strategies to control jitters generally involves three phases: (1) self-awareness and analysis, (2) individual experimentation and consistent application, and (3) revision and refinement. These techniques should eventually become completely automatic so that the mind is free of worry and fear and focused only on the present play and the present moment. Players perform best when they simply relax and let it happen. Players need to let their bodies do what they have trained to do over countless hours and years of practice. Players already know what and how they need to be at their best. All they need to do now is clear the way for the best performance to occur.

Self-Confidence

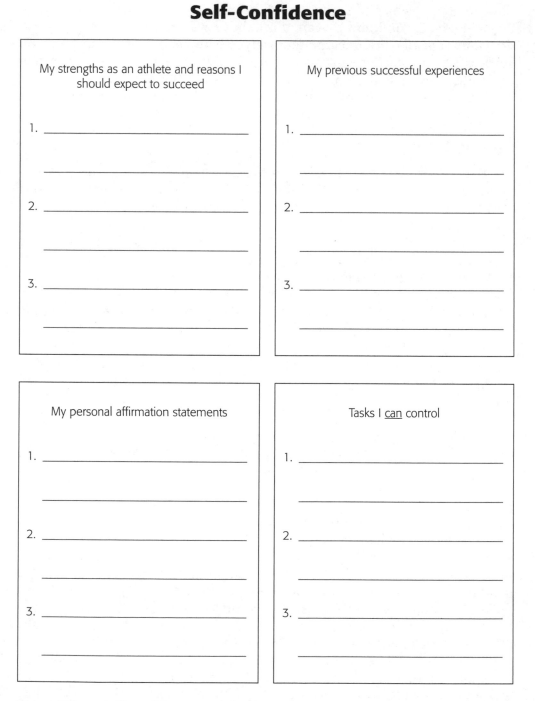

My strengths as an athlete and reasons I should expect to succeed

1. _____

   _____

2. _____

   _____

3. _____

   _____

My previous successful experiences

1. _____

   _____

2. _____

   _____

3. _____

   _____

My personal affirmation statements

1. _____

   _____

2. _____

   _____

3. _____

   _____

Tasks I can control

1. _____

   _____

2. _____

   _____

3. _____

   _____

Figure 22.2   Self-confidence worksheet.

Pregame and Prepractice Performance Plans

The importance of developing a consistent preperformance routine can't be overemphasized. Players frequently report that getting off their routine or not coming ready to play commonly precede poor performances. Typically, players engage in certain types of behavior for one contest, location, or situation and implement other strategies and behaviors for other matches. Players need to ask themselves these questions: Is my routine for home games the same or different than for away games? Do I feel, think, and behave the same for the big game as I do for the match against the last-place team? Do I follow the same procedure if I'm starting that I do if I'm coming off the bench? Unfortunately, for most players, the situation determines pregame preparation.

Most players experience their best performances when they're appropriately activated and ready for competition but also are free from negative thoughts, worries, doubts, or fears. Generally a psychological warm-up should include realistic and positive self-statements and reminders. These phrases should be based on actual strengths the player possesses. The statements must be grounded in reality and must be felt and believed by the player. Self-talk that increases worry should be eliminated and replaced with more performance-enhancing statements. Statements should reflect the benefits of hard training and preparation, readiness, ability, adaptability, and commitment to supreme effort.

It's also beneficial for players to mentally review their individual and team game plan. Players could replay previous best performances in their minds or review the tactical game plan the coach instituted for the match. Remember, the key to effective imagery is to use all the senses and the feelings associated with performance. Players should attempt to create or re-create the feeling of an outstanding performance. Players should use verbal and visual reminders of how they want to perform in the game.

Even in less than ideal situations, players need to develop the resources necessary to focus on reasons why they should be confident and optimistic. Shift the focus away from negative thoughts or images to ones that enhance confidence and increase feelings of control and commitment. Players may focus on the game plan, engage in tactical rehearsals, or focus on personal goals established for this particular event. Confident performers focus on what they want to have happen; others focus on what they fear might happen. Either way, performance is generally rooted in expectations and beliefs. Choose how you want to think, feel, and act and implement that plan consistently.

Coaches and players have discovered that specific, precompetition plans produce higher and more consistent performances. Precompetition plans allow players to focus on specific thoughts, images, feelings, and behaviors that enhance the likelihood for best performances. Precompetition plans allow players to control their internal and external environments rather than be controlled by circumstances or temporary personal or situational factors.

The pregame routine takes time to develop and should reflect the player's personality, needs, and unique characteristics. Figure 22.3 is a practical worksheet for players to carefully and specifically describe their individual preperformance routines. Although highly individualized, an effective pregame routine should include several important elements.

First, the player needs to clearly identify the common characteristics of previous best performances. What were you thinking, feeling, and doing or not doing? What words, images and descriptions describe your ideal pregame state? Have you considered food intake and timing? Travel to and from the field? Have you thought about physical warm-up time and sport-specific training? What are the psychological characteristics that coincide with these behaviors? What will you be doing, thinking, saying, and feeling in the last few minutes before the start of the match? What about the first few minutes of the game?

All these situations should be described and defined in detail. Players need to be in control; if they're not at the exact physical, emotional, or psychological state most conducive to optimal performance, they must be able to make the necessary adjustments. Self-responsibility and self-control are the cornerstones for optimal performance.

Develop realistic, positive, and meaningful self-statements that describe how you feel or want to feel for today's performance. These statements should be based on real strengths you have identified and should be extremely specific.

Develop a thought-stopping strategy when negative or worrisome thoughts enter your mind. Replace negative thoughts with constructive, powerful, performance-enhancing ones. In general, self-statements should be in the present tense and should reflect preparedness, commitment, ability, adaptability, and resolve.

Engage in a brief mental rehearsal of the game plan, both for yourself and as a member of the team. The key is to develop a feeling of greatness, confidence through preparation, and an ability to successfully execute the skills necessary for high levels of performance.

Perform this procedure constantly and faithfully. Don't use it only before the big game or critical matches. Pregame preparation is as essential to the game as is your first touch of the ball or runs made in support of teammates.

Combine previous best performance characteristics with specific phrases, behaviors, focus cues, and mental images of success. Write down this routine and include times, actual phrases, and specific images.

Environment/time	Thoughts	Feelings	Behaviors
Wake up			
Travel to competition			
Locker room changing and preparation			
On-the-field warm-up			
10 minutes before the game			
Player introductions			
2 minutes before the game			
Coach's final comments			
Game whistle			
Game			
Halftime			

Figure 22.3 Pregame performance plan.

Engage in "best friend" communication by talking to yourself with the same language and the same energy and support that you would use with your best friend or a valued teammate under the same circumstances.

View failures or setbacks as learning experiences and motivational incentives. There's nothing necessarily wrong with failing; if we don't attach negativity to failure, it can be just one of the many steps toward success. In fact, failure is necessary for ultimate triumph. Note the error, learn the lesson, make corrections, and move on physically, emotionally, and mentally.

VI

Growth Opportunities in the Coaching Role

CHAPTER 23

Learning and Developing as a Professional

Jeff Vennell and Peter Gooding

Professional coaches are a product of their experiences and individual personalities. *Mentoring* is a modern term for the process of an experienced person passing on wisdom and knowledge to a younger person. In some cases a person can be a mentor for others without even knowing it. In fact, that's what often happens with coaches—most young coaches begin their career watching older, experienced coaches, learning lessons and picking up valuable coaching tidbits to use with their own team when they become a head coach. While watching our mentors, we consciously examine and unconsciously absorb what works and what doesn't. Our mentors do certain things and have particular methods and styles that we observe, evaluate, learn from, and apply to our own coaching down the road.

Establishing Standards of Leadership

As coaches, we should stand up for what is ethically correct. Sometimes that means taking a lonely stand but, as professionals, if we think we're correct, we should voice our position intelligently and be grateful for the opportunity to express our view.

New Jersey high school coach Bob Nye (past president of the NSCAA) comes to mind. Bob once reported a player who was illegally playing outside soccer during the school season. This was something that happened often in the area, and Bob, who was then starting a new high school soccer program, thought it was wrong. He reported the case, the player was suspended, and the team experienced some rough paybacks in a match the next week. Even so, the team's players were able to stand up for their coach by their play on the field.

In the late 1960s, Peter Gooding inherited a team at Amherst College that paid little attention to the importance of captains. His previous experience in Europe, where captains acted as coaches on the field, was very different. In one of Coach Gooding's first games, an Amherst captain was ejected for fighting. At a subsequent team meeting, Gooding formally removed the player as captain. The whole team was aghast, and for several weeks they were willing to excuse Gooding only on the grounds that he didn't yet understand the American sporting culture. Gooding held firm and progressively demonstrated the importance of captains by involving them in team selection and management and halftime adjustments. By the end of the season, the players had an entirely different attitude toward team leadership. During the 35 years since the fighting incident, Amherst has never had another captain ejected from a game. In fact, rarely has a captain received a disciplinary card.

The requirements to be a successful coach are different from the requirements to be a successful player. Players need techniques, tactics, physical fitness, and psychological readiness to excel. Coaches need observational skills, intellectual skills, good methodology, effective teaching skills, and the ability to communicate.

Effective coaches are effective leaders of their teams and communities and within the game. Doug Williamson, a NSCAA national staff member, studied leadership and the traits of leaders at the Gallup Organization in Lincoln, Nebraska, where he worked in their Leadership Institute (now part of Gallup University). Drawing on Gallup's extensive research on the study of excellence in leadership and his own study and observation, Doug has written articles about leadership for *Soccer Journal* and created a session on leadership for the NSCAA premier level course. He has studied the challenges faced by effective leaders and learned a lot from the teachings of Donald O. Clifton, the former chairman of the Gallup Organization. One challenge is visioning, the ability to provide a clear, consistent picture of the direction the coach and team want to go. Setting individual and team goals is the key ingredient to setting a vision.

Good leaders know themselves and reflect regularly on their abilities. Gallup found that top-flight leaders emphasize their strengths and manage their weaknesses. Doug uses the following coaching example to illustrate how to apply this premise to training players. Once players reach the high school varsity level, dominant left-footed players should spend most of their time reinforcing left-sided abilities on the flank and not too much time trying to become more proficient with the right foot on the right side of the field. Emphasizing more effective left-sided play enhances the player's ability to be successful technically and tactically on the left side. Taking too much time on right-sided play will not emphasize left-sided strengths, which the player and the team needs.

As coaches, we need to stabilize values. We should establish and model the values on which we want to build our team. We should share our values with our players so they know where we stand and in the hope that they will model our values in their interaction and behavior. Significant research indicates that players prefer to play for a coach whose values they perceive clearly.

As professional coaches, it's our responsibility to set standards for ourselves and for our teams and to take pride in the program on and off the field. What you demand is what you get. The standards you get are the standards you set. The good coach learns how to reach players individually and collectively. This can mean taking players out of their comfort zone as we try to achieve new individual and team goals. For their part, players must want to work hard and be intense but controlled. They must be focused, driven, competitive, and set high standards for themselves and their teammates. They need to learn how to be coached, to accept advice, and incorporate changes into their game.

When we speak of coaches setting standards for their teams, a couple of coaches come to mind. Larry Briggs, the legendary University of Massachusetts coach, and past president of the NSCAA, was an enormously powerful influence without saying or doing very much. His strength of character principally dominated his program. The team's strong sense of fair play and excellent discipline were the result of the players not wanting to let Coach Briggs down. His impeccable behavior as a coach set a tone and a high standard most of his players tried to emulate.

Springfield College coach Irv Schmid (past president of the NSCAA) was not an outwardly motivating coach, but in his environment his method worked very well. Players played out of season on and off campus in amateur leagues, trying to prove to Coach Schmid (no one dared in those days to call him Irv, which took years to get used to) that they could play and play hard.

Another example of a coach setting high standards is the story of New Jersey high school basketball coach, George Cella, who won over 600 games. Cella believed that crowds should show respect for opponents and insisted that spectators be quiet when opponents shot foul shots. Cella would stand up and point toward any noise emanating from the crowd. If a spectator committed a second offense, which was rare, Cella would wave a hand at the offender, telling him to go home early. Coach Cella is a rare example of a coach who believes in respect strongly enough to apply his expectations to everyone in the arena, even the spectators.

Professionals should be conscious of their language and manners. You never know who is listening or watching, so pay attention to what you're saying and doing. Your reactions to successes and failures set the tone for those around you and contribute to the impression others have about you and your coaching. This doesn't mean you must be stalwart and serious all the time. Humor is a valuable coaching tool. Coaches need to be able to laugh at themselves and use self-deprecating humor at times. Using stories with humor and a message is an effective way to communicate.

Learning to Coach

Learning never ends. Coaches and organizations that don't improve actually move backward because the competition is moving forward. Coaches learn from each other, even when their coaching styles are remarkably different.

Joe Morrone, former University of Connecticut coach and past president of the NSCAA, is a coach many of us can learn from. When we were starting our coaching careers at Amherst and Williams, Joe was beginning his tenure at Connecticut after a successful coaching career at Middlebury College. The Little Three schools had traditional programs dating to the early 1900s with very good players and good teams for years. We were struck by the organizational and procedural strength of Joe's Connecticut program and with the quality of soccer they played. The commitment of the players to a team structure at the expense of individual freedom contrasted markedly with the Amherst and Williams teams. Some of our team-management organization changed after we observed Morrone's teams.

Coach Morrone set the standard in many areas, including recruiting, marketing a program, fund-raising, demanding that players adopt his principles, starting youth soccer programs, involving the community in the program (the Connecticut soccer boosters are still going strong), and raising the awareness of soccer on the campus and throughout New England. His style was surely his own, but his quest for excellence was an example for us.

Many coaches across the country have used their love for the game and coaching skills to develop soccer in their areas. In the Midwest, St. Louis University coaches Bob Guelker and Harry Keough coached several championship teams with rosters made up of graduates of the youth program developed in conjunction with the Catholic schools of St. Louis. On the west coast, NSCAA Hall of Fame inductee, Steve Negoesco, built a program that experienced unparalleled success. Jimmy Mills in Philadelphia also comes to mind. Of course, we could cite many other individuals who gave of their time in their communities to nurture their sport.

Fledgling coaches often observe that only after they start to think about the game as coaches rather than as players do they understand the game in a more comprehensive way. They must draw on varied resources as they transition from player to coach, making certain not to rely exclusively on their own experiences. They need to be open to ideas from other coaches and other teams and examine other coaching environments. Times change, and coaches sometimes need to adjust their approach based on what's occurring elsewhere.

Attending clinics is a good way to learn new ways to coach. For beginning coaches, clinics are tremendous sources for learning what and how to teach. But don't limit yourself only to clinics to learn more about coaching. High schools and colleges have many excellent coaches to learn from. While coaching at Virginia, U.S. National Team coach Bruce Arena's office bordered the visiting team's dressing room. Little did some of the Atlantic Coast Conference basketball coaches know that they had a wider audience than just their own team as they discussed pregame and halftime strategies.

The old adage that there's nothing new in soccer is true to a point. There are always new ways to present material. If nothing else, watching someone coach successfully will reinforce your own coaching methodology. Watch how master coaches make coaching points and from where they do most of their coaching (generally on the outside of the group). Listen to their voice projection; observe how they get and maintain group attention (for instance, youngsters listen better when kneeling on one knee than when standing). Watch how they introduce exercises (with a demonstration), the size of the spaces (larger is better than smaller at the start), the number of players in the spaces, and how they handle the age-old question of whether to stop the group or the individual who needs attention. Take note of how they handle players, which is the ultimate key to successful coaching. Don't limit yourself to just the teaching basics. Watch matches to see how teams are put together and what systems and tactics are used.

Contributing to the Profession

Contributing to professional journals is a good way for a coach to broaden horizons. Jeff Vennell began in this area by contributing to the *Soccer Journal* by reporting clinic sessions at the annual NSCAA conventions. Editors are there to help you through the rough spots, and having drafts reviewed by a colleague is a good way to start. With some confidence and experience, you'll be able to express what you do and what you believe about the game. Writing can also help you clarify your own thinking about how you prepare exercises and practices.

Don't underestimate the value of being able to express your thoughts clearly, both when writing and when speaking. For the coach, the dominant form of communication is the spoken word. We must be clear and concise in our instructions and conversations with players. This is true at all levels of the game but is particularly important for coaches who work in an academic environment.

You can improve the way you verbally present your ideas, but it takes work. Listen to yourself speak. Make an audiotape of a practice or presentation. Study (and borrow) from the styles of speakers who have entertained and educated you. Many NSCAA members recall the speaking expertise of early coaching giants like Glenn Warner (Navy), Whitey Burnham (Dartmouth), and Don Yonker (Drexel) all of whom were past presidents of the NSCAA. More recently, Cliff McCrath (Seattle Pacific) and the late Mike Berticelli (Notre Dame) honed their public speaking expertise and were noted for their ability to deliver the goods from podiums throughout the country.

Have you noticed that almost all successful coaches in a sport are involved in professional organizations? Formal coaching occurs at almost all levels in the United States, whereas in Europe it's generally found only at the senior amateur and professional level. Below these levels, usually a captain, teacher, or parent minds a team. Because there are so many active soccer coaches in the United States, it's inevitable that the professional associations will be bigger and more energetic and will exhibit a vitality that's rare in the rest of the world.

Good coaches have a great deal to contribute to the sport. Participating in local, state, and regional professional associations leads to learning more about the internal workings of organizations and encourages sharing ideas with other coaches. Our association with the NSCAA began as regional representatives and division representatives. We became more involved over the years as we joined the executive board and assumed leadership positions. By broadening professional involvement, a coach comes into contact with other serious coaches. We've found that a great deal of our soccer education emanated from colleagues after hours.

One of the most striking differences between U.S. coaches and those in England is the constant exchange of ideas American soccer coaches engage in, whether while sitting in a restaurant, talking at a game, or just hanging out. In England, soccer conversation seemed to center on controversy: Why was someone still playing at center forward when he hadn't scored in 10 matches? The fun in England was discussing who was playing where for the local professional team or who should be picked for England. We seldom talked about team tactics. In the United States, coaches are insatiable in their desire for information about tactics and training methods. This is a large reason why our soccer coaching has progressed so impressively.

Successful programs are usually headed by experienced coaches. One way a professional improves and develops coaching abilities is to volunteer to present clinic sessions. Start on the local level, where you can be confident of the environment, but also present at the next level. A new environment with many coaches in attendance is a different setting than a small clinic at the local or regional level. Realize that even at large gatherings, those in attendance might know little about the topic or how to properly teach or coach it.

Participation in the NSCAA Academy coaching programs has made better coaches and better athletic administrators. Get involved in your local soccer organization, join rules committees and officiating committees, offer clinics, and volunteer to attend or coach a practice session for youth coaches. You will be pleasantly surprised how good it makes you feel to give back to the game and how much your expertise is needed in your local environment. Promoting and marketing the game is part of the responsibility of a soccer coach.

Be a leader! Get involved with your local youth program and take advantage of articles and materials developed by national organizations. Remember, especially at the youth level, that the more organized and systematic the coaching becomes, the greater the risk of taking the game away from the children. Overcoaching is worse than no coaching for the young player, and the joyous experience, which should be the primary goal for youth soccer, is often lost among the cones, bibs, and drills.

Working With Assistant Coaches

Good programs usually have assistant coaches. The selection of an assistant coach is an important task for the head coach. Try to spread your search as wide as you can, but define the responsibilities you're looking for in an assistant coach. Recruiting ability is an important facet of an assistant coach at the collegiate level, though not at the secondary level. Knowledge about the game and playing experience are important, but being able to relate to athletes in your particular situation is more important. How much time will be required and what responsibilities—goal keeping, practice plans, scouting—will you delegate to an assistant? What balance do you want from your assistant?

Good head coaches want assistants who are loyal to the head coach and the program but who are willing to challenge the head coach in the correct environment (not on the field). In some cases, assistants are assigned to the program. Even so, the head coach has the responsibility to mentor and provide opportunities for the assistant to grow as a coach.

We assumed our head coaching positions because someone believed in us when we were coaching novices. Do you remember the person who gave you the opportunity to lead a team? When giving a new coach a chance, try to remember when you started out. It's your duty to provide the younger coach opportunities to take on increasing responsibilities.

Professional development outside the team is important, but the on-field chance to lead or plan is the best way to grow as a coach. This is particularly effective if the mentoring coach takes the time to review the strengths of the effort and points out where the assistant coach can try new or different ideas next time. Coaching confidence is built over time. An important factor for novice coaches to recognize is that they'll make some mistakes, but that's part of the growing process. The good coach falls down, gets back up, learns from the mistakes, and moves forward.

Evaluating Effectiveness

Improvement is not just an issue for assistant and younger coaches. Head coaches have many ways to assess their effectiveness. The first is probably the most obvious—the match result. Matches are a measure of where the team and team members stand in their development. Games are not a measure of a coach's or a player's self-worth but rather events that provides the coach a picture of the team's status in relation to its goals.

Performance reviews by others can also benefit the coach. Trust is a basic component of evaluations, and reviews should be based on goals set by the coach during preseason. Another set of eyes, especially if the reviewer is knowledgeable and impartial, can often offer a realistic perspective. Often a review by an athletic administrator involves other little things beyond "does the coach know the game" evaluation. Does the coach visibly support the school's sportsmanship values? Does the coach treat officials with respect? Does the coach communicate well with players and, at the high school level, with parents? Is the coach concerned with the academic progress of players? Does the coach meet deadlines for scheduling and equipment purchase, oversight, and return? Does the coach complete sport-information responsibilities, such as reporting game results? Is the coach prepared for practices? Does the coach take advantage of professional development opportunities? Does the coach have, or is the coach working on, a postgraduate degree? Does the coach read professional journals, receive and review newsletters, and use the Internet? How does the coach relate to support personnel such as office assistants, athletic trainers, and grounds crews?

If you're fortunate enough to have a relationship with a peer you can trust to effectively evaluate your coaching, take advantage of this special opportunity. Don't forget that asking for help or guidance from a more experienced colleague is a sign of maturity, not insecurity.

Developing a Relationship With the Institution or Organization

As athletic administrators, we have learned an important lesson as we liaison between coaches and administration. No surprises! Athletic directors don't want to coach your team, but they do need to know when a situation could arise in which their office could become involved. Most of the time, too much information is better than no information. Let the administration know in advance if you're having a problem with a team captain that might lead you to remove the player from the team.

Vennell once received a message from the ski coach that one of his captains had skipped out of practice at the ski area after taking only one of four required practice-training runs. Because the ski coach contacted him early in the process, Vennell could offer his perspective about the process and the coach's decision and, more important, could support the coach's decision when challenged by the player and his parents. Parents don't like bad news, and they don't accept surprises easily. Who does?

Sharing information about your program is critical in setting basic team standards. Many colleges and secondary schools issue student-athlete handbooks. These publications state school and athletic department policies for all the institution's athletic teams. Use these publications as a guide to establish expectations for your team. A preseason team meeting is a good time to articulate your standards and goals for the upcoming season.

Consider holding a mandatory preseason meeting with your players (and with parents at the secondary level) at which the following agenda items are addressed: introduction of assistant coaches; coaching philosophy; academic responsibilities; practice and contest schedules; criteria used to select the team (team size, how cuts are made, extent of the tryout period); inclement weather plans (where and when announcements of changes are available); how playing time is allocated; selection of captains and their roles; letters, awards, and qualifications; team rules; commitment, accountability, expectations, including college visits; travel policies; school and individual equipment; equipment room use and hours; distribution and collection of equipment; rules on drug and alcohol use and player commitment to say no to tobacco, drugs, and alcohol; conflicts with classes; athletic training services, injury prevention, injury care; communication with the coaching staff; and expectations of parents.

Coaches might also use this meeting to answer concerns of players and parents—for example, a player's concern about playing time or team rules. Players and parents are instructed that the player, not the parent, should talk to the coach. However, there are a few appropriate issues for parents to discuss with the coach, including treatment of their child and concerns about their child's behavior. Early identification of a problem is very important. Before confronting a player or, in severe cases, before separating a player from the team, the coach should contact the parents. Discuss the child's lack of effort or other negative behavior. Enlist parental support to change the behavior, reassuring parents you want to work with them to help the player improve and succeed. You might be surprised how much it can help when the player talks to mom or dad and learns that his or her parents support the coach.

Unfortunately, many parents have an increased sense of entitlement and often live vicariously through their children. Parents now schedule their children's lives from an early age. People other than parents often supervise children in structured activities, which is certainly different from the way it used to be when children often engaged in unstructured play. Unfortunately, that is not the norm today. Many parents end up managing their children's lives. It should not surprise us when their control enters into the child's hobbies and athletics as well.

It's difficult for parents to turn over control of their child's life to a coach two hours a day, but coaches can help parents learn that it's better for the child. Coaches can try to get students to take control of their lives, such as encouraging them to make telephone calls or send e-mails to college coaches concerning their interest in a particular institution rather than having their parents do it.

Communicating With the Media

As coach, you need to learn to deal with the print and visual media. Even the smallest programs have student newspapers. Establish honest relationships with the media at all levels. We've had success by volunteering to read student-publication pieces to be sure our ideas, and especially our quotations, are accurate. Yes, reporters are trying to sell their product, but with practice and skill, the good coach can use the media to promote the positive aspects of the program. Be willing to decline to answer questions if you think they're unfair. Ask for the question to be repeated if you want more time to consider your reply. Realize that your central responsibility is to the members of your team and that you should protect players' privacy. Know the confidentiality rules at your institution and your state's liability laws.

At Cranbrook and many other institutions, some parents don't want their children's pictures used in the media, including the school's Web site. A coach must respect a parent's desire to protect their child. Go on the offense with the media and get them to trust you. Alert them to the good news about your team so that when a possible controversial subject arises, they'll be willing to carefully hear your side of the issue.

All college coaches would love to have a sports information person assigned to their team. This is not the situation at most schools. Establishing a relationship with your local media representatives and the sports information director is important if you want to get maximum publicity for your team from a very busy office. Deliver rosters, statistics, and other information within the timeline and realize that being early is always better than being on time. As Web sites are used more and more, learn to create your team site, or submit material that your sports information director and local media can use to help make your soccer team number one in their efforts.

Ethical Conduct

Ethics—what you do when no one is watching and what you do when everyone is watching—are the fabric of who you are as a person and coach. Coaches should remember the tremendous effect their coaches and other role models have had on their lives. Take your role seriously. You have an important task to help young people mature. You will make a difference in their lives. Make that impression a positive contribution to their growth.

The NSCAA established a code of ethics, updated in May 1999. The code, which can be found on the NSCAA Web site (nscaa.com) and periodically in *Soccer Journal*, is used at NSCAA residential courses as a basis for discussions about coaching ethics. The code serves as a guide to conducting yourself as a professional soccer coach. Here are the 12 points.

1. Soccer is the players' game. The paramount concern of coaches is the holistic development, welfare, enjoyment, and safety of players.

2. Coaches bear responsibility for teaching players to strive for success while playing fairly, observing the laws of the game, and striving for the highest levels of sportsmanship.

3. Coaches will treat officials with respect and dignity and will teach players to do the same.

4. Opponents are worthy of being treated with respect. Coaches will model respect for opponents and expect their players to do likewise.

5. In both victory and defeat, the coach's behavior will model grace, dignity, and composure.

6. Coaches will adhere to the highest standards and the regulations of the institutions they represent: clubs, schools, sponsoring organizations, and sport governing bodies.

7. Coaches have a responsibility to promote the interests of soccer, including treating media with courtesy, honesty, and respect.

8. Coaches will model inclusive behavior, actively supporting cultural diversity while opposing all types of discrimination, including, but not limited to, racism and sexism, at all levels.

9. Coaches are responsible for taking an active role in educating players about drug, alcohol, and tobacco use, and preventing and treating abuse both in their own lives and in the lives of their players.

10. Coaches will refrain from all manner of personal abuse and harassment of others, whether verbal, physical, emotional, or sexual, and will oppose such abuse and harassment at all levels.

11. Coaches will respect the declared affiliations of all players and will adhere to all guidelines and regulations on recruiting established by the governing bodies with oversight of their teams and leagues.

12. Coaches will seek to honor those who uphold the highest standards and principles of soccer and will use appropriate protocol to oppose and eliminate all behaviors—violence, abuse, dishonesty, disrespect, and violations of the laws of the game and rules governing competition—that bring disrepute to the sport.

In relation to the code, we'd like to emphasize how important the coach's relationship with officials is. The treatment of officials is a tremendous problem in American sport. It starts in youth sports, including soccer, and has reached the point where in sections of the country there are not enough officials for matches. Coaches should not permit players to question officials' calls. Coaches need to learn that they, not the officials, are responsible for controlling the actions of their players. Coaches should also do their part to control the behavior of spectators toward officials. Coaches and spectators should realize that officials are not going to change their calls and learn that positive reinforcement goes a long way toward building the mutual respect that is not as evident as it should be in the game.

Developing as a professional coach is really about learning how to better meet the needs of players on and off the field and support the game we love. It's the coach's responsibility to challenge and lead players and teams. Although we might not be able to be all things to all players and teams, we can, as professional coaches, never cease to spend the time and effort to improve. Never forget to listen to players and realize that each one has tremendous potential to succeed. Remember that soccer is a game. Enjoy the journey and have fun as you grow as a professional.

CHAPTER 24

Mentoring the Next Generation of Coaches

Tony DiCicco

An incident that occurred at SoccerPlus Camps, my summer instructional program, shed some light on the mentoring process. One of my directors, a former professional player, was working with a young student. He was pushing the student hard, trying to get him to perform a skill a certain way. Finally, the student did it. Afterward, the instructor said nothing to the student, and they moved on to the next challenge.

At an appropriate moment, I pulled the coach aside and offered this feedback: "You just pushed that young player pretty hard, and he eventually performed the technique to a satisfactory level, but the real coaching, teaching moment passed without you taking advantage of it. To really take advantage of that moment, you needed to stop, walk over to him, give him a high five or handshake and say, 'I pushed you hard, you never gave up, you kept your head, and you got it right. I really respect that in a player—great job.' "

If the coach had done that, he would have bridged a gap with this player that would have taken the player–coach relationship to the next level. Instead, the coach, in his own mind was thinking, "I pushed him hard, and he did it. I'm sure he appreciates now why I rode him." In reality, the player was probably thinking, "Man, I'm glad I got that jerk off my back."

A common misconception in coaching is that demanding coaches get it done and receive respect. However, modern successful coaching requires just the opposite to get the best results. A "catch them being good" positive approach is inspiring the new model of champions to play with confidence and beyond self-imposed boundaries. Yes, a coach can be intimidating, demanding, or use a "crack the whip" coaching style, but only if he balances it with empathy and compassion to achieve an optimal player–coach relationship.

As coaches, our ability to mentor, learn from associates, and develop a coaching philosophy are all interrelated. Coaches can't successfully mentor until they have a coaching style and philosophy they're comfortable with. Their style must be constantly reviewed, adjusted, and proven to get results not only on the field but also in the area of character development in their players. Coaches are teachers and role models, facilitators of leadership development, and enhancers of performance skills.

Being a Mentor

What is mentoring? In its most basic form, the mentoring process involves a person with specific, hands-on experience helping, advising, and directing another, less experienced person.

A few guiding principles underlie the work of most mentors. First, a mentor should be a positive role model. Think of the role models who mattered in your life and how they acted or performed in public or within a close group, such as a team.

Second, mentors need effective communication skills, including the ability to listen. Effective listening starts with creating an environment in which a player or professional associate can ask questions and feel free to interact. Listening means being empathetic and patient. A problem with many listeners (particularly men) is that they want to find an immediate solution. In a counseling situation, don't try to find an immediate answer, don't try to fix things. Just listen. Confirm how the speaker is feeling and validate those feelings. Then you can begin to really communicate.

One of my star players on the women's national team was not playing to her level and wasn't enjoying the game. This was during the run to the 1999 Women's World Cup, and the media kept asking, "What's wrong? Mia hasn't scored in five, six, seven games. What's up?" Mia came to my office after a friendly game and was very upset. She didn't know what was going on; she thought that she was letting the team down, and she couldn't get any relief from the press.

If this had happened when I was a younger coach, I probably would have gone right to the solution: "We'll insulate you from the press and give you a game off so you can gather yourself." But I didn't go there. I stayed centered and listened to what Mia was saying. I showed empathy and shared that she probably thought that she was letting down the team, though, as I saw it, that wasn't the case at all. The team was concerned about her and wanted her to enjoy the game and enjoy them as teammates. Her teammates and our staff cared about Mia, and we wanted her to like the game, not just carry the load for the team. After our talk and later counseling, Mia started to have fun again in soccer, and the goals started to flow.

Third, most mentoring in coaching is informal. In many cases, an assistant coach learns from the head coach then mentors another even less experienced professional or group of professionals. So the process perpetuates itself. More formal mentoring relationships are created in business, such as when supervisors file evaluations of reports, or in school settings, where teachers evaluate and mentor students.

One of my early mentors in soccer was former U.S. National Team coach, Bob Gansler. I learned an enormous amount about soccer and team detail from attending the U.S. Soccer Coaching Schools and working with Bob and his colleagues. However, much of my coaching philosophy was developed earlier by my high-school coaches Bob Landers (soccer), Mill Mason (basketball), and Charlie Wrenn (baseball) and by college coach Irv Schmid at Springfield College. I also copied legendary coaches, such as John Wooden, and other coaches who served as models on how to teach and coach and win at the highest levels.

In almost every mentoring relationship, learning runs both ways. A mentor who isn't accepting of the best qualities in a coaching colleague might miss out on important learning opportunities.

I learned much from my assistant coaches during my head coaching time with the U.S. women. Coaches such as Lauren Gregg, Colleen Hacker, Jay Hoffman, and April Heinrichs served as mentors and professional associates. Learning was a two-way process; I believe my openness to others' ideas and avoiding imposing my own beliefs on the team contributed to our ultimate success. There were times when a player walked past me to ask a question of Lauren or Jay. That isn't easy to deal with as the head coach. But by staying true to our mission, resolute in my own abilities and direction, but vulnerable and open to new ideas, I did not undermine my strength as head coach—I solidified it.

Coaching Philosophies

Here are some of my basic coaching philosophies that became key mentoring points for coaching associates. Remember that players as well as staff are potential mentoring material.

Offer Feedback

Feedback leads to communication. If you're coaching or mentoring, you need to provide feedback. However, before offering advice, ask, "Can I offer you some feedback?" If the person says, "I really don't want it right now," then hold your comment and wait for a more appropriate time.

Because I was the national team coach, my players often wanted to speak to me to find out their status on the team. They wanted to know where they stood in terms of their roles, what they needed to do to improve their standing, and so on. If I avoided these sessions, I encouraged confusion, dissent, and discord among the team.

During the 1999 run to the World Cup, we played China in Hershey, Pennsylvania. Before the game, I met with each player. One of my meetings was with Tisha Venturini, a starter in the 1996 Olympics but now a reserve player. Tisha and I discussed her role. I thought that Tisha could score key goals for us in big games. Although she wouldn't get as much playing time as she previously enjoyed, I needed her to buy into my vision for her. Meanwhile she continued to impress on me that her play justified more playing time. That evening, with the game tied 1 to 1, Tisha subbed into the game and scored the winner in injury time. This is an example of feedback and communication working. In the World Cup group game against North Korea, she scored twice. In the final against China, she was one of my three substitutes. While she might not have agreed with my role for her, she clearly understood it, believed in the team vision, and ultimately thrived within it.

Catch Them Being Good

Catch Them Being Good is the title of a book I wrote with Dr. Colleen Hacker. In my opinion, this concept is vital in helping athletes achieve peak performance. However, it's not easy. The classic coaching model involves observing something wrong, stopping play, correcting it, and then restarting play. This method works, but it works better when it's used along with encouraging the positive. When you see something wrong, hold out until you see it done right; then stop play and applaud the good decision or performance. This is a powerful method to build confidence, motivate, and achieve ultimate success.

Our development of this coaching methodology began when we participated in a tournament in China. It was January of 1998. The teams in the tournament were Norway, China, and Sweden, our biggest rivals. Although we won the tournament and did not give up a goal, we played well below our standard. It was very frustrating for me, and my frustration led to negative coaching.

While still in China after the tournament, Carla Overbeck and Julie Foudy, our captains, asked to speak to me. They asked, "Are you going to cut us and bring in young players like some of these other teams are doing?" I smiled as I answered, "No, this is the team that will win the World Cup next year. I'm not planning to cut any of you. Some young players will challenge for spots, but this is the team that will regain World Cup Champion status." They looked at each other and then almost in unison said, "If you aren't going to cut us, then stop yelling at us!"

Clearly, I had crossed the line from being demanding yet supportive in training to being negative. Fortunately, my players and I had a wonderful working relationship, so they were able to approach me about my coaching demeanor, the demands on our schedule, and other issues.

Our next training camp was a couple of weeks away at the Olympic training facility in Chula Vista, California. When my staff and I arrived a day or so before training, we met and decided that we would coach only the positive things we saw and bite our lips when we saw negatives. We would wait to celebrate when it was done right. We called this "catch them being good" and the concept became part of every training session during our preparations.

The Challenge Coefficient

Challenging my players is really the foundation of my coaching, teaching, and mentoring. To facilitate growth, coaches need to create challenges. And they have to be real challenges, not token challenges. You might challenge players physically, such as meeting a fitness standard; technically, such as developing a greater range of play by perfecting long passing; or in other ways, such as speaking in front of a group or developing leadership skills. Whatever the challenge is, it should work on several levels.

Your role as mentor or coach is to make sure the person you're challenging achieves success. Once they experience success, they'll feel good about themselves. By overcoming self-doubt, a player develops a higher level of self-esteem and self-confidence. In most cases, this translates into improved performance.

Coach to Your Strengths

Know your limitations, but coach to your strengths. Many mentors, coaches, and players recognize their limitations but try to hide them instead of finding complementary abilities in others that neutralize these shortcomings.

I was not versed in sports psychology, but I knew the mental side of the game was as vital as anything else I was doing technically, tactically, or physically. So I found an expert, Colleen Hacker. She provided insights in this area that were beyond my abilities—yet taking advantage of her abilities did not undermine my own. Our teams won championships in the 1996 Olympics and the 1999 World Cup.

I see many coaches hire assistants who are clearly less knowledgeable than they are. They don't want to be overshadowed or upstaged, so they cheat their teams by hiring assistants who are less than the best. This doesn't make much sense, does it? In addition to Colleen, I also sought and took advantage of the expertise of Gregg, Hoffman, Jeff Tipping, and others who worked with our team. At times I left myself vulnerable, but my guiding principle was always to try to help the team get to the next level, not hold them back because of my own insecurities.

Less is More

When training and developing a team to achieve peak performance, you need to vary the level of intensity to maintain the freshness and enthusiasm of your players.

In 1995, when we arrived in Sweden to defend our world championship, we were fit and ready but slightly overtrained. For the first time, we had trained in a residency program. For many of these players, this was more training than they'd ever experienced. Certainly it was more than they had experienced in college, which has a very short season. The residency effects were negative. Nagging injuries, lost concentration, and inconsistent match efforts were signs of a team over their peak as we entered 1995 world championship play. We had a good tournament but not a great tournament. To win, we had to beat a great Norwegian team; We lost 1-0 in the semi-finals.

I think the 2000 Olympic team, coached by April Heinrichs, had similar symptoms. We opened play with a 2 to 0 win over Norway. We followed this victory with some average games (e.g., a tie against a relatively weak China team and a late controversial goal to win 1 to 0 over Brazil). In the final, we continued our roller-coaster play. We followed a superb effort in the first half against Norway with only sporadic brilliance in the second half, leading to a golden goal winner by Norway.

Sometimes less is more because it's better to balance tactics and training with rest. We might not have gone over every scenario many times because we trained less and gave extra time off, but our team was fresh and ready to compete and win gold in both the 1996 Olympics and the 1999 World Cup. It was a great lesson for me. During our preparations for the 1996 Olympics, we had Olympic athletes speak to the team. Some of them had won a medal, and some hadn't. Those who hadn't won a medal expressed a common sentiment: "If I had it to do all over again, I would have trained less in the final month."

Clearly, there's a time to overtrain players in the preseason, knowing there's ample time to build them back up, but as you get closer to competition, remember that less is often more.

Imprint Versus Perfect

I trained in three sports as a young athlete in high school and college. Some training sessions were awesome, and some were boring. In the boring sessions, we went over the same thing again and again to try to reach perfection.

Don't read me wrong. I love perfection, but I'm also realistic. I know that, in soccer, perfection is inconsistent at best. I learned to apply a coaching methodology of imprinting rather than drilling for elusive perfection. I recommend that younger coaches consider this approach to training. If we didn't get it quite right on one day, we didn't keep doing it. We made sure that everyone was clear on what needed to be done and then gave it a few days off before imprinting the next level of execution.

In the 1999 World Cup, I can honestly say we did not play our best. The pressure outside the game on this team to market the event was staggering. If they and the event were successful, it would lay the groundwork for a professional league. So the team had to perform and win.

We all felt the pressure, and it clearly affected our performance. However, we competed wonderfully in every game and fought through all kinds of adversity without retaliation. I am very proud that we were the least-carded teams in both the 1996 Olympics and the 1999 World Cup.

A key was our ability at restarts. We were recognized as having deadly set piece plays that led to many goals. The press asked, "How long do you practice corner kicks and free-kick plays?" The truth was far less than one would suspect. Why? Because, all those corner kicks and set pieces had hours of training done over months of training. It was a continual layering to imprint the basic, subtle nuances of each free-kick opportunity. We imprinted layers rather than attempting to rush perfection. This provided the edge we needed to turn difficult games against Nigeria and North Korea our way. Imprinting won us a game with two second-half corner-kick goals in the quarterfinals against an excellent Germany team.

Make Use of Failures

Use failures as seeds to future success. Coaching is not always about success. I often counsel that one of the wonderful maturities in life is to understand that failure, although never pleasant, can be a useful tool. Many people avoid failure by never performing to near their personal potential. By never taking the risk, they are never exposed to the negatives and emptiness of failure. However, they are also never exposed to the richness and exhilaration of ultimate triumph.

The best example I ever saw of using failure as fertilizer was our 1995 World Cup team. We went to Sweden as defending World Cup champions. Our goal was to win the gold medal, but we were beaten by Norway, the best team in the tournament and the eventual champions. We finished with a bronze medal, which, in our minds, was a failure.

After the Norway game, no one pointed fingers. People could have suggested that my substitutions in the semifinal loss to Norway were ill chosen. No one did, but I thought my substitutions did not help us. Someone could have claimed that Briana Scurry needed to make that save. No one did, but if you asked Bri, she would have told you that she needed to make that save. No one said Mia Hamm needed to score in games like that, but if you asked Mia, she would have agreed she needed to get it done. It was a display of character that no one on the team pointed to anyone else for that loss. Each player looked inward and said to herself, "I should have been better, I can be better, and I will be better for the Olympics next year."

For the 1996 Olympics the following year, we improved dramatically because each player had bettered herself and, collectively, we were a different team. In 1995, Norway was the best and deserved to be champions. In 1996, at the first ever Olympics for women's soccer, the U.S. was clearly the premier team and deserved to be gold medallists.

The semifinal loss to Norway in 1995 motivated us. As my own personal motivation, I carried a picture of the Norwegians accepting the trophy. Every player held something dear and near from that loss for motivation. In every fitness session, team meeting, friendly game, or training session, that loss was never far from our thoughts. It pushed us to another level.

The choices that these women made were the best examples of turning failure into seeds for success that I ever saw or experienced. It was a wonderful lesson and an example of the vitality of the human spirit.

Chemistry: The 12th Player

People often ask me how I deal with bench personnel. We all witnessed the self-destruction of a good U.S. team during the men's tournament in the 1998 World Cup. Players didn't seem to be supporting each other. Those on the bench seemed to resent the players on the field. When things went wrong, everyone looked for someone else to blame instead of looking internally.

Clearly, reserves can make or break the collective team morale. My staff, particularly Colleen Hacker, and I spent a lot of time communicating with the reserves. At the national team level, they are all stars, and they want to play. In fact, I would be concerned if I had a player who seemed willing to sit out. However, the reserves needed to understand that they had to fight for playing time but also support my final decisions on playing time—not an easy task.

On the women's national team, coaches have always stressed positive chemistry. We did not want complainers. We wanted players to understand their roles while trying to expand those roles. I met regularly with my players and also had my assistant coaches (Gregg and Hoffman) and Hacker talk with the nonstarters, if only to let them vent their frustrations.

Every player on the team, veterans and rookies, shared such team responsibilities as taking out water, balls, training vests, or equipment to training sessions. My philosophy is that if all players share the demands of the game on the field, they also share team demands off the field.

Three of my players, Tisha Venturini, Shannon MacMillan, and Tiffany Roberts, had been starters in the Olympics. Now they were reserves for the 1999 World Cup. This situation was a potential powder keg. We spent a lot of time with the reserve group, especially these three, but it wasn't a hard sell. They needed to know where they stood, what was expected of them, and that they had a chance to change all of that with performances.

They were model team members during the entire Cup. In fact, Shannon played brilliantly, and the press started asking her and me if she was going to start. With every excellent game she played, the questions grew. Finally, Shannon came to me and said, "I know you're getting hammered with questions about me starting, and I want to play every minute, but whatever you decide, I support." What more can a coach ask of a player? Tisha and Tiffany were equally as supportive, and each of their playing opportunities was marked by inspired efforts.

Getting to that point requires some effort. Each player needs to know that team chemistry demands a contribution, an action. It isn't something that just happens. Without positive chemistry you can still win, but not over time and not with sustained excellence.

Layers of Leadership

No matter how effectively a coach instructs players, a team cannot thrive without leaders. When I looked at players, I looked for outstanding qualities such as speed, technical skill, toughness, or leadership. Positive leadership on a team is an undervalued commodity. Coaches have a responsibility to nurture and develop leaders on their team.

The women's national team was blessed with two captains and many leaders. Carla Overbeck was our captain and our number one leader, followed closely by co-captain and 2003 World Cup U.S. captain Julie Foudy. Along with the rest of the leadership in the team, these players developed a culture that has survived the test of time. Our team's culture centered on such fundamentals as maintaining fitness levels, competing at every practice, and acting professionally.

To their credit, the veterans never undermined the newcomers, making the team stronger. A young player would be welcomed onto the team, but if she didn't buy into these unwritten rules of conduct on and off the field, she would almost certainly be weeded out.

The key to this culture was positive leadership. When a player made a mistake, the team didn't come down on her. She was supported. However, if a player showed up unfit for training camp, she was told in no uncertain terms to pick it up or move on.

Every day features leadership moments that the coach must recognize and celebrate. This is how to perpetuate positive leadership. Also, give players leadership responsibilities and expect them to accept them and act on them.

When the WUSA launched, I was proud to see so many women's national team players thrown into leadership roles on their teams and handle those responsibilities so well. Great leaders are special, but great team-wide leadership is made, not born.

Create a Theme

One of the lessons I'd pass on to those seeking my input on coaching successfully is to develop a coaching motto or theme that reflects your coaching philosophy. Before every women's international game, I wrote on the blackboard the motto, "Play hard, play fair, play to win, HAVE FUN!" My players always read these words just before going out onto the field.

This motto, which has evolved during my years as head coach, sums up my belief in sport and competition as clearly as I can express it. I attribute it to my wonderful teachers and coaches, who were my role models as I developed into the person and coach I wanted to be.

If you emulate your mentors, do it in your own unique way. Merge your own ideals with your personality and ideas you received from your mentors. Later, you'll be in position to pass these ideals on to others in the profession, and the process will be perpetuated.

"Play hard" has meaning for me in that the journey between events was so special. The Olympics and the World Cup were awesome, but the six months that we trained and lived together was my favorite time as a coach. This is where we established our objectives, dreams, and goals to achieve ultimate success. Let's face it—no one sets goals to be nearly successful. So what's the difference between those who reach success and those who consistently come up short? In my mind, it's a decision that a coach or athlete makes to push herself or himself to new levels of performance. It doesn't happen overnight. The twisted, curving road to success is laced with setbacks.

During these phases in training, coaches have wonderful opportunities to build self-esteem and self-confidence in players. Doing so is a key part of any coach's job description. Don't get me wrong—sometimes, usually early in the preseason, a coach might want to tear his or her team down a few notches. If done knowingly and with a real plan, this tactic can bond the players. The coach builds players back up individually and collectively. The key ingredient of this rebirth is building individual and collective team confidence.

In my opinion, the real value of athletics is that we learn so much about our players and ourselves. Sport allows an artificial environment that is very important for a relatively short period of time. The 1996 Olympic games were tremendously important to my players and me. It was one of the most important thing in our lives that year, but it still was not the most important thing. The 1996 Olympics and 1999 Women's World Cup were awesome groundbreaking events, but they were still sport. Sport is not a matter of life or death, but because it is so important to us, it elicits similar emotions and reactions that give us great insight into ourselves. The most beneficial byproduct of sport and competition is character development.

Family and the Coaching Profession

One of the toughest factors for coaches is finding a balance between their obligations to the profession and their families. I can only offer a glimpse into my situation following the 1999 World Cup as evidence that sometimes a balance can be struck.

The most difficult professional decision of my life was when I resigned from the women's national team after the 1999 World Cup. I have missed it every day since I made that decision. However, I can also say it was absolutely the right decision for my family and myself, and I am glad I was able to make it. Actually, I had a lot of help from my four sons and my wife, but my youngest son, Nicholas, was the real dealmaker. Even during the 1999 World Cup, Nicholas wanted to know when I was going to leave coaching. After the quarterfinal game against Germany, Nicholas, seven at the time, came up to me in the locker room while I was talking to President Clinton and said, "Two more games, dad, and then you're going to quit, right?"

Later in the fall, after I decided to coach through the 2000 Olympics, I was sitting at breakfast with my family and said, "I've decided to coach through the Olympics." Nick looked at me and asked, "Dad, are you going to coach or are you going to be my dad?" That afternoon I called Hank Steinbrecher and told him my decision to resign from the team. What other decision could I make?

Perhaps, in retrospect, keeping long-range life goals in the forefront will help coaches develop the right perspective in relation to achieving harmony between the "two teams": the family unit and the soccer team family.

Final Thoughts

Play fair and play to win was all about character development. I wanted to win but not by cheating. My players and I held ourselves to a higher standard—win by playing hard, by finding ways to win, and winning with flair. We touched a cord in America because we played the way Americans appreciate sport being played. The team conveyed a blue-collar work ethic. Yes, the team had loads of talent, but it played with resilience and a fighting spirit. The team demonstrated an ability to seize victory from the jaws of defeat.

HAVE FUN is capitalized because in my mind it's the most important ingredient to sport. I don't care what level you play—the game has to be fun. When it wasn't fun for my players, they let me know it. I am eternally grateful they could trust my response. When the game is fun, learning is enhanced. When the game is fun, it becomes a lifelong endeavor rather than a fleeting flash in the pan.

As coaches, we have amazing opportunities to change lives, inspire, guide, suffer and survive setbacks, and witness the heart of champions. We just have to be centered, sensitive, sensible, and ready to facilitate and observe the magic happening around us every day. The team is a sacred entity. As mentors, it's our responsibility to pass on our most valuable messages and experiences to our players and our coaching colleagues, whatever their levels of experience may be.

CHAPTER 25

Looking to the Future of Player Development

Glenn Myernick

Ironically, when I was asked to contribute to this book, I was in the midst of reading Sir Stanley Matthews' autobiography *The Way It Was*. During an extraordinary career that spanned four decades (1930s to 1960s), Matthews was considered one of the first footballers to make specialized training, diet, and total lifestyle part and parcel of his daily routine. Throughout the book, Matthews offers many examples of how simple, routine, and straightforward the team's daily training regimen was. A typical day of training for most clubs consisted of lap work, the most fundamental form of calisthenics, and a "free play" scrimmage. The ball often did not make an appearance until the scrimmage. He describes how it was naturally assumed that every team practiced the same way and that every team played from the then standard playing form of the WM system. Matthews also pointed out that for years on both the domestic and international scene, any deviation from the training routine or system of play was considered radical and revolutionary.

Although daily training methods have evolved, and systems of play have shifted from the attack-minded days of Mr. Matthews to the conservative, defensive-oriented schemes of today, the pillars of the game remain the same: technical, tactical, physical, and psychological.

In this chapter, we'll look at some of the current trends in the game, examine their effectiveness in affecting player development, and offer some examples of areas that could benefit from a fresh approach in the evolution of soccer in America.

Current Trends in Youth Soccer

Nationwide soccer has evolved into an organized, systematically governed sport that functions from the national governing body (U.S. Soccer) down through regional, state, and local associations. Many of us who have seen soccer slowly carve out its own identity in our sporting culture applaud the way the focus is correctly shifting from quantity to quality.

At every level, coaches must take a critical approach to player development, constantly assessing the quality of what we're doing and the appropriateness of our intent. We should remind ourselves that we're merely the voice of the game and the facilitators of the environment. No convoluted approach can replace investing in the basics of the game.

Over time, the coaching community has adopted a progressive system of training and competition that recognizes the different stages of player development. A multitude of books and coaching materials expertly outline and define a philosophy and approach that is appropriate at each level. However, somewhere between our ideology and methodology, we lose our focus and allow adult intentions to interfere with youth and adolescent needs.

Let's look at some of the main areas in which the game has improved over recent years and examine the ones that need to be reevaluated with regard to effectiveness and quality.

Improvements

Player participation in soccer has significantly improved. At every level, more individuals are playing. Opportunities for boys, girls, men, and women of all ages to participate in the game at an appropriate skill level and desired level of competitiveness abound.

As soccer becomes more accepted as part of the American sports scene, there are increasing opportunities to participate in, watch, and read about the game on both the domestic and international fronts. The sport has slowly developed its own identity and become a part of the fiber of our society. The possibility of a professional career is a vital component in player development and the development of a soccer culture.

Although there's a great deal of room for improvement, we have slowly implemented training philosophies and competitions that are age appropriate. We're becoming much more sensitive to coaching children as children and not as adults. Coaching education programs that address the needs of coaches working with youth players are positively affecting the work done at this critical stage of development.

Through time and evolution the average player has become much more proficient at the basic skills of the game. This raises the standards at each level. As novices strive for improvement, the gifted and motivated strive for excellence.

Increased knowledge of nutrition, sports medicine, weight training, and sport-specific physical conditioning methods have all combined to make today's soccer players the fittest, fastest, and most athletically gifted generation of players. Through improved physical conditioning programs, players are capable of playing the game at a faster pace for longer periods of time.

As the game evolves in the U.S., we're seeing more coaches at every level of the game with richer playing experiences than the generation before them. That experience combined with coaching education and access to player-development trends around the world has led to more players understanding the subtleties and nuances of the game at an earlier age.

Areas Needing Improvement

Although more children are playing soccer, the attrition or dropout rate is a concern. First we must understand why children stop participating and then address those factors to retain more players. Several nationally recognized and prominent sport foundations have conducted studies to determine the cause of player dropout. While many of the contributing factors are common to most youth activities, the overriding reason for leaving the sport was they simply weren't having fun. These findings indicate that children want to play soccer to have fun, develop skills, and be with their friends and play. The implications are clear. If coaches don't create an environment that gives players what they want and need, the coaches and the sport will lose the players.

Clearly contributing to the dropout factor are parents whose well-meaning intentions are simply inappropriate and misguided. A critical task for any youth coach is educating the parents about the importance of their role in nurturing and supporting the development process. Parents who embrace their role will positively influence and accelerate their child's growth and enjoyment of the sport.

In addition to player retention, retention of experienced youth coaches is an area of concern. Identifying talented and effective youth coaches and retaining them to hone and polish their coaching at a level that most positively and appropriately affects the players is a vital component in player development. I have no doubt my kindergarten teacher, Mrs. Cook, could have taught any subject to any age student with great success, but taking her out of the most important link in the educational chain would have been a disservice to her students and the process. Mrs. Cook was a master kindergarten teacher. My point is that not every coach can coach the national team, and not every coach is capable of effectively coaching 10-year-old children.

For quite a few years, the soccer community has bemoaned the disappearance of "street soccer" or pickup games. Players who regularly play soccer outside the formalized practice setting are overwhelmingly the exception, not the rule. History is quick to point out that the greatest players developed their instincts, soccer savvy, and style away from the formal practice setting. They then learned how to become effective team players at organized practices. We need to find a way to encourage free play away from formal practices.

Too many youth coaches are overcontrolling individuals who simply inhibit and stifle the creative instincts of promising young players. A very important responsibility of every youth coach is to encourage, motivate, and inspire players to play or practice outside of the formal training setting. Players are much more willing to experiment and exercise their creative instincts away from the watchful and often overly critical eye of the coach.

Although the coaching community is well aware of this missing link in the developmental process, we have failed to address it effectively. There are hundreds of soccer fields across the country that see activity only during formal practices. On any day, you can drive by empty soccer fields and wonder, why aren't the kids out here playing? We have unwittingly created this environment, and it's buoyed by the fact that some concerned parents are unwilling to allow their young children to be unsupervised at a local playground or training field. The middle ground lies somewhere in the realm of "semi-supervised spontaneity." In other words, the league or the community needs to provide some form of safe supervision for children at designated times. The players need to then organize themselves into teams and simply play. No coaching! In the beginning, such activity might require some adult intervention, but in time the hope is that the group becomes self-reliant.

In assessing the current state of the game, we need to refer to the pillars as a measuring stick of where we are in our evolution as a soccer nation. It's commonly accepted that the most vital component in improving any nation's overall soccer standard is an all-around effective and comprehensive youth program. We have made significant strides in the areas of physical, tactical, and mental preparedness, but in spite of some very intensive efforts at the youth level, technical and creative levels of play at the next level have hardly progressed. Are we spending enough time on appropriate technical training at every level of development?

Let's look at the arts and some other sports to examine the amount of time dedicated to polishing and perfecting technique. On a recent trip to Houston to visit our daughter, we met an accomplished ballet dancer, Kelly, who told us about her training regimen and the number of hours dedicated each day to refining and polishing basic technique. On average, the company practices five to six hours a day with a mixture of basic ballet movements (technical training) and performance rehearsals (scrimmaging). Without polished and refined technique, how could we expect the artist to be capable of interpreting the music and transforming technique into skill? I asked Kelly to speak with several members of the Houston Ballet Orchestra to inquire how much time they spent polishing their craft. On average, the musicians practiced two to three hours a day individually plus rehearsals. To take a sport example, aspiring young golfers spend several hours a day perfecting 1 or 2 clubs out of the legal 14.

Although the game is the greatest teacher, most players are not spending time with the ball on their own away from the formal practice setting. Coaches must intervene. Development occurs at every level. Technical training and the refinement of basic ball skills will always be the foundation for how the game is played and interpreted.

Other chapters in this book cover technical training, but I feel the need to address its vital importance here. Without sound, appropriate technical training at every level, the game simply becomes an athletic contest that's not pleasing to the eye.

The masters of the game (Pele, Maradona, Cruyff, Best, Matthews, Puskas, Di Stefano, Beckenbauer) were naturally gifted athletes, but they worked to perfect the techniques of the game. Through perfect technique, they acquired unparalled confidence. With this confidence firmly in place, they transformed impeccable technique into glorious skill.

The value of playing small-sided games at every stage of development is well documented. As the game has evolved, leagues and organizations have instituted a progressive system of competitions that begin at three on three and build to eleven on eleven. These leagues have truly enhanced player development. Players of all ages enjoy the increased ball contacts and spirited challenges that small-sided games provide. During my travels across the country to compare players at every age to their international counterparts, one thing I've observed is how capable our players are to solve problems in a game.

A typical practice involves small-sided play in a relatively tight space. Often the number of touches is limited to one, two, or three. Eventually the touch restriction is removed, and some free play occurs. The value of these exercises is clear: playing faster in less time and space means tighter ball control, more ball contacts, and other benefits.

My observations and comparisons led to the following question: Is the balance between small-sided games, which use small goals and touch restrictions, and free play to full-size goals in matchlike conditions appropriate? Small-sided games have several limiting factors. Vision is limited to a small area; reading the game is limited to only several teammates and opponents; no dribbling occurs if touch restrictions are in effect; no real shooting takes place if small goals or cones are used; long passing, distance shooting, and heading are generally not required; and covering ground defensively and moving as a team is limited.

The variables of any training session are content, duration, and intensity. What are we going to do? How long are we going to do it? How hard will we work? And, keep in mind, whom am I coaching? If coaches don't dedicate enough training time to replicating competitive conditions, why should they expect players to be comfortable meeting the demands of the real game?

Stages of Player Development

The overall progress of the game at the youth level has been steady. For the most part, more and more appropriate training conditions and competitions are evolving. Creating the proper environment at each stage of development is the role of coaches and administrators.

Player development is a constant source of conversation among coaches. Recently a colleague of mine, Bob Jenkins, a national staff coach for U.S. Soccer, put together a clear, simple document outlining the various stages of player development. The following section borrows some of Bob's thoughts and combines them with my own.

The coach is the facilitator for what will take place each day at practice, including content, duration, and intensity. The common bond between past, present, and future generations is simple—they all love to play soccer. Go to any training field at any stage of development (youth to senior) and ask, "What do you want to do today?" Whether you ask a six-year-old or a world-class international player, the answer will be, "Let's play!"

Let's examine the various stages of player development and the degrees of emphasis that separate them. The development of a player spans three general stages: youth (6 to 12), junior (13 to 17), and senior (18 and older). Within these stages, there will be some overlapping based on emotional and athletic maturity.

A player's chances of success at the senior level are significantly improved if he or she masters the fundamentals of the game at the youth and junior levels. The emphasis at the youth level should be fun and comfort with the ball. At the junior level, the emphasis is having fun, refining ball skills, and developing a keener insight into the game. This insight allows the player to understand the imposed demands of fitness, mental strength, and results. The development of the individual should remain the focus within the concept of team development. At the senior level, fun and enjoyment are byproducts of properly investing time at the earlier stages. A commitment to excellence with a focus on results is a culmination of the entire process. If a player's experience and investment at the youth and junior levels has been distorted, he or she will find success and enjoyment more difficult at the senior level.

Youth

The youth stage should be a period of exploration and self-discovery. Players should be in constant contact with the ball and develop a comfort zone that's both challenging and rewarding on their own terms. Balance, agility, and the ability to guide the ball with both feet through dribbling and passing are forms of competition.

When they play games, they should be left alone. The game is theirs to interpret in childlike terms. Developing a relationship with the ball while interacting socially and athletically with teammates and opponents is a sufficient challenge. To burden the child with adult interpretations of the game only hinders the natural development process.

As the child progresses through the latter stages of the youth level, the aim is to provide training and game environments that promote the continued growth of ball skills, an increasing game awareness, and an appreciation for expressing oneself within the concept of the team.

The small-sided game is simply the most effective forum for maximizing ball contacts, meeting challenges, and making decisions with an appropriate number of variables, such as teammates and opponents.

Games are a forum for players to test their ball skills and game awareness and should be considered an additional means of development rather than the objective. Training and games should be guided, not directed, by the coach. The overall objective of activities at this level should be soccer that's free-flowing and coach-guided and encourages all players to participate in attacking and defending while gaining an appreciation of broad concepts. Players should not play positions.

Junior

As players move to the junior level, they should possess a comfortable relationship with the ball and an insight into the game that allows them to cope with the increasing pace and demands of the game.

As a player's understanding of the game increases, it should be the goal of the player and coach to transform expanded techniques into a wider range of skills. The competitive shift from small-sided games to 11 v 11 should be a logical, smooth progression. The ideas and principles that apply to smaller games continue to apply to bigger games. If the players' ideas and understanding of the game are sound, they'll have no problems adjusting to the 11-v-11 environment, even if physically challenged at first.

The barometer for measuring success is the ability of players to stand on their own merit. The outcome of the game is still largely determined by skill and game insight.

Senior

Players who have been exposed to an environment that address their needs and abilities over the long term should be prepared for this next stage of the game. At this point, winning is the focus of the game. The emphasis is for players to pull together all the components of the game in order to be as competitive as possible, both as individuals and as a team, and get a positive result.

If ball skills are insufficient or players lack basic concepts of team play, they will struggle to have a positive impact on the game. Ill-prepared players will have difficulty continuing their careers at this level. At this level, performance should determine the result. There's still a measurable focus on development, but now the emphasis is on developing through match experience.

At this stage, motivated and gifted players need to have better and more opportunities for preprofessional development. At this critical stage of development (15 to 18), technique needs to be challenged and transformed into skill. Thus, the daily demands of the player must increase.

For those talented, motivated potential pros, the current state of high school and club soccer simply does not provide a challenging environment, nor enough quality competition. More of our talented, aspiring young players need to develop a profile that includes much higher standards in all aspects of play than can be found in our current system. Trying to refine and polish their game while expanding their ability to meet the demands of the game at a higher level requires daily training and competition against players of similar talents and aspirations.

Recently, many progressive clubs have united their attempts to provide more meaningful competition for motivated players. Across the country, several of the more high-profile clubs have become very creative in developing additional programs to provide supplemental opportunities for motivated, aspiring youth players.

The most visible program that identifies talented players and brings them together is the U.S. Soccer Residency Program at the IMG Academy in Bradenton, Florida. Under the direction of John Ellinger, the residency program has expanded from 20 players in 1999 to 30 players in 2002. Many of the players are graduates of the U-14 program and comprise the nucleus of our U-17 national team.

In the future it would be ideal to have a residency program in every state that mirrors the residency program at the national level. These programs need to be staffed by coaches who truly understand the development process at this transitional stage. Certainly the program is not for everyone, but our most motivated and capable players are entitled to and need these programs.

Collegiate Soccer

In spite of the limited and restrictive nature of college soccer, well over 75 percent of the players in our professional leagues come through this traditional system. As the college game has evolved, dozens of quality institutions have increased revenues and upgraded facilities, staffing, and support for their soccer programs. Most notably, the growth and emphasis in the women's game has been remarkable.

There are many talented coaches with outstanding facilities and the ability to develop players. Unfortunately, the current system with its academically rooted compass simply is incapable of providing a year-round environment conducive to maximizing player development at yet another critical stage of growth. The reality of the situation is that quality coaches and facilities can't make up for limited training opportunities and an insufficient number of quality competitive matches.

As long as college soccer relies on the major revenue producing sports, little will change. For college soccer to become a year-round, meaningful component in the development of potential pros, significant legislation must be enacted.

College soccer in and of itself is a wonderful opportunity for a player to pursue his or her educational goals and play some soccer at the same time. Many college traditionalists will argue that it's not the role of college soccer to produce professional players. I could not agree more. For those players who truly aspire to maximize their potential and have careers as professionals, there simply must be another avenue to get them there.

The Professional Game

As the sport slowly evolves, it's incumbent on the professional sector to provide the environment for tomorrow's pros. The greatest asset any professional league or franchise has is its players. With each passing year, only minimally increased revenues have been earmarked for player development at the professional level. To become a serious contender in the global soccer market, the pro sector must commit itself to investing in the future generations of players.

Having been involved with our national team programs for nearly 15 years, I have seen the steady progress we've made in all age groups. However, I'm also aware that the depth of our national teams is not as extensive as it should be given the number of players participating.

Don't underestimate the value of being in a professional environment and having to compete for a place on a daily basis. Professionally trained coaches who clearly understand the appropriate levels of emphasis in the various developmental phases can have a very positive effect on young, talented players.

The professional club culture of progressing from one age group to the next under the careful guidance of experienced coaches is a tried and true reality in the soccer nations of the world. Young aspiring pros who can rub shoulders with, observe, and emulate senior pros mature faster.

Although there's always room for improvement at every stage of development, I and many of my colleagues believe that the single biggest void in our growth as a soccer nation is at the preprofessional sector. Until a significant effort is made to invest in the professional development of preprofessional players, I believe we will plateau and stagnate as a developing soccer nation.

The formula seems clear. Better development means better players. That leads to a better product, more fans, more corporate interest, and more television exposure and revenues. These ideas are not new, but looking at the failure of the NASL and the lack of investment made in future generations makes one draw comparisons.

The efforts and commitment that the owners have shown are greatly appreciated by coaches, fans, and players. However, no one should have a greater appreciation for investing in the future than the owners themselves. Youth teams, reserve teams, and experienced coaches at all levels require a significant commitment of resources. The future is now.

Technology

As we continue to develop a soccer culture, technology plays an integral part in our evolution. There's a saying, "Information is power." As technology makes the world seem smaller and puts information at our fingertips, fans, coaches, and players can scan the globe to follow the sport.

From a coach and player perspective, technology will continue to enhance player development. Each generation becomes more visually oriented and stimulated. The use of technology to capture player performance and create feedback will become more prevalent at all levels. At the professional and collegiate levels, better technology will become available to be used in the physical testing and evaluation of both fit and injured players.

The important thing to remember is that technology should not be viewed as a shortcut or substitute for dedicating oneself to mastering all the components of the game.

Summary

We're all products of our daily environments. Creating the best possible environment for each player on a daily basis is the responsibility of the coach.

The game is meant to be very simple, requiring minimal intrusions from the coach. That's why soccer is called a player's game. If coaches at each stage of development clearly understand what the players want and need, we will retain more players and produce better footballers.

At the youth and junior levels, coaches must be steadfast in their commitment to what is right and appropriate for developing young players. Our motivated, talented, aspiring young players require challenging environments to stimulate them to fulfill their potential. The professional sector has an obligation to invest in its own product in order to grow the sport and future generations of entertaining players. At every level we should strive to uncover original creative talents, not replicate the ones who came before.

Possibly the two greatest gifts coaches can give their players are respect and passion for the game. The future of player development should be a combination of positive lessons learned from the past mixed with an attainable vision.

Coaching is a rewarding and honorable field. To think as a coach while letting your heart be guided by the purest intentions of the game is an inspiring challenge.

Unlike most traditional American sports, soccer is a free-flowing, spontaneous game that requires players to think for themselves. The coaches, administrators, and referees often overestimate their importance to the game. The players and their abilities, as well as how they interpret the game, are most important.

Don't forget about Sir Stanley. His shining example of passion and love for our game was evident right up until his passing in 2000. As we close this chapter on the future of player development, let Mr. Matthews stand as the measure of commitment, dedication, and pride that is required if one truly wants to achieve greatness in our game. He was an original!

ABOUT THE NSCAA

Based in Mission, Kansas, the National Soccer Coaches Association of America (NSCAA) is the largest coaches' organization in the United States. Since its founding in 1941, it has grown to include more than 16,000 members who coach both genders at all levels of the sport. In addition to a national rankings program for colleges and high schools, the NSCAA offers an extensive recognition program that presents more than 10,000 individual awards every year. It fulfills its mission of coaching education through a nationwide program of clinics and weeklong courses, teaching more than 3,000 soccer coaches each year. For more information about becoming a member of the NSCAA, visit the NSCAA Web site (www.nscaa.com) or write to the following address:

National Soccer Coaches Association of America
6700 Squibb Road, Suite 215
Mission, Kansas 66202

ABOUT THE CONTRIBUTORS

Joe Bean took the reins of the Wheaton College men's soccer program in 1969. Since then, Wheaton has won 473 matches, including an NCAA Division III national championship in 1997, a second-place finish in 1999, a 21-1-0 record in 1998, and a 17-0-3 record in 1996 with number one national and regional rankings. Wheaton set a national record by going 66 consecutive matches without a loss from the start of the 1996 season to November 14, 1998. Bean received the 1984 and 1997 NSCAA Division III Coach of the Year awards after he led Wheaton to NCAA Division III national crowns.

Miller Bugliari has been head varsity coach at Pingry School (New Jersey) for more than 35 years. In that time his teams have a record of 611-82-49. Bugliari's teams have consistently won numerous county and state soccer championships and have been invited to several tournaments in areas outside of New Jersey. He has been twice selected as NSCAA National Coach of the Year and is heavily involved in coaching education within the New Jersey Youth Soccer Association. He is a former president of the NSCAA and served on the Governor's Fitness Counsel.

Tony DiCicco is the former head coach of the U.S. women's national team program and was the commissioner of the WUSA until it ceased operations in September 2003. DiCicco led the U.S. women's national team to a 103-8-8 record and established a winning percentage of .899, the best ever in U.S. soccer history. In 1996, he led the team to the first-ever gold medal in Olympic women's soccer. In 1999, he spearheaded the signature Women's World Cup champions. He has served as the goalkeeper specialist for the NSCAA and holds both the U.S. Soccer "A" license and the NSCAA Advanced National Diploma.

Anson Dorrance is the head women's soccer coach at the University of North Carolina, where he has coached since 1978. He is a former USA women's national coach and is the most successful coach in the women's game—a four-time National Coach of the Year—whose college team has won 17 NCAA championships. Dorrance led the United States to victory in the first-ever Women's World Championship in China in 1991. Anson Dorrance's renowned girls' soccer camp can be accessed on the Internet through www.ncgsc.com.

Peter Gooding has been a fixture in athletics at Amherst College (Massachusetts) for more than three decades, starting his tenure as the men's soccer coach in 1968. Although he guided the men's soccer team to several ECAC tournament appearances, the growing demands of his other positions at Amherst forced him to relinquish his coaching duties in 1989. However, with the position vacant in 1997, he returned to coaching and led the Jeffs to an NCAA regional appearance in 1998. He served as president of the NSCAA from 1990 to 1991 and director of coaching from 1987 to 1989, and he is a senior staff coach for the NSCAA Academy Program. Gooding was presented the 2001 Honor Award by the NSCAA.

Barry Gorman was named the men's head soccer coach at Penn State University in 1988. He is the winningest PSU soccer coach and has won four conference championships while advancing to the NCAA tournament ten times. He is the first men's coach in Penn State history to win the Big Ten Championship twice (1993 and 2002). Gorman was the 1992 and 1999 NSCAA Mid-Atlantic Coach of the Year. His collegiate coaching record stands at 222-106-23. Gorman was appointed president of the NSCAA in 2002.

Lauren Gregg was a two-time NSCAA All-American (1981 to 1982) and captained the University of North Carolina to three national titles. After a playing career that included membership on the U.S. national team (1986 to 1988), she began coaching at the University of Virginia (1986 to 1995) where she led the team to seven consecutive NCAA appearances and was voted NSCAA Coach of the Year in 1990. Gregg also served as coach of the U-21 women's national team from 1997 to 2000. In 1999 she helped coach the U.S. team to the World Championships in Pasadena, California.

Dr. Colleen Hacker is the assistant dean and a professor in the School of Education at Pacific Lutheran University in Tacoma, Washington. She is also the sports psychology consultant for the U.S. women's national soccer team and a member of the NSCAA Academy coaching staff. In addition to her work with those organizations, she works with professional, international, and Olympic athletes in a variety of sports. Dr. Hacker is much in demand as a speaker to corporations, business groups, and civic organizations, both nationally and internationally.

Jay Hoffman is in his third decade of coaching soccer. He is currently with the U.S. Paralympics, a division of the U.S. Olympic Committee, in preparation for the 2004 Paralympic Games in Athens, Greece. His experiences range from collegiate coaching at SUNY-Fredonia to coaching in both the North American Soccer League and Major Indoor Soccer League. Hoffman has also served as assistant coach for the U.S. U-17 and U-20 men's national teams and head coach of the U-20s. In 1998 and 1999, he led the U.S. women's Pan Am team to a gold medal, was an assistant with the U.S. Women's World Cup champions, and was head coach for the Boston Breakers of the WUSA.

Schellas Hyndman is the head coach at Southern Methodist University. Before arriving at SMU in 1984, he coached seven seasons at Eastern Illinois University. While at EIU, Hyndman earned NSCAA Division I Coach of the Year honors for directing his team to a third-place finish in the NCAA Tournament. Hyndman's teams have qualified for the NCAA playoffs in 25 of 26 seasons. He currently serves on the NCAA Division I Tournament Committee, is vice-president of the NSCAA, and is a member of its Academy coaching staff.

Mike Jacobs is an assistant coach at Duke University. *College Soccer News* named him one of the top assistant coaches in the country in 2002. He began his coaching career in 1994 when he became the youngest Division I head coach. Holding a USSF "A" license and an NSCAA advanced national diploma, Jacobs has served on the NSCAA Division I Great Lakes Regional Rankings Committee and has chaired the NSCAA Division I New York Regional Rankings Committee.

Jim Lennox is one of the country's leading clinicians and is director emeritus of the NSCAA Academy program, having served on its academy staff since 1983. He is currently the director of coaching for the Connecticut Junior Soccer Association.

Tracey Leone is the women's soccer coach at Arizona State University but will go down in history as the coach who led the United States to the first-ever FIFA U-19 Women's World Championship. She was a three-time NSCAA All-American at North Carolina under coach Anson Dorrance. Leone was a member of the 1991 U.S. women's team that captured the Women's World Championship in China. Following two years as assistant coach at Creighton, she built Clemson into a national powerhouse, leading the team to an 87-36-3 record in six years, including six NCAA Tournament berths.

Dr. Jay Martin has been soccer coach at Ohio Wesleyan University for 26 years. In that time his record is 447-91-33, including a NCAA Division III national championship in 1998. Martin, who also serves as athletic director at OWU, has been honored 13 times as NSCAA regional Coach of the Year and NSCAA National Coach of the Year on two occasions. He is a former president of the NSCAA, has been a consultant for the MLS Columbus Crew, served as chair of the NCAA Soccer Committee, and most recently assumed the editorship of *Soccer Journal*.

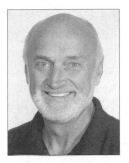

C. Cliff McCrath is considered one of soccer's greatest humorists and also one of its most successful coaches. During his 43-year coaching tenure, including Wheaton College (Illinois), Gordon College (Massachusetts), and Seattle Pacific University (since 1970), his teams won 541 college matches. The former Wheaton NSCAA All-American is a 19-time conference coach of the year and was NSCAA coach of the year in 1978. His teams have appeared in 34 postseason tournaments, with Seattle Pacific clinching five NCAA Division II titles. McCrath was inducted into the U.S. Soccer Hall of Fame in 1993.

Ron McEachen has been a fixture on the American coaching scene for nearly 30 years. Currently the head coach at Skidmore, he has compiled a 213-120-49 record. McEachen was an NSCAA All-America choice both at Mitchell College and at West Virginia and played professionally in the North American Soccer League and American Soccer League for seven seasons (1971 to 1978). He has been a United States Soccer Federation staff coach and has been a member of the NSCAA since 1983 and a member of its Academy staff.

For more than 20 years, **Peter Mellor,** the 2003 U.S. national team's goalkeeper coach and coordinator, has worked to develop soccer throughout the world. He holds a CONCACAF goalkeeping diploma, a full English coaching certificate, U.S. Soccer Federation "A" and "B" licenses, and a national certificate in recreational management. His experience has taken him to World Cups and Olympics around the world. In the off-season, Mellor directs soccer clinics for coaches and athletes at all levels of the game.

Al Miller's first coaching position was at SUNY-New Paltz, and in 1970 he took over the reins at Hartwick College. In 1973 he guided the Philadelphia Atoms to the North American Soccer League title in the team's first year. Over his career he has been a featured clinician and public speaker. He was one of the first American coaches awarded the coveted USSF "A" License and served as U.S. national team coach in the 1970s.

Joe Morrone's coaching resume includes 11 years at Middlebury College and 28 years at the University of Connecticut. He accumulated 422 career victories and an NCAA Division I title in 1981. In 1991, *Soccer America* acknowledged his involvement in promoting soccer by naming him one of the 20 most influential persons in U.S. soccer for the past 20 years. He was inducted into the NISOA Hall of Fame in 1977 and the NSCAA Hall of Fame in 2002.

Glenn Myernick has contributed to American soccer as both a player and coach. He has been captain of the team at Hartwick College and was the recipient of the Hermann Award. He later enjoyed the longest career of any American player in the North American Soccer League while playing for Portland and Dallas. Myernick has coached various U.S. national teams, Hartwick College, and the Colorado Rapids of the MLS. Most recently he served as an assistant to Bruce Arena with the U.S. national team at the 2002 World Cup in Korea.

George Perry is the men's soccer coach at Wabash College and currently serves as the resident youth coaching expert for the NSCAA. As a senior NSCAA Academy staff member, Perry has offered countless National Youth Diploma courses both in his region and at the annual NSCAA convention sites. He has also instructed or administrated at every level of NSCAA residential courses. Those interested in helping upgrade the coaching of youth soccer in their community should contact Perry at perryg@wabash.edu.

Chris Petrucelli began his coaching career at Old Dominion University as an assistant coach in 1985. In 1991, he was named head coach for the women's team at Notre Dame. Petrucelli was selected as NCAA Division I Coach of the Year in both 1994 and 1995, winning the NCAA Division I Championship in 1995. In 2001 he led the University of Texas to the Big 12 title and the school's first appearance in the NCAA tournament. Petrucelli has served as NCAA Division I Rules Committee chair and has been a senior member of the NSCAA Academy staff.

John Rennie has more than 30 years of coaching experience and is one of the winningest coaches in collegiate men's soccer. As the head coach at Duke University, Rennie leads one of the most successful programs in the country. He was voted Atlantic Coast Conference Coach of the Year five times, South Region Coach of the Year three times, and National Coach of the Year in 1982. Rennie was the inaugural chairman of the NCAA Division I Soccer Coaches Committee and a former USSF national coaching staff member, and he has coached for the South Region Olympic Development Program.

Steve Sampson played college soccer at San Jose State for NSCAA Hall of Fame member Julie Menendez. He later coached at Santa Clara where his Bronco team shared the 1989 NCAA Division I title with Virginia. Sampson was named coach of the U.S. national team in 1998. He also served as director of coaching for the California Youth Soccer Association South. In the fall of 2002, he became the first American-born coach selected to manage another country's national team, when he took over the reins of the Costa Rican national team.

Tim Schum coached men's soccer for 31 years, 29 at Binghamton (New York) University. Over his last 20 years at Binghamton the team participated in 16 postseason tournaments and captured six conference championships. He is a member of the NSCAA Academy coaching staff and helped establish youth soccer organizations in the Binghamton community.

Layton Shoemaker coached collegiate soccer for 30 years, 23 of them at Messiah College in Pennsylvania. His 1978 and 1981 teams won the National Christian College Athletic Association national titles. The 1986 and 1988 Messiah teams advanced to the final four of the NCAA Division III championships. Three times he was national coach of the year. He has chaired the NSCAA Ethics Committee since 1997. He is most proud of the fact that during a 49-game stretch from 1987 to 1989, Messiah's players never received a yellow card!

Charlie Slagle is the CEO of the Capital Area Soccer League (CASL), one of the largest nonprofit soccer leagues in the United States, a position he has held since August 2001. Before joining the CASL, Slagle spent 21 years coaching the Davidson College Wildcats, where he racked up over 200 victories and a 1992 appearance in the Men's Soccer College Cup. Slagle was named National Coach of the Year in 1992, has served as chairman of Division I coaches for the NSCAA, and currently holds a position on the NSCAA men's and women's soccer rules committee.

Jeff Tipping serves as the director of coaching education for the NSCAA and is one of the country's leading clinicians. Previously, Tipping was head men's coach at Muhlenberg College from 1986 to 2001, where he established one of the nation's most competitive Division III programs (225-71-21). As a player, Tipping led Hartwick College to the NCAA Division I title in 1977 and later captained the American Soccer League's Pennsylvania Stoners to the league championship in 1980.

Jeff Vennell's coaching career began at Williams College before he moved on to Kenyon College. During his stay at Kenyon, Vennell was also the school's director of athletics while serving on several soccer advisory committees, including the NCAA Division III Men's Championships and the Eastern College Athletic Conference (ECAC) Championships. From 1987 to 1999, Vennell was the director of athletics at the University of Rochester. He currently serves as athletic director at the Cranbrook Schools in Michigan.

Tony Waiters has had a long and distinguished playing and coaching career in England, Canada, and the United States. He played professionally in England and was selected to the national team. Later he moved to Canada where he coached the national team to an Olympic berth in 1984 and to the Mexico World Cup in 1986. Currently, Waiters is a senior member of the NSCAA Academy staff and was honored for his work in developing the Academy's goalkeeping curriculum at the 2003 NSCAA Convention.